AMERICAN

SLAVERY AND FINANCES.

BY THE

HON. ROBERT J. WALKER, M.A.

COUNSELLOR AT LAW IN THE SUPREME COURT OF THE UNITED STATES,
LATE LAW REP. MI., SENATOR OF THE UNITED STATES,
SECRETARY OF THE TREASURY, COMMISSIONER TO CHINA
GOVERNOR OF KANSAS, ETC., ETC.

LONDON:
WILLIAM RIDGWAY, 169, PICCADILLY, W.
1864.

American Slavery and Finances
Originally published by
William Ridgway
London, England
1864

Reprint edition published by
The University of Illinois Library
Urbana, Illinois
2009

ISBN 978-1-60841-088-0

PREFACE.

The present volume contains the various pamphlets published by me here during the last six months. The subject discussed relates to the present rebellion in America, and embraces Jefferson Davis and Repudiation—Recognition—Slavery—Finances and Resources of the United States.

R. J. WALKER.

London, March 1, 1864.

JEFFERSON DAVIS.
REPUDIATION,
RECOGNITION AND SLAVERY.

LETTER

OF

HON. ROBERT J. WALKER, M.A.

COUNSELLOR AT LAW IN THE SUPREME COURT OF THE UNITED STATES,
LATE LAW REP. MI., SENATOR OF THE UNITED STATES,
SECRETARY OF THE TREASURY, COMMISSIONER TO CHINA,
GOVERNOR OF KANSAS, ETC. ETC.

SECOND EDITION.

LONDON:
WILLIAM RIDGWAY, 169, PICCADILLY. W.
1863.

JEFFERSON DAVIS.

REPUDIATION, RECOGNITION, AND SLAVERY.

London, 10, *Half Moon Street*, *Piccadilly*,
July 1*st*, 1863.

SOON after my arrival in London from New York, my attention was called, by some English, as well as American friends, to an article which had appeared more than a month previously in the London "Times" of the 23rd of March last. In the Money Article of that date, is the following letter from the Hon. John Slidell, the Minister of Jefferson Davis at Paris.

My dear Sir,

I have yours of yesterday. I am inclined to think the people of London confound Mr. Reuben Davis, whom I have always understood to have taken the lead on the question of repudiation, with President Jefferson Davis. I am not aware that the latter was in any way identified with that question. I am very confident that it was not agitated during his canvass for Governor, or during his administration. The Union bank bonds were issued in direct violation of an express constitutional provision. There is a wide difference between these bonds, and those of the Planters' bank, for the repudiation of which, neither excuse nor palliation can be offered. I feel confident that Jefferson Davis never approved or justified that repudiation. What may have been his private opinions of the refusal to consider the State of Mississippi bound to provide for the payment of the Union bank bonds, I do not know.

Yours truly,

JOHN SLIDELL.

It is due to the Editor of the "Times" here to state, that, in his money article of the 23rd March last, he refers to the controversy of that press with Jefferson Davis on that question, in 1849, and, as regards the suggestion of Mr. Slidell, that it might have been Reuben Davis who was the repudiator in 1849, instead of Jefferson Davis, the Editor remarked, "it is to be feared that the proof in the other direction is too strong." Indeed, the Editor might well be astonished at the supposition, that Jefferson Davis, who subscribed the repudiation letter in question of the 25th May, 1849, as well as a still stronger communication of the 29th August, 1849, should have been confounded, during a period of near fourteen years, by the press of Europe and America, with Reuben Davis, and that the supposed mistake should just now be discovered, especially as Reuben Davis never was a Senator of the United States from Mississippi, or from any other State.

I was asked if it really was Reuben or Jefferson Davis who was the author of the letter in question advocating the repudiation of the Union bank bonds of Mississippi, their recollection being, that it was the latter. I said that the repudiation letter in question of the 25 May, 1849, was subscribed and published at its date in the "Washington Union," by Jefferson Davis as a Senator of the United States from Mississippi, which position he then held, that he was personally well known to me for nearly a fourth of a century, as was also Reuben Davis, and that the latter never had been a Senator of the

United States from Mississippi, or any other State, as was well known to me, and would be shown by reference to the Journals of the United States Senate. I stated, that I had represented the State of Mississippi in the Senate of the United States from January, 1836, until March, 1845, when, having resigned that office, I was called to the Cabinet of President Polk, as Secretary of the Treasury of the United States, and remained in that position until the close of that administration in March 1849. I added, that I was in Washington city, the Capitol of the Union, and residing there as a Counsellor at Law in the Supreme Court of the United States when the first repudiation letter of Jefferson Davis communicated by him to the Editor of the "Union" (a newspaper of that city,) was published on the 25th May, 1849, in that print, and very generally throughout the United States. It was remarked by me, that it was well known to myself personally, and I believed to every prominent public man of that date, especially those then in Washington, that Mr. Jefferson Davis was the author of that letter then published over his signature, and that he defended its doctrines, with all that earnestness and ability for which he was so distinguished. I was also residing in Washington, when, Mr. Jefferson Davis, published, over his signature, as a Senator of the United States from Mississippi, his well-known second repudiation letter, dated at his *residence*, "Brierfield, Miss.," August 29, 1849. This letter was addressed to the Editors of the "Mississippian," a newspaper published at Jackson, Mississippi, and was received by me in due course of mail. This letter extended over several columns, and was an elaborate defence of the repudiation of Mississippi. This letter also was generally republished throughout the United States. These views of Mr. Jefferson Davis attracted my most earnest attention, because, after a brief interval, he was one of my successors in the senate of the United States, from Mississippi. I had always earnestly opposed the doctrine of repudiation in Mississippi, and the Legislature of 1840-41, by which I was re-elected, passed resolutions by overwhelming majorities, (hereafter quoted,) denouncing the repudiation either of the Union Bank, or Planters' bank bonds.

At the period of the conversations before referred to, late in April or early in May last, I was, on this recital of the facts, strongly urged to make them known in Europe, to which my consent was given.

After some investigation, however, the necessary documents fully to elucidate the whole subject could not be obtained here. It was necessary, therefore, to write home and procure them. This has been done, and I now proceed to a narrative of these transactions from the authentic historical public documents.

The first letter of Mr. Jefferson Davis before referred to, of the 25th of May, 1849, was published by him as a Senator of the United States from Mississippi, over his signature in the "Union," a newspaper published at Washington city. That letter is in these words:

"Daily Union," Washington City. May 25, 1849.

"*Statement furnished by Jefferson Davis, Esq., Senator of the United States.*

"The State of Mississippi has no other question with bondholders than that of debt or no debt. When the United States Bank of Pennsylvania purchased what are known as the Union Bank bonds, it was within the power of any stock-dealer to learn that they had been issued in disregard of the constitution of the State whose faith they assumed to pledge. By the constitution and laws of Mississippi, any creditor of the State may bring suit against the State, and test his claim, as against an individual. To this the bondholders have been invited; but conscious that they have no valid claim, have not sought their remedy. Relying upon empty (because false) denunciation, they have made it a point of honour to show what can be shown by judicial investigation; *i.e.*, that there being no debt, there has been no default. The crocodile tears which have been shed over ruined creditors, are on a par with the baseless denunciations which have been heaped upon the State. Those bonds were purchased by a bank then tottering to its fall—purchased in violation of the charter of the bank, or fraudulently, by concealing the transaction under the name of an individual, as may best suit those concerned—purchased in violation of the terms of the law under which the bonds were issued, and in disregard of the constitution of Mississippi, of which the law was an infraction. To sustain the credit of that ricketty bank, the bonds were hypothecated abroad for interest on loans which could not be met as they became due.

"A smaller amount is due for what are termed Planters' Bank bonds of Mississippi. These evidences of debt, as well as the coupons issued to cover accruing interest, are receivable for State lands; and no one has a right to assume they will not be provided for otherwise, by or before the date at which the whole debt becomes due.

"JEFFERSON DAVIS."

To this letter the London "Times," in its money article, of the 13th July, 1849, replied as follows:—

"The case of Mississippi stands thus: In 1838 "the State issued bonds for five millions of dollars, to "establish the Union bank. These bonds were dated "June, 1838, bearing five per cent. interest from date, "and it was stipulated with the bank that they should "not be sold under their par value. On the 18th "August following, the bank sold all these bonds to "the United States Bank for five millions of dollars, "payable in five equal instalments in November, "January, March, May, and July, but without in-"terest. The money was punctually paid to the Mis-"sissippi Bank, and the Legislature of Mississippi, "on the terms of the sale being communicated to "them," resolved, '*That the sale of the bonds was "highly advantageous to the State, and in accordance "with the injunctions of the charter, reflecting the "highest credit on the Commissioners, and bringing "timely aid to an embarrassed community.*' In "little more than two years, however, the Mis-"sissippi bank became totally insolvent, having lost "the entire five millions invested in it by the State. "Immediately on this having transpired, the Gover-"nor of the State sent a message to the Legislature "recommending them to *repudiate*, (this was the "first time the word was used) their obligations, being "founded on the plea, that as the bonds were issued "with interest payable from the date, and they had "been sold to the United States Bank for their nomi-"nal amount only, the stipulation that they should "not be disposed of below their par value, had been "departed from. He further urged that although "the bonds had been sold ostensibly to Mr. Biddle,

" the President of the United States Bank, the sale " was actually to the bank itself, which, by its charter " could not legally purchase them. Hence although " Mississippi had received the money for the bonds, " it was thus proposed to refuse to repay it, on the " ground that the purchaser had no right to buy " them. The Legislature however, was not quite pre- " pared for this, and accordingly in responding to the " Governor's message, they resolved. '1st. That the " State of Mississippi is bound to the holders of the " bonds of the State sold on account of the bank for " the amount of principal and interest. 2nd. That the " State of Mississippi will pay her bonds, and preserve " her faith inviolate. 3rd. That the insinuation that " the State of Mississippi would repudiate her bonds " and violate her plighted faith, is a calumny upon " the justice, honour and dignity of the State.' But " after this, the pecuniary condition of the State be- " came rapidly worse, and the disposition to pay " diminished in proportion. Accordingly a joint com- " mittee of the Legislature appointed in 1842, re- " ported that the State was not bound to pay the " bonds, advancing the reasons before mentioned, and " also another, namely, that the bonds had not been " sanctioned in the manner required by the constitu- " tion, since although the provision that no loan should " be raised, unless sanctioned by a law passed through " two successive Legislatures had been complied with, " and the bonds had been legally authorized, the act " also prescribed certain conditions regarding the " Bank of Mississippi, which conditions had been " altered by a subsequent act, that had only passed " through one Legislature.

" In addition to the five millions thus repudiated, " Mississippi owes two millions which she recognizes. " It has always, however, been a difference without " distinction, since she pays no dividends on either. " From the period of repudiation up to the present " moment, all representations of the bondholders have " been treated with disregard. About a year and a- " half back, however, one of the citizens of Mississippi, " a Mr. Robbins, admitted the moral liability of the " State, and proposed that the people should dis- " charge it by voluntary contributions.

" The next step is the appearance of the letter from " Mr. Jefferson Davis, with whom we are now called " upon to deal. This statement which was trans- " mitted by him to the 'Washington' Union, in reply " to our remarks of the 23rd February last runs as " follows :—(Here the Times inserts Mr. Jefferson Davis repudiation letter before quoted.)

" The assurance in this statement that the Planters' " bank, or non-repudiated bonds are receivable for " State lands, requires this addition, which Mr. Jef- " ferson Davis has omitted, that they are only so " receivable upon lands being taken at three times its " current value. The affirmation afterwards, that no " one has a right to assume that these bonds will not " be fully provided for before the date at which the " principal falls due, is simply to be met by the fact " that portions of them fell due in 1841 and 1846, " and that on these, as well as on all the rest, both " principal and interest remain wholly unpaid.

" Regarding the first part of the statement no " comment could be made which would not weaken its " effect. Taking its principle and its tone together, it "is a doctrine which has never been paralleled. Let it "circulate throughout Europe, that a member of the "United States Senate in 1849, has openly proclaimed "that at a recent period the Governor and Legisla- "tive Assemblies of his own State deliberately issued "fraudulent bonds for five millions of dollars to 'sus- "tain the credit of a rickety bank;' that the bonds "in question, having been hypothecated abroad to in- "nocent holders, such holders have not only no claim "against the community by whose executive and re- "presentatives this act was committed, but that they "are to be taunted for appealing to the verdict of the "civilized world, rather than to the judgment of the "legal officers of the State by whose functionaries "they have been already robbed; and that the ruin "of toil-worn men, of women, of widows, and of chil- "dren, and the 'crocodile tears' which that ruin has "occasioned, is a subject of jest on the part of those "by whom it has been accomplished, and then let it "be asked if any foreigner ever penned a libel on "the American character equal to that against the "people of Mississippi by their own Senator."

To this reply of the London "Times," which, (except in portions of Mississippi,) was generally approved throughout the Union, Mr. Jefferson Davis responded in a very long letter, dated from his residence, Brierfield, Mississippi, Aug. 29, 1849, addressed to the Editors of the "Mississippian." He begins as follows:—"The *London Times* of July 13, 1849, contains an article which most unjustly and unfairly attacks the State of Mississippi and myself because of a statement I made in refutation of a former calumny against her, which was published in the same paper." This article of the London "Times" Mr. Davis denounces as "a *foreigner's slander* against the government, the judiciary, and people of Mississippi;" "very well for the high tory paper as an attack upon our republican government;" as "untrue;" "the hypocritical cant of stock-jobbers and *pensioned presses*" "reckless of reputation;" "hired advocates of the *innocent* stock dealers of London Change;" "a calumnious imputation." These are pleasant epithets which Mr. Jefferson Davis applied to the "London Times" and the "London Change." But Mr. Jefferson Davis was very indignant, not only with London, but with all England, for he says, "With far more propriety might *repudiation* be charged on the *English Government*, for the reduction of interest on her loans when she consolidated her debts; for the income tax which compels fundholders to return a part of the interest they receive on their evidences of public debt, for the support of the Government which is their debtor." According, then, to Mr. Jefferson Davis, the London Times and the London Change are great reprobates, and it is not Mississippi but "THE ENGLISH GOVERNMENT" which has repudiated their own public debt.

From such angry epithets and fierce denunciation, the reader will be prepared to find very little argument in Mr. Jefferson Davis's second letter. He denies that Mississippi received the money. But a bank of which she was the sole stockholder, and whose directory was all appointed by her, received it. They received it also for her exclusive benefit, for she, *as a State*, was to derive large profits on the stock of the bank, which was hers exclusively, and was paid for entirely by the proceeds of these bonds. Mississippi then, as a State, through her agents appointed by her received this money. All governments must act through human agency, and the agency in this case which received the money, was appointed entirely by the State. But this is not all. The Bank, which was exclusively a State bank, and based entirely on the proceeds of these State bonds, with no other stockholders, was directed by the charter to loan this money, the proceeds of these bonds, only to "the citizens of the State," sec. 46, and so the loans were made. The State, then, through an agency appointed exclusively by itself, received this money, the proceeds of the State bonds, and the State, through this same agency, loaned this money to "the citizens of the State," who never repaid the loans. The State then received the money and loaned it out to its own citizens, who still hold it; and yet this money, obtained on the solemn pledge of the faith of the State, her citizens still hold, and the State repudiates her bonds on which the money was received, and Mr. Jefferson Davis sustains, indorses, and eulogises this proceeding. Never was there a stronger case.

Mr. Jefferson Davis reiterates in this letter his arguments contained in his previous communication of the 25th May, 1849, so fully answered by the Editors of the London "Times" in their money article before quoted of the 13th July, 1849. He elaborates, particularly, the legal position, that the bonds were invalid, because he says not sanctioned by two successive Legislatures as required by the Constitution of Mississippi. This statement is erroneous, because the loan in the precise form, in which the bonds were issued, was sanctioned by two successive Legislatures in perfect conformity with the Constitution. This is shown, as will be proved hereafter, by reference to the laws passed by the State, and such was the decision on this very point by the highest judicial tribunal of Mississippi, in 1842 and 1853. But let us suppose that there was some technical legal informality as to the law, would that justify the repudiation of these bonds? The Legislature had passed laws in 1837 and 1838 authorising the issue and sale of these bonds, those acts had been all signed and approved by the Governor of the State, the bonds had been signed by the Governor and Treasurer of the State, the broad seal of the State had been affixed to them by the Governor, they were placed in the hands of the authorities of the State for sale, they were sold by them, and the full amount paid over to the agency appointed by the State, and by that agency the money was loaned to the "citizens of the State" and still retained by them. When the sale of these State bonds in August, 1838, together with all the facts and documents were placed by the Governor before the Legislature in 1839, they ratified and highly approved the sale as before quoted by the "Times," and again still more decidedly in 1841.

And yet the State on the technical grounds stated by Mr. Davis, repudiated their bonds. It was unconstitutional to return the money which they had borrowed and used! Could anything be more absurd or dishonourable than this? The law says if a man borrows money without certain legal authentications he shall not be forced to repay, but if he receives and uses the money, and then interposes such technical pleas, he is justly deemed infamous. He has violated his honour. And is the honour of an individual more sacred than that of a state or nation? State and national debts rest upon faith, they repose upon honour, the obligation is sacred, and must be fulfilled. It can never be illegal or unconstitutional to *pay a debt*, where the money has been received by a state or a nation. And, where a State, acting through its supreme Executive and Legislature, has issued its bonds and affixed its seal, and they have passed into the hands of *bona fide* holders, the obligation must be fulfilled. For a state or nation, having issued its bonds under its highest legislative and executive sanction, to say, that her own functionaries mistook some of the formalities of the law, and refuse payments, is a fraud upon the *bona fide* holders, and can never be sustained before the tribunal of the world. But when, besides the Legislature and Executive of the State, its highest judicial tribunals have declared the bonds perfectly constitutional and valid, and to have been sold in accordance with the terms of the law, for such repudiation of such bonds it is difficult to find any language sufficiently strong to mark the infamy of such a transaction.

If indeed the formalities of the Constitution had not been complied with, and this were not a mere pretext, how easy would it have been to have passed a new act in conformity with the constitutional formalities, assuming the debt, or providing for the issue of new bonds to be delivered to the holders on the return of those alleged to be informal. But the truth is, this alleged unconstitutionality was a mere pretext for repudiating a just debt, it never occurred to the Legislatures which passed these laws in 1837 and 1838, or to the Governor who signed them, and was rejected by the Legislature in 1839, and again, in the most solemn form in 1841.

And now let me trace the history of this transaction chronologically. The original act chartering the Bank, with the 5th section authorising the loan, was passed by the Legislature Jan. 21st, 1837, and again, in strict compliance with the provisions of the Constitution, reenacted in the same words on the 5th of February, 1838. Now the bonds issued are in strict conformity with this law, and an exact copy of the form of the bonds prescribed by the law. If then, the supplemental act of the 15th February, 1838, was unconstitutional, null, and void, as contended by the repudiators, then the whole original act remained in full force, and the bonds were valid under that law, and such was the unanimous decision of the High Court of Errors and Appeals of Mississippi, as will be shown hereafter. It was contended before the Court, (and by Mr. Davis in his last letter,) that, under the original law, certain acts were to be performed before the bonds could issue. But here again, it is plain on the face of the law, and so the High Court of Errors and Appeals of Mississippi unanimously decided, that these acts were not required to be performed as *conditions precedent* to the issue of the bonds, and that the issue and sale of the bonds were perfectly valid before these acts had been performed. The bonds then are in exact conformity with a law, which was passed by two successive Legislatures, precisely as provided by the constitution.

In 1836 there was great pecuniary embarrassment in Mississippi, attributed by many to what was called the *specie circular*, and soon followed a suspension of the banks. Under these circumstances, there was an almost universal demand in Mississippi for relief measures. As a consequence, the attention of the Legislature was absorbed almost exclusively in the consideration of remedies for the existing embarrassments. The result was, the enactment, on the 21st January, 1837, of the law, creating the Union Bank of Mississippi. This bank was based upon loans to be obtained upon bonds of the State, the proceeds of which, when sold, were to constitute the capital of the bank, which money, by the terms of the charter, was to be loaned to the "*citizens of the State*," to relieve the existing embarrassments.

The fifth section of the Act, was the only one, in which any authority was given for a loan by the State, and any power to pledge its faith. That section, entire, was as follows:—

"That in order to facilitate the said Union Bank for the said loan of fifteen millions five hundred thousand dollars, the faith of this State be, and is hereby pledged, both for the security of the capital and interest, and that 7500 bonds of $1000 each, to wit: 1875 payable in twelve years; 1875 in fifteen years; 1875 in eighteen years; and 1875 in twenty years, and bearing interest at the rate of five per cent. per annum, shall be signed by the Governor of the State to the order of the Mississippi Bank, countersigned by the State Treasurer, and under the Seal of the State; said bonds to be in the following words, viz.:

"$2000. Know all men by these presents, that the State of Mississippi *acknowledges to be indebted* to the Mississippi Union Bank in the sum of two thousand dollars, which sum the said State of Mississippi *promises to pay* in current money of the United States to the order of the President, Directors, and Company in the —— year —— with interest at the rate of five per cent. per annum, payable half-yearly, at the place named in the indorsement hereto, viz.: —— on the —— of every year until the payment of the said principal sum: in testimony whereof the Governor of the State of Mississippi has signed, and the Treasurer of the State has countersigned these presents, and caused the seal of the State to be affixed thereto, at Jackson, this —— in the —— year of our Lord.

Governor.
Treasurer."

The whole act, of which this section was a part, was passed by the Legislature and approved by the Governor in 1837, and the entire section as to the loan as required by the provision of the Constitution of the State, was referred to the action of the next succeeding Legislature. That succeeding Legislature was chosen in November, 1837, and assembled, at its regular session, in January 1838. After full discussion in both houses, this act of 1837 was passed by large majorities in both branches of the Legislature, and approved by the new Governor, A. G. McNutt, on the 5th of February, 1838. The act of 1837, including the 5th section, before quoted, was thus re-enacted by the succeeding Legislature, without any change whatever. There was then a full, complete, and undisputed compliance with the requirements of the Constitution, and, under this act, thus sanctioned by two successive Legislatures, it is conceded, that the faith of the State was pledged, and that the bonds might be issued and sold. But it is contended by Mr. Jefferson Davis, in his first, as well as his second letter, before quoted, that the bonds are invalid, because of the supplemental act of the 15th of February, 1838. Now, it will be observed, that no change whatever was made by this supplemental act, in this 5th section of the original act, before quoted, by which alone the faith of the State was pledged for the payment of these bonds, and which section alone, as required by the Constitution, had been referred to the action of the succeeding Legislature. No change whatever was made by the supplemental act in that section of the original act, the bonds were issued and sold in precise conformity with its provisions, and, indeed, these bonds, thus actually issued and sold, are a precise and literal copy of the form of the bonds as given in the original act, as before quoted. The supplemental act changed only some of the "*details*" of the charter of the Bank, but made no alteration whatever in the 5th section. This supplemental act, which is now denounced by Jefferson Davis as unconstitutional, was passed, after the fullest investigation of this question, as to the power of the Legislature, with favourable reports as to the Constitutional power by the joint Committee of both houses. The Committee reported to the Senate, that, by a "a supplemental bill" "it is competent for this Legislature to alter and amend the details of the bill, incorporating the subscribers to the Mississippi Union Bank, passed at the last session of the Legislature of this State."—(*Senate Journal*, 103.)

The report of the Committee to the House was as follows:—"The said Committee are of the opinion, that it is within the province of the Legislature to amend or change the details of the said Mississippi Union Bank Charter," &c. (*House Journal, p.* 117.) Such was the opinion of the joint Committee of both houses of the Legislature, which reported this supplemental act, which act was passed by the vote of 22 to 3 in the Senate, (Journal, 320,) and 55 to 22 in the House (Journal, 329-30.) It would appear, then, that in the opinion of an overwhelming majority of both branches of the Legislature of Mississippi, the supplemental act was constitutional; and the act was approved by A. G. McNutt, the Governor of the State, and thus became a law on the 15th of

February, 1838. Indeed, the idea that a subsequent Legislature could change none of the details of a Bank charter, because there was embodied in the act a separate and distinct section authorizing a loan of money by the State, seemed to me never to rise to the dignity of a question. Such, we have seen, was the view of the Legislatures of 1838, 1839, and 1841, and such was the unanimous decision, hereafter quoted, of the Chancellor and Circuit Judge of Mississippi, and of the Supreme Judicial Tribunal, the High Court of Errors and Appeals of the State, in two decisions, on this very point, and in favour of the constitutionality of this law. One of these decisions was made in January, 1842, and the other in April, 1853. These decisions were conclusive against the State, and binding upon the Legislature, the Governor and the people, for the following reasons. The Constitution of the State of Mississippi contains the following clause:

"Article II. *Distribution of Powers.*

"Sec. 1. The powers of the Government of the State of Mississippi shall be divided into three distinct departments, and each of them confided to a separate body of magistracy; to wit, those which are legislative to one, those which are judicial to another, and those which are executive to another.

"Sec. 2. No person or collection of persons, being of one of these departments, shall exercise any power properly belonging to either of the others, except in the instances hereinafter expressly directed or permitted."—It is not pretended that any exception was made for this case. The contrary has always been held by the Courts of Mississippi. Indeed, as late as October Term, 1858, this very question was decided by the High Court of Errors and Appeals of Mississippi, when it was ruled by the Court that "The Legislature may not, therefore, exercise powers which in their nature are judicial." — Isom. *v.* Missis. R. R. Co. 7. George 314.

In the 9th section of the 7th article of the Constitution of Mississippi is found the provision on which Mr. Jefferson Davis relies, requiring the assent of two successive Legislatures to pledge the faith of the State. Immediately succeeding this provision is the following: "The Legislature *shall direct* by law in what Courts suits may be brought against the State."

These two consecutive sections of the *same article* of the Constitution, being in *pari materia*, are to be construed together. Indeed, it is a well known historical fact, that this 9th section, as regards the pledge of the faith of the State, which is now perverted to a wholly different purpose, was intended to give greater solemnity and a higher credit to the bonds of the State, as was likewise the provision in the same Constitution of 1832, sanctioning by name the Planters' bank bonds of the State (now unpaid,) in consequence of which, they were sold at a premium of thirteen and a half per cent. In pursuance of the provision of the Constitution before quoted, the Legislature of Mississippi, in 1833, passed an act, designating the Court of Chancery, as the one in which suits might be brought against the State, with the right of appeal by either party to the High Court of Errors and Appeals. That act was passed in 1833, in pursuance of this *mandatory* provision of the Constitution before quoted. That act provided, that, if the decree of the Court should be against the State, the Governor *shall issue* his mandate to the Auditor to draw on the Treasurer to pay the decree, but "no execution whatever shall ever issue on any decree in Chancery against the State of Mississippi whereby the State may be dispossessed of lands, tenements, goods and chattels."—*Howard's Dig.* 523, 524.

Here, then, are the two consecutive provisions of the Constitution in *pari materia*, the one designating the mode by which the bonds of the State might be issued, and the other, the judicial tribunals in which all disputes as to such bonds might be *definitively* settled, and payment made, if the decree were against the State. That Constitution vested the *whole judicial power of the State* in the Courts, it vested nothing but "legislative power" in the Legislature, and it prohibited the Legislature and Executive from exercising judicial power; it adopted the great fundamental principle of constitutional government, separating the executive, legislative, and judicial power. Indeed, it is the great doctrine of American law, that the concentration of any of these two powers, in any one body or functionary, is dangerous to liberty, and that the *consolidation* of all of these powers, creates a despotism. The interpretation of a law, and particularly of a constitution, which is made the "supreme law," the *lex legum*, has uniformly been regarded, as exclusively a judicial, and not an executive or legislative function. In this case, however, it has been made clear by an express provision of the constitution separating these functions, and designating, under its mandate, the *Courts* in which *suits* shall be brought against the State, and the form of the decree to be rendered, and requiring payment to be at once made. A suit is a judicial act, and so is the decree of a Court. Well, then, the highest judicial tribunals of Mississippi, have twice decided this question; they have declared this supplemental act constitutional, these bonds valid, and the sale of them to be in conformity with the law; and, in a suit on one of these very bonds, after the fullest argument, the Court entered a decree of payment, overruling every point made by Jefferson Davis, and yet the State still repudiates, as well, after the first decision, in 1842, as the second in 1853. It is difficult to imagine a more palpable infraction of the constitution, or a clearer violation of every principle of justice than this.

The State prescribes certain forms under which her bonds may issue, she adds to this, in the very *next scotion*, a provision *commanding* the Legislature to designate the judicial tribunals in which suit may be brought on such bonds against the State—those tribunals are designated by the Legislature, namely, the Court of Chancery, with appeal to the High Court of Errors and Appeals of the State; both those tribunals, (including the Chancellor,) have unanimously decided against the State, and a decree is entered for payment of the bonds. And yet the State persists in repudiation, and Jefferson Davis defends her course. When the High Court of Errors and Appeals of Mississippi first decided this question, it was composed of Chief Justice Sharkey, and Justices Turner and Trotter (one of the framers of the Constitution). When, again, in 1851, suit was brought against the State on one of these repudiated Union Bank bonds, and a decree for its payment rendered by the Chancellor, that decree, on full argument on appeal, was unanimously confirmed by the highest judicial tribunal of the State, composed entirely of different judges, namely, Chief Justice Smith, and Justices Yerger and Fisher. Here then are eight Judges, all chosen by the people of Mississippi, concurring in 1842, as well as in 1853, as to the validity of these bonds, and yet Jefferson Davis justifies their repudiation. The Judges of Mississippi all take an oath to support the constitution, and it is made their duty to interpret it, and especially this very clause: the Legislature is confined to law making, and forbidden to exercise any judicial power; the expounding this supplemental law, and the provisions under which it was enacted, is exclusively a judicial power, and yet the Legislature *usurps* this power, repudiates the bonds of the State, and the acts of three preceding Legislatures, and the decision of the highest tribunals of the State, Jefferson Davis sustains this repudiation, and the British public are asked to take new Confederate bonds, issued by the same Jefferson Davis, and thus to sanction, and encourage, and offer a premium for repudiation. These so-called Confederate bonds are issued in open violation of the constitution of the United States, they are absolute nullities, they are tainted with treason, they never can or will be paid, and yet they are to be thrust on the British public under the sanction of the same great repudiator Jefferson Davis, who applauds the non-payment of the Mississippi bonds, and thus condemns hundreds of innocent holders, including widows and orphans, to want and misery. Talk about *faith*, about *honour*, about *justice*, and the *sanctity of contracts.* Why, if such flagrant outrages, such atrocious crimes, can be sustained by the great public of any nation, small indeed must be the value of their bonds, which rests exclusively on good faith.

Suppose some astute lawyer could find some informality in the law authorizing the issue and sale of the bonds representing the British consols; would any member of either House propose in Parliament to repudiate such bonds, and would not such a motion cause his immediate expulsion? Yet, this is what the Legislature of Mississippi has done, what Jefferson Davis approves and applauds, and what *he says*, the "English Government" *has done.*

The London "Times" has heretofore quoted the proceedings of the Legislature of Mississippi in 1839, approving the sale of these bonds and eulogizing the transaction. It has also referred to the Message of Governor McNutt, of 1841, nearly three years after the sale of the bonds, first recommending their repudiation, and to the resolutions of the

Legislature of Mississippi of that date, affirming the legality of these bonds and the duty of the State to pay them. As these resolutions are of great importance, and ought to have closed the whole controversy, I will state, (what is shown by the Journals of the Senate and the House), that they passed both Houses, in great part *unanimously*, and for the remainder, by large majorities. [Sen. Jour. p. 312,] [House Jour. p. 416-17, 249, 324 to 329].

The objections made by Governor McNutt in 1841, were as follows:—.

"1st. The Bank of the United States is prohibited by its Charter from purchasing such stock either directly or indirectly.

"2nd. It was fraudulent on the part of the Bank, inasmuch as the contract was made in the name of an individual, when in fact, it was for the benefit of the Bank, and payment was made with its funds.

"3rd. The sale was illegal, inasmuch as the bonds were sold on a credit.

"4th. Interest to the amount of about $170,000 having accrued on those bonds before the purchase money was stipulated to be all paid, the bonds were in fact sold at less than their par value, in direct violation of the Charter of the Bank." (House Journal, p. 25).

It will here be remarked, that the great objection now urged by Jefferson Davis against these bonds, namely, that the act under which they were alleged to have been issued was unconstitutional, is *not enumerated* by Governor McNutt. Surely if such an objection existed to the payment of the bonds, it must have found a place in this celebrated message. Is not this conclusive proof, that this constitutional objection was a mere afterthought and pretext of Jefferson Davis and his associate repudiators?

Let us examine the Governor's objections—As to the 1st and 2nd. The Bank did not make the purchase—The contract was made by an individual, although the performance was guaranteed by the Bank. As this is a mere technical objection, surely the Bank guarantee, even if void, could not affect the contract itself. 2nd. The transaction, even if made by the Bank, was not in *stock,* but a *loan* made upon *bonds.* 3rd. The right of the Bank to do this act, is immaterial, if the money was paid, as in this case, the bonds received, payable to bearer, and passed for value, into the hands of *bonâ fide* holders. What an objection to the refunding the money—that, although it was received, the purchaser of the bonds had no right to buy them, and therefore the *bonâ fide* holders should lose the money. It might have been in violation of its Charter for the Bank to purchase the bonds, but it was "*fraudulent,*" when the money was received by the State, to retain it, on the allegation, that the Bank could not legally make the purchase, especially when the bonds, in the meantime, had passed into the hands of *bonâ fide* holders. As to the 3rd objection. As the money was paid, before the objection was made, and the Union Bank authorised to draw *at once* for the amount, at a point beyond the limits of the State, which it did do, and realized a large premium on the exchange, and profit on the transaction, the objection is as unfounded in law, as it is in morals or good faith; especially as the bonds were payable to bearer, upon their face, in exact conformity to the law, and had passed, for value, into the hands of *bonâ fide* holders. Besides, there was no such restriction in the Charter. The only restriction in the supplement was, that they should not be sold *below par.* Suppose the bonds for five millions of dollars had been sold for five millions and a half, payable in sixty days, and the money paid at the time, it is equally absurd and fraudulent to contend, that for such a reason, the whole money could be retained, and bonds repudiated. As to the 4th objection, the original 5th section which passed two successive Legislatures, did not require that the bonds should not be sold for "less than their par value." If then, as contended by Jefferson Davis, the supplemental act containing this provision, was unconstitutional, null and void, then no such restriction existed, and the sale was valid under the original act. But the truth is, the bonds were not sold *below par*, but *above par* as shown by the High Court of Errors and Appeals of Mississippi in the decision hereafter quoted by me. Indeed, all these four objections of the Governor, as well as those of Jefferson Davis, are shown, in that decision to be as unfounded in fact, as they were in law or morals.

But suppose the bonds were sold below par, that is that the State had lost $170,000, or less than four per cent., on bonds for five millions of dollars. Was that a just or valid ground for repudiating the whole, principal and interest? The plea of *usury* is always disgraceful, even if true, especially where the security was negotiable to bearer and had passed, for full value, into the hands of *bonâ fide* holders. But if such a plea is disgraceful to individuals, what shall be said when it is made on behalf of a State? And what shall be thought of those who make such an objection? What of a Governor, or of a United States Senator, who urges such objections on behalf of a State? Do we not feel as if the State were some miserable culprit, on trial, and some pettifogging lawyer was endeavouring to screen him from punishment, by picking a flaw in the indictment. Yet such are the pleas in behalf of a State, urged by Governor McNutt and Senator Jefferson Davis. On reference to the letter before referred to, of Jefferson Davis, it will be found that he does not confine himself to the Constitutional objections. In his first letter, before quoted of 25th May, 1849, Mr. Jefferson Davis says, "Those bonds were purchased by a Bank then tottering to its fall--purchased in violation of the Charter of the Bank, or fraudulently by concealing the transaction under the name of an individual, as may best suit those concerned, purchased in violation of the terms of the law under which the bonds were issued, and in disregard of the Constitution of Mississippi, of which the law was an infraction." These positions are deliberately repeated by Jefferson Davis, in his second letter, before referred to, of the 29th August, 1849. That is, the State should pay *none* of the money received, because the purchaser, as alleged, had no right to buy the bonds—and because the sale was, as erroneously stated, an infraction of the law, that is, *usurious*, or a sale below par. He insist the money was not received by the State, because, he says, "Mississippi had no bank, and could not have a bank of issue, because forbidden by the tenth section of the first article of the United States Constitution—'no State shall emit bills of credit.'" Surely Mr. Davis must have known, that in the case of the bank of Kentucky, a State bank of issue owned exclusively by the State, it was decided by the Supreme Court of the United States, that such a bank was constitutional, and no politician of the Secession school can object to that decision.—II Peters, 257.* But however this might be, what kind of a plea is this? Why, if, as alleged, by Mr. Davis, Mississippi had violated the Federal Constitution, by establishing a bank of circulation, that therefore the *bonds* of the State should be repudiated. Is it not incredible that a Senator should assume such a position on behalf of his State? But, if this be sound, it clearly follows, that, in as much as the Confederate bonds are issued in plain violation of the constitution of the United States, those bonds should be repudiated; so also if they were sold below par, or if there be any other technical objection. Nor will it avail that the bonds may have passed into the hands of *bonâ fide* holders, for, Mr. Jefferson Davis says, in his letter of the 29th August, 1849, "If the bonds have passed into the hands of innocent holders, the fact does not

* A similar decision was made by the same Court in the case of Darrington *v.* State Bank of Alabama, 13 Howard, 12. But if the Bank could not issue notes, it would still be constitutional, as a Bank of exchange, discount, and deposit, like the Bank of Commerce, New York, and many others having no circulation.

vary the legal question, as the purchaser could not acquire more than the seller had to dispose of." And again, he says, referring to the alleged inability of the first purchaser to buy the bonds, "The claim of foreign holders is as good, but no better than that of the first purchaser." It is difficult to say, which is most astounding, the law, or the morals of this position. At all events "the foreign holders" of Confederate bonds, are informed by Jefferson Davis, that this is the law. Indeed it is a singular coincidence, that one of the objections made to the payment of the Union bank bonds by the Governor, was, as he alleged "the monstrous assumption of power on the part of the bank, in seeking to monopolize the *cotton crop* of the State, and becoming a *factor* and *shipper* of our great staple." —(Senate Journals, 29.) Why, this is what is being attempted by these Confederate cotton bonds, although the State rights strict constructionists of slavedom, would in vain look for any clause in their so-called constitution, authorizing any such transactions in cotton. And here, let me say, that the objection of a Senator from Mississippi to the payment of her bonds, that, in issuing them, her Governor and Legislature had violated *their own constitution*, proposes to cure one fraud, by commiting another, far more stupendous. The bonds were issued by the highest Legislative and Executive functionaries of the State, the broad seal of the State attached, the bonds sold, and the money received. In such a case, there is a legal, as well as a moral estoppel, forbidding such a plea, for, by the English, as well as by the American doctrine, an estoppel excludes the truth, whenever such proof would enable the party, who obtained money on false pretences, to commit a fraud on third persons, by disproving his own averment. This is not a mere technical rule, but one which is based upon experience, and sustained by the most exalted morality.

I have given the several objections made by Governor McNutt and Senator Davis to the payment of these bonds, with one exception. This will be found in the following extract from the executive message of Governor McNutt, p. 502, "The bank, I have been informed, has hypothecated these bonds, and borrowed money upon them of the Baron Rothschild; the blood of Judas and Shylock flows in his veins, and he unites the qualities of both his countrymen. He has mortgages on the silver mines of Mexico and the quicksilver mines of Spain. He has advanced money to the Sublime Porte, and taken as security a mortgage upon the holy city of Jerusalem, and the sepulchre of our Saviour. It is for the people to say, whether he shall have a mortgage upon our cotton fields and make serfs of our children." I trust the Baron will have the good sense to smile at such folly, and realize, how universally, at least throughout the North, the malice and dishonesty of these suggestions was condemned and repudiated. We have no such prejudices, worthy only of the dark ages, against "God's chosen people," "the descendants of the patriarchs and prophets," and the "countrywomen of the mother of our Lord."

Mississippi was the *first* repudiating state; A. G.

McNutt, the *first* repudiating Governor, and Jefferson Davis, the *first* repudiating Senator. As another evidence of the incredible extent to which the public sentiment of that day was debased, I quote the following passage from Governor McNutt's message of 1840, proposing to repeal the Bank Charters, and to *legalize* the *forgery* of their notes—"The issuing of paper money, in contravention of the repealing act, could be effectually checked by the abrogation of all laws making it penal to forge such paper."—Sen. Jour. p. 53. Surely, nothing, but the fell spirit of slavery, could have dictated such a sentiment.

But this whole question has been twice unanimously decided by the highest judicial tribunal of Mississippi, against the State, and every point made by Governor McNutt and Jefferson Davis, overruled by the Court. One of these decisions was in January term, 1842, more than seven years before the date of Jefferson Davis' letters, and the other was at April term, 1853, nearly four years subsequently.

The first decision at January term, 1842, is in the case of Campbell et al *v.* Mississippi Union Bank, 6 Howard, 625 to 683. In this case it was pleaded "that the charter of the Mississippi Union Bank was not enacted and passed by the Legislature, in compliance with the provisions of the Constitution of the State, in this, that the supplemental act of 15th February, 1838, the same being a law to raise a loan of money, on the credit of the State, was not published and submitted to the succeeding Legislature according to the provisions of the Constitution in 9th section, 7th article." Here the direct constitutional question was presented, requiring the decision of the Court. The case was most elaborately argued on both sides The able and upright circuit Judge, Hon. B. Harris, had decided that the supplemental act was constitutional, and the bonds valid, and the High Court of Errors and Appeals of Mississippi, after full argument on both sides, unanimously affirmed that decision. In delivering the opinion of this highest judicial tribunal of the State, and the one designated by the Legislature in 1833, under the *mandatory* clause of the Constitution, Chief Justice Sharkey said,

"The second plea, is, in substance, that the act sup-
"plemental to the charter of the Union Bank, was
"not agreed to by a majority of each House of the
"Legislature, and entered on the Journals with the
"yeas and nays, and referred to the next succeeding
"Legislature after publication in the newspapers,
"according to the provisions of the 9th section of the
"7th article of the Constitution; but the said supple-
"mental act made material alterations in the original
"act, and was only passed by one Legislature, and
"that no loan of money can be raised on the faith of
"the State without the assent of two Legislatures
"given in the manner prescribed by the Constitution."
—"I shall then proceed to notice the Constitutional
"provision, and to inquire by an application of it to
"the Bank charter, whether the position can be sus-
"tained. The 9th section of the 7th article, (of the
"Constitution) is in these words. 'No law shall ever

" be passed to raise a loan of money on the credit of " the State, for the payment or redemption of any " loan or debt, unless such law be proposed in the " Senate or House of Representatives, and be agreed " to by a majority of the members of each House, and " entered on their Journals, with the yeas and nays " taken thereon, and be referred to the next succeed- " ing Legislature, and published for three months " previous to the next regular election, in three news- " papers of the State, and unless a majority of each " branch of the Legislature, so elected after such " publication, shall agree to pass such law, and in " such case, the yeas and nays shall be taken, and " entered on the Journals of each House.'

"The 5th section of the original act provides— " 'That in order to facilitate the said Union bank for " the said loan of fifteen million five hundred thou- " sand dollars, the faith of this State be and is hereby " pledged both for the security of the capital and " interest,' &c. It appears that the original charter " in which this provision is contained, was passed in " accordance with the provision in the Constitution. " The supplemental act makes no alteration whatever " in regard to this section. It changes in some " respects the mere details of the original charter, in " the mode of carrying the Corporation into successful " operation, and authorizes the Governor to subscribe " for the stock on the part of the State. The object " of the pledge is not changed, on the contrary, the " supplemental act was passed in aid of the original " design. In applying the constitutional test to the

"5th section, I am not able to perceive any reason "which to me seems sufficient to justify the conclu- "sion that it is unconstitutional."

"The plea presents no bar to the action."

Justices Turner and Trotter concurred.

Mr. Howard, the distinguished State reporter, gives, in the heading of the case, the following as the decision of the Court. "The act supplemental to the Charter of the Union Bank, being in aid of the Charter, and changing the same only in some of the mere details, is a constitutional act."

The supplemental act, we have seen, was not, in the language of the Constitution, a law "*to raise a loan of money on the credit of the State,*" that act had already passed two successive Legislatures, and was unchanged by the supplement, which merely modified some of the details of the Bank Charter; such was the the fact, and such the decree of the inferior Court, such was the unanimous decision of the highest judicial tribunal of the State, to which *the final adjudication* had been assigned, by a mandatory provision of the Constitution.

Surely this decision should have settled the question. But it did not. Jefferson Davis, notwithstanding his professed desire to submit this question to the final decree of the Courts of the State, persisted, as we have seen, in 1849, in repudiating these bonds, at a period more than seven years after this decision of 1842, and still persevered, after the second similar adjudication of 1853.

The Governor, A. G. McNutt, who had signed the laws authorizing these bonds, and the bonds themselves, anticipating the decision of the Court (as he indicates in his message,) in favour of "the holders of certain bonds heretofore issued to the Planters' and Union Bank," recommends the Legislature, in his message of January, 1842, to create a "revenue court," the judge of which shall be appointed "by the Executive or Legislature" to which such cases should be transferred.—Sen. Jour. p. 22. Thus the case, on the bonds, was to be taken from the high tribunal, (where it was then pending,) created by the Constitution, and chosen by the people, and transferred to a revenue judge to be appointed by the repudiating Governor or Legislature of 1842, of course a mere executive parasite, or legislative minion, placed on the bench to repudiate the bonds. Fortunately, such an appointment was forbidden expressly by the Constitution, and would have been disregarded by the Court; so this attempted usurpation failed.

The Governor says in that message, "It never was intended by the framers of the Constitution, that every public creditor should be permitted to harass the State at pleasure by vexatious suits—Neither the judgment of a Court nor the decree of the Chancellor *can be obligatory on the Legislature*," &c. —p. 17.

In conformity with this recommendation of the Governor, the Legislature passed a series of resolutions, declaring that "the Legislature is the exclusive judge of the objects for which money shall be raised and appropriated by its authority," &c.—that the Legislature has no right to "levy or appropriate money for the purpose of executing the object of a law, by them deemed repugnant to, or unauthorized by the Constitution," that the "Supplemental (Union Bank) Bill is unconstitutional," that "the bonds delivered by said Bank, and by it sold to Nicholas Biddle on the 18th August, 1838, are not binding upon the State," &c.—Acts of 1842, ch. 127. But, unfortunately for these positions, the Constitution of the State had deprived the Legislature of all "judicial power," it had vested this power exclusively in "the Courts," it had, in the very case of all bonds of the State, required and commanded the Legislature to designate the *Courts* in which such cases should be decided; it had, by the Act of 1833, passed in obedience to the imperative mandate of the Constitution, referred all such cases to the decision of the Court of Chancery, with appeal to the High Court of Errors and Appeals, it had made their decision conclusive, it had already appropriated the money, to pay *all such decrees*, and made it the *duty* of the Governor to command the Auditor to draw his warrant on the Treasurer for payment; this was the constitution and the law when these bonds were issued and sold in 1838—such was the *contract* of the State, in regard to which, the Federal Constitution declares, "no State shall pass any law impairing the obligation of contracts"—which clause has been uniformly held by all the Federal as well as State Courts, to apply to contracts of a State—and yet, in flagrant defiance of the highest duties and the most sacred obligations, the Legislature passed these resolutions, to nullify the anticipated decisions of the Court. We have seen, however, that this Executive and Legislative usurpation was ineffectual. The Court stood firm, not a single Judge wavered, and, by a unanimous decree, reversed the Legislative and Executive repudiation – vindicated the majesty of the Law and the Constitution—upheld the sacred cause of truth and justice—resisted the popular phrensy, and defied the unprincipled demagogues, by whom the people of the State had been deceived and deluded. It was a noble spectacle, when those three upright and fearless Judges, Sharkey, Turner, and Trotter, entered the temple of justice, and declared to the people, by whose ballots they were chosen, that the State was bound to pay these bonds, and decreed accordingly. The same sublime scene, was re-enacted, by a similar decree, in a suit against the State, on one of these bonds, by the same Court, in 1853, then composed of different Judges—Smith, Yerger, and Fisher. And not one Judge or Chancellor of the State ever wavered. Amid all this heaven-daring iniquity, thank God! the judicial ermine was unstained. Whilst constrained to denounce the repudiating Legislature, Governor, and *Senator* of Mississippi, let me point to another green spot amid the moral waste and desolation of that dreadful period.

With scarcely an exception, the *Bar of Mississippi* was true to the cause of honour, law and justice. They knew the objections of McNutt and Davis were wretched pretexts, and they vindicated the reputation of that noble profession, which, in all ages, has been the champion of Constitutional liberty. They were men of the same stamp as their illustrious English ancestry, Hampden, Sidney and Russell, whose names cover the map of my country, and whose deeds have exalted the character of man; and although the blood of our anti-repudiating heroes, did not flow like that of the British martyrs, as a sacrificial offering on the altar of freedom, they sacrificed ease, and affluence, and ambition, and political preferment, and endured obloquy and reproach. I rejoice in the recollection, that, during this contest, they should have selected a sentence from my address against repudiation, and placed it on their banners, and at the head of their presses in these words,—"The honour of the nation and of every State is the birthright of every American—it is the stainless and priceless jewel of popular sovereignty—it has been preserved unsullied, in all times that are past, through every sacrifice of blood and treasure, and it must be maintained." Aye! and it will yet be maintained. The time will come, when repudiation will be repudiated by Mississippi—when her wretched secession leaders, the true authors of her disgrace and ruin, will be discarded, when her insolent slave holding oligarchy will be overthrown, when the people will break the chains of their imperious masters, and labour, without regard to colour, will be emancipated. *Secession*, *repudiation* and *slavery*, are the same in principle and had the same leaders. Jefferson Davis carried the repudiation banner in 1849, as he now does that of secession and slavery. Secession is a repudiation of law, of constitution, of country, of the flag of our forefathers, and of the Union purchased by their blood. Driven at home, within a circle of fire, which narrows every day, it is crouching before foreign rulers, and imploring their aid to accomplish the ruin of our country. It appeals to their ambition, their avarice, their fears, their hatred of free institutions and of constitutional government. It summons them to these English shores, it unsheaths the imperial sceptre in the House of Commons, denounces the Ministry of England, and dictates the vote of Parliament on the most momentous question in the history of the world. Why, when these sentiments were uttered, I almost expected to see the shades of Burke and Fox, and Pitt and Chatham, and Peel and Wellington, rise in the midst and denounce the degenerate bearer of such a message. What! the British Commons become the supple tools, the obsequious minions, the obedient parasites, to do the bidding of a foreign master, and tremble when his envoy should stamp his foot and wave the imperial banner in the halls of Parliament. From whom was this message, and to whom? Was it to the England of Trafalgar and tho Nile? Was it to the descendants of the men who conquered at Agincourt and Cressy, and changed for ages at Waterloo the destiny of the world? Why Nelson would speak from his monument, and the Iron Duke from his equestrian statue, and forbid the degradation of their country. But there stood the Confederate messenger, delivering the mandate of a foreign Power to the House of

Commons, describing England as a crawling reptile, exalting the Government he professed to represent, as controling the Continent, and fearing lest the Imperial Eagle alone should swoop down upon his prey. And such language, such sentiments! Was I in Billingsgate, that ancient and illustrious institution, so near the House of Parliament? Why, the whole code of morals and of international law was repudiated in a sentence, and our demagogues distanced in the race. Did the envoy echo the voice of his master, when he announced that the American Union must be dissolved by foreign intervention, because, if re-united, it would be too strong and bully the world—therefore France and England combined must strike us when we were supposed to be weak and divided. It is not the author of such ignoble sentiments, that would lead the banner of France, or of England, any where, except to humiliation and disgrace. "Non talis auxilii, nec defensoribus ipsis"—No, when, England seeks leaders, it will not be the sycophants of power, those who worship alternately democracy and autocracy, who slaver over despotism one day with their venom, and the next with their still more loathsome adulation.

But there was a change. The Ministry, and one of an order supposed to be our most deadly foe, spoke. There were some opinions especially, as to the results, in which no American could concur—there was deep devotion to England — but there was also the voice of reason, of justice, of international law —it was not so cosmopolitan as I expected, but the argument of felon force and robber violence was discarded. The scholar, the statesman, the gentleman — the philanthropist addressed the English Commons. Yes, and the nobility of nature also spoke, one who could rise above the reputed prejudices of his order, and do justice to a kindred race of simple Republicans, though they may know neither diadems nor coronets. Such examples exalt and dignify the character of man. They teach us republicans a useful lesson—that those who differ from us as to some of the forms of Government, may most sincerely support that system, which in their judgment will best promote the welfare and happiness of the people. That indeed is the only question. Let England and America work out the problem in peaceful and friendly rivalry. Time and experience will decide the question. If, when slavery is extinguished in our Union, and the only aggressive element of our system is extirpated, we should run a grand and peaceful career of honour and glory, and prosperity, we will want no other argument than the results. The blasphemous doctrine of the divine right of kings was discarded by England in the revolution of 1688. The British throne reposes now on the alleged basis of the welfare and happiness of the people. What form of Government will best promote that end—this is the only question. I believe it is ours—but only with slavery extinguished, and universal education—Schools—*Schools*—SCHOOLS—common schools—*high schools* for all. Education the criterion of the right of suffrage, not property. I do not believe in a Government of ignorance, whether by the rich, or poor, the many, or the few. With the constant and terrible opposing element of slavery, we have certainly achieved stupendous results in three-fourths of a century, and to say that our system has failed, because slavery now makes war upon it, is amazing folly. Why predict, that, when re-united, and with slavery extinguished, we would *bully the world.* Who were our bullies? Who struck down Charles Sumner the senator of Massachussetts, the eminent scholar and orator, on the floor of the Senate, for denouncing the horrors of slavery? A South Carolina Member of Congress, whilst all slavedom approved the deed. Who endeavoured to force slavery on Kansas by murder and rapine, and the forgery of a constitution? Who repealed the Missouri compromise, in order to force slavery upon all the territories of the United States? Who are endeavouring now to dissolve the Union, and spread slavery over all this wide domain! Who conspired to assassinate the American President on his way to Washington? Who murdered in Baltimore the men of Massachusetts on their way to the defence of the Capitol of the Union? Who commenced the conflict by firing upon the starving garrison of Sumpter, and striking down the banner of the Union which floated over its walls? Who, immediately thereafter, announced their resolution to capture Washington, seized the National arms, and forts and dockyards, and vessels, and arsenals, and mints and treasure, and opened the war upon the Federal Government? There is a plain answer to all these questions. It is the Lords of the whip and the chain and the branding iron, who are our bullies; who insist upon forced labour, and repudiate all compensation to the toiling millions of slaves—who repudiate, among slaves, the marital and parental relation, and class them by law as chattels—who forbid emancipation—who make it a crime to teach slaves to write or read—aye, even the Bible—who keep open the interstate slave-trade—(more horrible than the African, making Virginia a human stock farm,) tearing husband from wife, and parents from children—founding a Government boldly announcing the doctrine of *property* in man, based avowedly on the divinity, extension, and perpetuity of slavery —these are our bullies, and when they are overthrown, we shall commence a new career of peaceful progress and advanced civilization. And why sow the seeds of international hatred between England and America? Is war really desired between the two countries, or is it supposed that we will yield to foreign intervention without a struggle? No, the North will rise as one man, and thousands even from the South will join them. The country will become a camp, and the ocean will swarm with our privateers. Rather than submit to dismemberment or secession, which is anarchy and ruin, we will,—we must fight, until the last man has fallen. The Almighty can never prosper such a war upon us. If the views of a foreign Power have been truly represented in Parliament, and such an aggression upon us is contemplated, let him beware, for in such a contest, the political pyramid resting upon its apex, the power of one man, is much more likely to fall, than that which reposes on the broad basis of the will of the people.

But, let me resume the debate. When the ministry had closed, the earnest opponents of slavery, and true friends of England and America, discussed the question. Seldom have such great speeches been heard on any occasion, and the impression made was most profound.

What is it England is asked to recognize? It is a Confederacy, claiming to be a *league of Sovereign and Independent States*, like the old American Confederacy of 1778, abandoned when we formed a nation in 1787. When England, in 1783, recognized the old Confederacy, the recognition was of *each of the several States by name*, as sovereign and independent. Now, applying those principles on the present occasion, to the several seceded States by name. Is Virginia independent? Why all her coasts and sea ports are held by us, so is Norfolk, her commercial capital, more than half her area and white population, and nearly half her territory has been organized as a new State of the Union, and, by the almost unanimous vote of her people, has abolished slavery. Are North and South Carolina, Georgia, Florida, Alabama, and Texas, independent? Why, their whole coast and large portions of the interior are held by our army and navy. Is Tennessee independent? Two-thirds of her territory, as well as her political and commercial capitals, Nashville and Memphis, are held by us. The same thing is true, to a great extent, as to Arkansas. As to Mississippi—her whole sea coast, and her whole river coast, for 500 miles, with the exception of a single point, is held by us, and more than half her territory.* As to Louisiana, we hold three-fourths of her territory, all her sea coast, all her river front on both banks of the Mississippi, except one point, and her great city, New Orleans, the commercial capital of the State and of the South, with four times the population of any other southern city, and with nearly half the free population of the State.† More than three-fourths of the population, as well as area of Louisiana, is held by us, with her political and commercial capital, and yet it is proposed to acknowledge Louisiana as one of these *sovereign and independent States*. How can the so-called Confederacy, claiming to be a league of sovereign and independent States, be recognized as independent, when the States composing that league are not independent? How is Richmond to be reached by an English envoy, or is the blockade to be broken, which is war? How as to slavery? The 331,000 slaves of Louisiana, the three millions of slaves of the seceded States, are emancipated by the proclamation of the President, under the war power uniformly recognized as Constitutional by the Supreme Court of the United States. If these are States of our Union, or are retained by us, slavery has ceased, and the *three millions of slaves are free*. But, if you

* That point, Vicksburg, is now in our possession.

† That point, Port Hudson, is now taken by us, and the whole Mississippi river held by our Government.

acknowledge the Confederate independence, then, these three millions of slaves, so far as England is concerned, are slaves still, and will remain so for ever. To refuse recognition, is to admit the freedom of these slaves— to recognize, is to remand them to bondage, so far as England can accomplish that purpose. Nor is this all—it is to spread slavery over an almost boundless territory, claimed by the South. It is impossible then to escape the conclusion, that, in recognizing the Confederacy, England ranges herself on the side of slavery, and does all she can to maintain and perpetuate it in America. Nor is this all. She violates a great moral rule, and a well settled principle of international law, to maintain and perpetuate slavery in the South. By the law of Nations, the recognition of national independence, is the acknowledgment of the fact of independence. But, we have seen, that the States composing this so called league, are not independent, but are held, to a vast extent by our army and navy, including two-thirds of their area. Never was independence acknowledged under such circumstances, except as an act of war. The acknowledgment then of the Confederate independence, in the present posture of affairs, is, in fact, *a declaration of war by England against the United States without cause or justification.* It would be so universally regarded in the United States, and would instantly *close all dissensions in the North.* If any suppose, that, England, without any just cause, should thus strike us with the iron gauntleted hand, and that we will not resist, let the history of the past answer the question. Nor would the union of France, in such an act, change the result, except that nearly all the loss and sacrifice would fall upon England. Including the slaves and free blacks, there is not a single seceded State, in which an overwhelming majority of the people are not for the Union. Now, by the Federal Constitution, slaves are mentioned only three times, and then not as slaves, but as "*persons,*" and the Supreme Court of the United States, have expressly decided, that slaves, so far as regards the United States, *are persons, and not property.* Groves *versus* Slaughter, 15 Peters, 392. *All persons*, in every State, owe a paramount allegiance to the United States, the rebel masters, as well as their slaves—the Government has a right to their services to suppress the rebellion; and to acknowledge the independence of the South, is to ignore the existence of the slaves, or to treat them, as the South do, as chattels, and not persons. In acknowledging, then, Southern independence, the independence of the *masters*, England expressly recognizes the doctrine of *property in man.* Such a war, proclaimed by England and France against the United States on such grounds, would be a war of their *Governments*—not of their *peoples*, and could have but one termination. As to our recognition of the independence of Texas, it was long after the decisive battle of San Jacinto,—when the Mexican army was destroyed or captured, together with the President, when by treaty he had acknowledged the independence of Texas, and after the Mexican Government, by accepting the advantages stipulated by their President, had, in fact, and in law, ratified the recognition. It was after all this: when the contest was over, not a Mexican vessel on the coast of Texas, nor a Mexican soldier upon her soil, that we recognized the independence of Texas. The case, therefore, is widely different from the present. Let it be remembered, that we hold, not only the mouth of the Mississippi, its great city, the whole of the west bank of that imperial river, but all the east bank, except two points,* thus dissevering Texas, Louisiana, and Arkansas from the rest of the South. Now the area of these three States, is 373,000 square miles, and that of all the remaining seceded States, 396,000 square miles. In holding then the west bank of the Mississippi, we have severed the great artery of the South, which is death.

Returning from this episode, I resume the narrative.

We have seen the repudiating Executive message and repudiating Legislative resolutions of Jan. 1842, and their failure to influence the decision of the Court. And now, we approach another act in the drama. The Court having affirmed the Constitutionality of the Union Bank bonds, and the act of 1833 having directed their payment; the Legislature

* Both these points now in our possession.

of 1844, enacted a new law, in these words—"That hereafter, no judgment or decree of any Court of Law or Equity having jurisdiction of suits against the State, shall be paid by warrants on the Treasurer, or otherwise, without an appropriation by law, any former law or usage to the contrary notwithstanding." The "law and usage" were plain, to pay such decrees, as required by the Law and Constitution; but both were disregarded, and the act of 1833, for all practical purposes, repealed. It remained in part, on the statute book, only to invite to the gambler's game of "odd I win, even you lose"—That is, if, under the act of 1833, there should be a decision in any case in favour of the State, it should be conclusive, but if against the State, the money should not be paid, where (as in the case of these bonds) the Legislature differed from the Court, and had already repudiated its decision. Such was the action of the Legislature in 1842 and 1844. In 1842, it repudiated, in advance, the decision of the Court on these bonds, and, after that decision, repealed so much of the law as required the payment of the decrees of the Court. Now, with a full knowledge of these facts, is it not amazing, incredible, that, several years subsequently, Mr. Jefferson Davis should have declared in his first letter of 1849, "By the constitution and laws of Mississippi, any creditor of the State may bring suit against the State, and test his claim as against an individual; but, conscious that they have no valid claim, they have not sought the remedy," and he repeats this averment, substantially, in his second letter. Now who would have supposed, that more than seven years before the date of Mr. Davis's letters, the highest judicial tribunal of the State, the one designated by the law and the constitution, had already unanimously decided that these bonds were valid, and that the State Legislature, instead of paying the money, had *repealed the appropriation.* But there came a new Court, all chosen by the people, under the wretched system, in many of the States, of an elective judiciary, but unknown to the independent Federal judicial system. A suit was brought in 1851, under the act of 1833, on one of the Union Bank State bonds and coupons before the Chancellor. After elaborate argument, the Chancellor decided against the State, and entered a decree for the payment of the money. The State, as authorized by the law, appealed from this decision to its own High Court of Errors and Appeals, elected by the people.

Surely, it was supposed, that this new Court, so recently chosen by the people, after the Legislative repudiation, would be governed by "*a proper regard for the public interest and public opinion.*" Before the Chancellor, as well as the High Court, all the objections made by Governor McNutt and Senator Davis were earnestly pressed by the Attorney General of the State and Associate Counsel, but in vain; the decision of the Chancellor was against the State, and it was unanimously affirmed by the High Court. This case will be found reported by the State reporter, Johnson *v.* the State, April Term, 1853—3rd Cushman, 625 to 882, (257 pages).

In this case, the bond sued on is given in the record, and will be found an exact copy of that, (heretofore quoted,) under the original act, which had passed two successive Legislatures, the principal as well as coupons, being payable in Federal currency.

On the reverse side of the bond is the following:—

"£450. sterling. The President, Directors, and Co. of the Mississippi Union Bank, do hereby designate the agency of the Bank of the United States in London, as the place of payment of the within bond and interest, and hereby assign and transfer the same for value received to the bearer, principal equal to £450. sterling, and guarantee the payment of the same at the place designated.

S. Gwin, *Cashier.*

H. G. Runnells, *President.*

Mississippi State Bond, No. 91.

Redeemable February 25th, 1850."—As to the place where the bonds was made payable, there could be no objection, for the original, as well as the supplemental act, gave full authority to make the bonds payable abroad. But, as to the objection, that they were said to be payable in sterling, at the rate of four shillings and sixpence to the pound, the answer was, as shown. 1st. That this was the true rate of exchange. 2nd. That the bond was payable in Federal currency, and this was all the bond holder ever asked from the State. As to the allegation, that the bonds were sold below par, the Court showed most conclusively from the facts, and agreed case, that they were sold above par, and their constitutionality was fully affirmed.

The argument of the Attorney General (Glenn) for the State, embraced 32 printed pages; in addition to which, was an elaborate argument by his associate Mr. Stearns. The opinion of Chief Justice Smith embraced 45 pages, the concurring opinion of Justice Yerger 27 pages, and Justice Fisher concurred. The State was not satisfied, but moved for a re-argument, that of Wharton, for the State, embracing 54 pages, and that of Mays, on the same side, 32 pages; but the Court adhered to their decision, and unanimously affirmed the decree of the Chancellor against the State. The decision of the Court in the heading of the case, is thus given by the reporter.

"The bonds might have been legally issued to the bank, by the Governor on the 5th June, 1838, pursuant to the provision of the original charter of the bank, and the faith of the State pledged for the purpose of raising the capital." "The supplement was not void in consequence of not having been passed in conformity with the provisions of the constitution contained in the 7th article, 9th section of that instrument." "The object of the original pledge of the faith of the State, was not changed by the supplemental charter, but it was passed in aid of the original charter." "Campbell *v.* Union Bank, 6 Howard, 625, *cited and confirmed.*" "The liability of the State, under the operation of the charter of the Bank, attached so soon or whenever the bonds were legally executed to the Bank, and the execution of the mortgages, was neither a condition precedent to the pledge of the faith of the State, nor the condition on which the State bonds were to be executed and delivered." "It does not appear from the facts that the bonds were sold for less than their par value. Held that the sale was neither illegal nor void." "If the commissioners in the sale of the bonds received 'sterling money of Great Britain' at the rate of four shillings and sixpence to the pound, that is not such an act on their part, as would avoid the bonds." Here then the whole case was again fully decided in 1853 by the very tribunal, to which Jefferson Davis, in 1849, invited the bond holders. And did he or the State, then yield or pay the obligations. Not at all, but they adhered to the repudiation of these bonds, disregarded and defied the decision of the Court, and have never paid one dollar of principal or interest, and never will, so long as slavery exists in Mississippi.

And now, after the almost unanimous passage of the supplemental Act in 1838, the sanction of the Legislature in 1839 and 1841, the decision of the

Circuit Court and Chancellor, and of the High Court of Errors and Appeals, how strange is the assertion of Mr. Slidell, that "The Union Bank bonds were issued in direct violation of an express constitutional provision." It is a well settled principle of American law, so adjudicated by the State Courts, as well as by the Supreme Court of the United States, that, 1st. To authorize the Court to decide that a law is unconstitutional, the repugnance to the Constitution must be "*plain and palpable.*" 2. That the interpretation given by the *highest Court of a State*, to a State law, or constitution, "*is conclusive.*"* But the truth is, as is proved by Mr. Slidell's own letter, (having never resided in the State), he knew nothing of the subject, or he never would have spoken of Jefferson Davis as "Governor," or alluded to "his administration," when he never held that office. But it is of some moment, at least to the unfortunate bondholders, that the Minister of Jefferson Davis at Paris, *avers now*, that these bonds are *unconstitutional.*

But, Mr. Slidell says, "There is a wide difference between these bonds, and those of the Planters'

* The Supreme Court of the United States, in 2nd Peters, 492, decided that "the judicial department of a State Government is the rightful expositor of its constitutional law"—and the same tribunal has uniformly maintained that such decision is conclusive—5 Cr. 22; 9 Cr. 87; 10 Wheat. 152, 454; 6 Wheat. 119; 4 Pet. 124; 6 Pet. 291; 8 Pet. 220; 16 Pet. 455; 7 How. 812.

bank, for the repudiation of which, neither excuse nor palliation can be offered."

Now, in a subsequent letter, I will prove conclusively, from authentic documents, that the State of Mississippi has, *most effectually*, repudiated those bonds also, and that Jefferson Davis has sustained that repudiation.

In the case, also, of another slave holding State, I will prove, from the public documents, that Jefferson Davis volunteered to sustain her in the repudiation of her State bonds, in a case more atrocious if possible, than that of Mississippi. As Jefferson Davis is now at the head of a slave holding rebellion, endeavouring to destroy the Government of my country, and is now also engaged in selling worthless Confederate bonds in this market, I have deemed it my duty to make this publication.

R. J. WALKER.

Note.—Since this pamphlet went to press, the supposed menacing message from the Continent, has been officially contradicted. Surely, however, I had a right to conclude, after such solemn assurances from a Member to the House, that, although acting in the character of a Confederate messenger, and avowing such ignoble sentiments, he spoke the truth on that point.

R. J. W.

JEFFERSON DAVIS.

REPUDIATION,

RECOGNITION AND SLAVERY.

LETTER

No. II.

OF

HON. ROBERT J. WALKER, M.A.

COUNSELLOR AT LAW IN THE SUPREME COURT OF THE UNITED STATES,
LATE LAW REP. MI., SENATOR OF THE UNITED STATES,
SECRETARY OF THE TREASURY, COMMISSIONER TO CHINA,
GOVERNOR OF KANSAS, ETC. ETC.

LONDON:
WILLIAM RIDGWAY, 169, PICCADILLY. W.
1863.

those bonds? The principal and interest now due on those bonds exceed $5,000,000, (£1,000,000,) and yet, for a quarter of a century, the State has not paid one dollar of principal or interest. 2. The State, by act of the Legislature (Ch. 17), referred the question of taxation for the payment of those bonds to the vote of the people, and their decision was adverse. As there was no fund available for the payment, except one to be derived from taxation, this popular vote, (to which the question was submitted by the Legislature,) was a decision of the State for repudiation, and against payment. 3. The State, at one time, (many years after the sale of the bonds), had made them receivable in purchase of certain State lands, but, as this was "at three times its current value," as shown by the London *Times*, in its article heretofore quoted by me, this was only another form of repudiation. 4. When a few of the bondholders commenced taking small portions of these lands in payment, because they could get nothing else, the State repealed the law, (Ch. 22), and provided no substitute. 5. The State, by law, deprived the bondholders of the stock of the Planters' Bank ($2,000,000), and of the sinking fund pledged to the purchasers for the redemption of these bonds when they were sold by the State. Surely there is here ample evidence of repudiation and bad faith.

The bonds issued by the State of Mississippi to the Planters' Bank, were based upon a law of the

State, and affirmed, by name, in a specific provision of the State constitution of 1832. The State, through its agent, received the money, and loaned it to the citizens of the State, and the validity of these obligations is conceded by Mr. Slidell and Mr. Davis.

These bonds were for $2,000,000, bearing an interest of six per cent per annum, and were sold at a premium of 13½ per cent. For those bonds, besides the premium, the State received $2,000,000 of stock of the Planters' Bank, upon which, up to 1838, the State realized ten per cent dividends, being $200,000 per annum. In January, 1841, the Legislature of Mississippi *unanimously* adopted resolutions, affirming the validity of these bonds, and the duty of the State to pay them. (Sen. Jour. 314.) In his message to the Legislature of 1843, Governor Tucker says, "On the 1st of January, 1838, the State held stock in the Planters' Bank for $2,000,000, which stock had prior to that time yielded to the State a dividend of $200,000 per annum. I found also the first instalment of the bonds issued on account of the Planters' Bank $125,000, due and unpaid, as well as the interest for several years on said bonds." (Sen. Jour. 25.) The Planters' Bank, (as well as the State), by the express terms of the law, was bound for the principal and interest of these bonds. Now, in 1839, Mississippi passed an Act (Acts, ch. 42), "to transfer the stock now held by the State in the Planters' Bank, and invest the same in stock of the Mississippi Railroad Company." By the first section of this act, the Governor was directed to subscribe for $2,000,000 of Stock in the Railroad Company for the State, and to pay for it by transferring to the Company the Planters' Bank Stock, which had been secured to the State by sale of the Planters' Bank bonds. The 10th section released the Planters' Bank from the obligation to provide for the payment of these bonds or interest. Some enlightened members, including Judge Gholson, afterwards of the Federal court, protested against this act as unconstitutional, by impairing the obligation of contracts, and as a fraud on the bond-holders.

They say in this protest, "The money which paid "for the Stock proposed to be transferred from the "Planters' Bank to the Mississippi Railroad Com- "pany, was, under the provisions of the charter, "obtained by loans on the part of the State, for the "payment of which, the Stock, in addition to the "faith of the Government, was pledged to the holders "of the bonds of the State. By the terms of the "contract between the Commissioners on the part "of the State and the purchasers of the bonds, the "interest on the loans is required to be paid semi- "annually out of the semi-annual dividends *accruing* "*upon the said stock*; and the surplus of such divi- "dends, after paying the said interest, is to be con- "verted into a *sinking fund* for the payment and "liquidation of said loans. The bill, as the title

" purports, simply provides for the transfer of the " Stock now held by the State in the Planters' Bank, " and that the same shall be invested in the Stock " of the Mississippi Railroad Company, leading from " Natchez to Canton, which has banking privileges " to twice the amount of capital stock paid in. The " transferring of the Stock and dividends to another " irresponsible corporation, and the appropriation of " the same to the construction of a road, is a viola- " tion of and impairing the obligation of the contract " made and entered into with the purchasers or " holders of the bonds of the State, under a solemn " act of the Legislature. If it should be thought " that a people, composed of so much virtue, honour, " and chivalry, as the noble and generous Missis- " sippians, would disdain, and consequently refrain " from repealing or violating their plighted faith, it " may be answered, that the faith of the State, " solemnly and sacredly pledged by an Act of the " Legislature, with all the formality and solemnity " of a constitutional law, is violated by the provisions " of this very bill under consideration. The faith of " the State is pledged to the holders of the bonds, " by the original and subsequent acts incorporating " the Planters' Bank as solemnly as national or " legislative pledges can be made, that the stock and " dividends accruing thereon shall be faithfully ap- " propriated to the redemption and payment of said " loans and all interest thereon, as they respectively " become due; the appropriation of this fund to "another purpose, is therefore a violation of the "faith of the State." House Jour. 443.

Thus, was it, that the stock of the bank, which for so many years had been yielding a dividend far exceeding the interest on the loan, and which stock had been pledged for the redemption of the loan, was diverted to the building of a railroad, which never did or could yield a single dollar, and the Company soon became insolvent. By another clause of this act of 1839, the Planters' Bank which, by the loan act, was made responsible (together with the State,) for the payment of these bonds, was released from the obligation to make such payments.

And now what is the answer of Jefferson Davis on this subject? He says in his letter of the 25th May, 1849, before quoted—

"A smaller amount is due for what are termed "Planters' Bank bonds of Mississippi. These evi-"dences of debt, as well as the coupons issued to "cover accruing interest, are receivable for State "lands; and no one has a right to assume they will "not be provided for otherwise, by or before the "date at which the whole debt becomes due." To this the London *Times* replied in its editorial of the 13th July, 1849, before quoted, as follows:—

"The assurance in this statement that the Planters' "Bank, or non-repudiated bonds, are receivable for "State lands, requires this addition, which Mr. Jef-"ferson Davis has omitted, that they are only so "receivable upon lands being taken at three times

"its current value. The affirmation afterwards
"that no one has a right to assume that these bonds
"will not be fully provided for before the date at
"which the principal falls due, is simply to be met
"by the fact, that portions of them fell due in 1841
"and 1846, and that on these, as well as on all the
"rest, both principal and interest remain wholly
"unpaid."

Mr. Davis' "palliation and excuse" for the non-payment of these bonds was: 1st. That the principal was not due. If this were true it would be no excuse for the non-payment of the semi-annual interest. But the statement of Jefferson Davis as to the principal was not true, as shown by the *Times*, and as is clear upon the face of the law. Then, as as to the lands. The bonds, principal and interest, were payable in money, and it was a clear case of repudiation to substitute lands. But when, as stated by the *Times*, this land was only receivable "*at three times its current value*," Mr. Davis' defence of the repudiation of the Planters' Bank bonds by Mississippi, is exposed in all its deformity. When, however, we reflect, as heretofore shown, that the law authorising the purchase of these lands by these bonds was repealed, and the bond-holders left without any relief, and the proposition for taxation to pay the bonds definitively rejected, it is difficult to imagine a case more atrocious than this.

The whole debt, principal and interest, now due by the State of Mississippi, including the Planters' and Union Bank bonds, exceeds $11,250,000 (£2,250,000). Not a dollar of principal or interest has been paid by the State for more than a fourth of a century on any of these bonds. The repudiation is complete and final, so long as slavery exists in Mississippi. Now, would it not seem reasonable that, before Mississippi and the other Confederate States, including Florida and Arkansas, ask another loan from Europe, that they should first make some provision for debts now due, or, at least, manifest a disposition to make some arrangement for it at some future period. If a debtor fails to meet his engagements, especially if he repudiates them on false and fraudulent pretexts, he can borrow no more money, and the same rule surely should apply to states or nations. Nor can any pledge of property not in possession of such a borrower, or, if so, not placed in the hands of the lender, change the position. It is, (even if the power to pay exists,) still a question of good faith, and where that has been so often violated, all subsequent pledges or promises should be regarded as utterly worthless.

The *Times*, in reference to the repudiation of its Union Bank bonds by Mississippi, and the justification of that act by Jefferson Davis, says:—

"Let it circulate throughout Europe, that a "member of the United States Senate in 1849 has "openly proclaimed, that at a recent period the "Governor and Legislative Assemblies of his own

"State deliberately issued fraudulent bonds for five "millions of dollars to 'sustain the credit of a "rickety bank;' that the bonds in question, having "been hypothecated abroad to innocent holders, "such holders have not only no claim against the "community by whose executive and representatives "this act was committed, but that they are to be "taunted for appealing to the verdict of the civilized "world rather than to the judgment of the legal "officers of the State by whose functionaries they "have been already robbed; and that the ruin of "toil-worn men, of women, of widows, and of chil- "dren, and the 'crocodile tears' which that ruin "has occasioned, is a subject of jest on the part of "those by whom it has been accomplished, and then "let it be asked if any foreigner ever penned a libel "on the American character equal to that against "the people of Mississippi by their own Senator."

Such was the opinion then expressed by the London *Times* of Jefferson Davis and of the repudiation advocated by him. It was denounced as *robbery*, "the ruin of toil-worn men, of women, of widows, "and of children." And what is to be thought of the "*faith*" of a so-called Government, which has chosen this repudiator as their chief, and what of the value of the Confederate bonds now issued by him? Why, the legal tender notes of the so-called Confederate Government, fundable in a stock bearing eight per cent. interest, is now worth in gold at their own capital of Richmond, less than ten cents on the dollar, (2*s* on the £,) whilst in two-thirds of their territory such notes are utterly worthless; and it is TREASON for any citizen of the United States, North or South, or any ALIEN resident there, to deal in them, or in Confederate bonds, or in the cotton pledged for their payment. No form of Confederate bonds, or notes, or stock, will ever be recognized by the Government of the United States, and the cotton pledged by slaveholding traitors for the payment of the Confederate bonds is all forfeited for treason, and confiscated to the Federal Government by Act of Congress. As our armies advance, this cotton is either burned by the retreating rebel troops, or seized by our forces, and shipped and sold from time to time, for the benefit of the Federal Government. By reference to the census of 1860, it will be seen, that three-fourths of the whole cotton crop was raised in States, (now held by the Federal army and navy,) touching the Mississippi and its tributaries, and all the other ports, are either actually held or blockaded by the Federal forces. The traitor pledge of this cotton is, then, wholly unavailing; the bonds are utterly worthless; they could not be sold at any price in the United States, and those who force them on the London Market, in the language of the *Times*, before quoted, will only accomplish *"the ruin of "toil-worn men, of women, of widows, and of chil-"dren."*

But the advocacy of repudiation by Jefferson Davis has not been confined to his own State, as I shall proceed to demonstrate in my next letter.

R. J. WALKER.

JEFFERSON DAVIS.

REPUDIATION

OF

ARKANSAS BONDS.

LETTER III.

OF

HON. ROBERT J. WALKER, M.A.

COUNSELLOR AT LAW IN THE SUPREME COURT OF THE UNITED STATES,
LATE LAW REP. MI., SENATOR OF THE UNITED STATES,
SECRETARY OF THE TREASURY, COMMISSIONER TO CHINA,
GOVERNOR OF KANSAS, ETC. ETC.

LONDON:
WILLIAM RIDGWAY, 169, PICCADILLY. W.
1864.

this very question was brought directly for adjudication, affirming the constitutionality and validity of these Bonds. When it is recollected, also, that this was the Court designated by the constitution and laws of Mississippi, as the tribunal to which the ultimate decision of this question was referred, the wretched character of this pretext must be at once perceived. Mr. Davis's two repudiating letters, were published by him in the spring and summer of 1849, yet one of these decisions by the highest judicial tribunal of Mississippi, quoted by me, affirming the validity and constitutionality of these very Bonds, was made in 1842, and again unanimously re-affirmed in 1853. But, still, Mr. Davis adhered to the same position. As to the Planters' Bank Bonds, however, the repudiation of which was shown to have been justified by Mr. Davis, there never was, even a pretext, that they were illegal or unconstitutional. Nor is there any force in the suggestion, that these questions were decided before Mr. Davis came into public life. They were *continuous* questions, constantly discussed in the press and before legislative and judicial tribunals. And, we have seen, even as late as 1853, four years succeeding Mr. Davis's repudiating letters, the second decision was made by the highest judicial tribunal of Mississippi, re-affirming the validity and constitutionality of these Bonds.

But I will now cite another instance of the advocacy of repudiation by Mr. Jefferson Davis, still more flagitious than that of Mississippi. It was that of the State Bonds of Arkansas, the validity and constitutionality of which never has been disputed. A brief history of this transaction is as follows. In 1830, James Smithson, an eminent and wealthy citizen of London, in the kingdom of Great Britain, died, bequeathing, by his last will and testament, the whole of his property to the United States of America, in trust, to found at Washington, under the name of "the Smithsonian Institution," an establishment "for the increase and diffusion of knowledge among men." After some delay, the Congress of the United States, in 1836, passed an Act, accepting the trust, and pledging the faith of the Government for the faithful application of the money to the noble purpose designated by the illustrious donor. Under this Act, Richard Rush, one of our most distinguished citizens, who had been minister to England and to France, and had held the position of Secretary of State and of the Treasury, at Washington, was sent by the Government to London, to obtain from the Court of Chancery the fund, amounting to over $500,000. It is usual, in the proceedings of the English Court of Chancery, when funds, under circumstances like these, are bequeathed to trustees for scientific or charitable purposes, not to part with the money to the trustee, except upon his filing in Court absolute security for the faithful fulfilment of the trust. In this case, however, the High Court of

Chancery in England, considering that to imply any laches or neglect of a trust so sacred, on the part of the Government of the United States, was an idea not to be entertained, did, by their decree, without any security, hand over all the money to the Government of the United States, to be appropriated to the purpose designated by the donor, receiving only the pledge given by the Congress of the United States, for the faithful appropriation of the money. Now, if there ever was any obligation, that would be considered sacred by the whole civilized world, it was this, and most faithfully has the Government of the United States executed this trust. Nay, it has done much more; it has granted forty acres of ground, belonging to the Government, in the city of Washington, gratuitously, for the erection of the buildings for this noble Institution, which grounds, with the buildings upon them, erected by the Government, are worth largely more than the whole bequest. Not only has the Government done this, but, upon the whole fund received from Mr. Smithson, it has always punctually paid an interest of 6 per cent. in gold upon the whole sum, and pledged its faith for a similar perpetual payment. It has also largely aided the Institution by contributions to its museum, collections, and library, and by the gratuitous services of public officers in its behalf. Such was the Bill passed by Congress in 1846, and which has always been most faithfully executed. So that the Institution is now established upon a permanent basis, and is fulfilling all the great and noble purposes proposed by the illustrious donor. Now, in 1837, this fund was received by the Government of the United States, and invested by the Secretary of the Treasury, Mr. Woodbury, in the 6 per cent. Bonds of the State of Arkansas at par, to the extent of over half a million of dollars. During the same year, Arkansas invested this money in a bank, entitled, "The Real Estate Bank of Arkansas;" and of which the State was the great stockholder. In 1839, this Bank, having loaned out these funds to the citizens of Arkansas, became absolutely and totally insolvent, and has never been able to pay one cent. on the dollar to any of its creditors. In 1839, the State of Arkansas failed to pay the interest on its Bonds, and from that day to this has never paid one dollar either of interest or principal on any of these most sacred obligations.

On the 4th of March, 1845, I became Secretary of the Treasury of the United States, and having taken the deepest interest in this Smithsonian fund, and in its faithful application to the noble purpose of the donor, and inasmuch as one of my predecessors had invested these funds in these Bonds, and the Government had made itself directly responsible for the faithful execution of this trust, I endeavoured to reclaim, as far as possible, this money from the State of Arkansas, and to induce Congress to appropriate its own monies to redeem the pledge of the

Government, and fulfil this trust. My first official action on this subject was as follows. By Act of Congress, 5 per cent. of the nett proceeds of the sales of the public lands in the United States in Arkansas, was payable to that State, for certain purposes designated in the Act. There was, also, an Act of Congress in force, authorizing the Secretary of the Treasury, where there were mutual debts and credits between the Government and any other person, to offset any debt due by any creditor to the United States, against any debt, so far as it would go, due by the United States to such creditor. I interpreted this Act as authorizing me to withhold this 5 per cent. fund from the State of Arkansas, and appropriate it, as far as it would go, in payment of the interest which had accumulated on the Bonds of the State of Arkansas, in which my predecessor, Mr. Woodbury, on behalf of the Government, had invested the Smithsonian Fund; thus saving a small portion of the interest which had accrued on these Bonds. For this act I was violently denounced by the Senators and Representatives of Arkansas in Congress, as also by the Legislature and Governor of the State, and strenuous efforts were made, unsuccessfully, first to induce me to revoke my action, and, secondly, to have it overruled by the Government. But I adhered to it, and declared openly, that if such a breach of trust were consummated, and my action overruled in the premises, I would resign my seat in the

Cabinet. My official action, however, was sustained by an almost unanimous public sentiment of Congress, and of the country. Indeed, beyond the limits of the State of Arkansas, and the circle of the repudiators of Mississippi, my course was sustained and approved.

Now, then, let us see what was the action of Mr. Jefferson Davis on the question of these Arkansas Bonds. On reference to the journals of the House of Representatives, of the Congress of the United States, it appears that Mr. Jefferson Davis took his seat in that body, as one of the members elect from the State of Mississippi, on the 8th of December 1845—p. 56. When the Bill was pending for organizing the Smithsonian Institution, and making good for both principal and interest, the sum bequeathed by Mr. Smithson that had been invested by the Government of the United States in these Arkansas State Bonds, Mr. Jefferson Davis, on the 29th April 1846, as appears by the official proceedings of the House, page 749, moved an amendment: "To add at the end of the "section the following"—"*Provided, however,* That "if the Governor of the State of Arkansas shall "make it appear to the satisfaction of the Attorney-"General of the United States, that he has used "suitable means to obtain from the Real Estate "Bank of the State of Arkansas, payment of the "debt due by said Bank to the State of Arkansas, but "without success, then, and in that case, and until "the arrears due by the said Real Estate Bank shall "have been received into the Treasury of the State "of Arkansas, the said State shall be and is hereby "declared to be absolved from the promises on the "face of her bonds by which the said State here- "tofore pledged her faith for the due payment of "the principal and interest of said bonds." Now, then, it will be remembered, that the legality and constitutionality of these Arkansas State Bonds, never has been disputed. These bonds were issued by the State, under direct authority of law, signed by the Governor, with the broad seal of the State attached, and recognised by the Government of the United States, by the investment of this sacred fund in these obligations. Nay, more, this fund thus received by the State from the Government on these bonds, had been invested, under the law of the State of Arkansas, in a Real Estate Bank created by that State, and the money loaned to the citizens of the State. That State Bank, however, in 1839 became utterly and notoriously insolvent, and never did or could pay one cent in the dollar on its obligations. And, more especially, never did it pay, after 1839, one single cent of the principal or interest upon these State obligations. Now, then, this Institution, in 1846, being absolutely and totally insolvent, its funds having been wasted and squandered without the possibility of recovery, either in whole or in part, Mr. Davis offers this resolution to authorize the State to repudiate its bonds, and that the Government should look only to this insolvent Bank for the payment of the principal and interest on these bonds amounting then to over 700,000 dollars. It was not alleged by Mr. Davis, or by any other person, that these bonds were unconstitutional. No such pretext was ever made even by the State of Arkansas. It was a most atrocious case of open repudiation. And here, it matters not, so far as this question is concerned, what may have been the obligation of the Government of the United States, to make good these funds. That is a totally distinct and independent question. The true and real issue in this case is this, was not the State of Arkansas bound to pay these bonds, both interest and principal as it fell due, in which bonds, by the request and authority of the State, the Government of the United States had invested this Smithsonian fund? This obligation of the State of Arkansas, both moral and legal, is undisputed and indisputable; and yet, Mr. Davis moved the resolution before quoted, absolving the State from the payment of the principal and interest of these bonds, except so far as the assets of her own Bank, then notoriously bankrupt, should avail to make good these obligations. That is, the Congress of the United States, by solemn act was to authorize the State of Arkansas to repudiate her solemn obligations. Recollect, this was not a case of Mississippi Bonds, of which State Mr. Davis was then a Representative in Congress, but it was the case of Arkansas, another State, having on the floor of Congress its own Senators and Representatives. But it is a very remarkable fact, that Mississippi for many years had then repudiated her own bonds, that Mr. Davis justified and sustained that repudiation, and that now, he appears on behalf of Arkansas to induce Congress, by solemn act, to authorize that State to repudiate her obligations also. Thus was it, that Mr. Davis travelled out of his own State into another to make the Government of the United States a party to the repudiation of her bonds by the State of Arkansas. Let me not be misunderstood. I do not mean to say, that Mr. Davis proposed or intended that the Government of the United States, should repudiate its faith, plighted to the British Court of Chancery, to make good this fund. That is not the question. It is entirely collateral. But, what he did do was this, and there stands his own resolution offered by himself in the Congress of the United States, which, if carried into effect, would have released the State of Arkansas from these bonds, or, in Mr. Davis's own words, "The said State shall be and is hereby "declared to be *absolved from the promises* on the "face of her bonds, by which the said State heretofore "*pledged her faith* for the due payment of the "principal and interest of said bonds."

Why should Congress release Arkansas from the payment of her State obligations? Why thus justify the repudiation of her bonds? Can any other reason be assigned than this, that Mr. Jefferson Davis was looking to the repudiated bonds of Mississippi, and was endeavouring to establish a precedent, by solemn act of the Congress, by which, if adopted as a principle, Mississippi, and every other defaulting State, could be justified in the repudiation of their bonds also. It is to the credit of the Congress of the United States, that Mr. Davis's resolution was rejected without a division, and without a count. When it is recollected, that at this very time, I, as Secretary of the Treasury, was appropriating the 5 per cent found payable by the Government to the State of Arkansas towards the liquidation of these bonds against the protest of that State, the further meaning of these movements will be clearly perceived. Had this resolution of Mr. Davis's passed the two Houses of Congress, absolving the State of Arkansas from the payment of these bonds, I could, of course, as Secretary of the Treasury, no longer have withheld that fund from the State, and appropriated it, so far as it went, towards the liquidation of the interest accrued and accruing on these bonds. It appears, then, by conclusive and official evidence, that Mr. Jefferson Davis's repudiation of State obligations, was not confined to his own State, nor even to the State of Arkansas; but that he desired to make the Government of the United

States, by solemn act of Congress, a party directly sanctioning such atrocious violations of State faith and State obligation.

R. J. WALKER.

AMERICAN

THANKSGIVING DINNER,

AT

ST. JAMES' HALL, LONDON.

THURSDAY, NOVEMBER 26TH, 1863.

LONDON:
WILLIAM RIDGWAY, 169, PICCADILLY. W.
1863.

THE NATIONAL THANKSGIVING DAY.

A PROCLAMATION BY THE PRESIDENT OF THE UNITED STATES OF AMERICA.

The year that is drawing toward its close has been filled with the blessings of fruitful fields and healthful skies. To these bounties, which are so constantly enjoyed that we are prone to forget the source from which they come, others have been added, which are of so extraordinary a nature that they cannot fail to penetrate and soften the heart which is habitually insensible to the ever-watchful providence of Almighty God.

In the midst of a civil war of unequalled magnitude and severity, which has sometimes seemed to invite and provoke the aggressions of foreign States, peace has been preserved with all nations, order has been maintained, the laws have been respected and obeyed, and harmony has prevailed everywhere, except in the theatre of military conflict, while that theatre has been greatly contracted by the advancing armies and navies of the Union.

The needful diversions of wealth and strength from the fields of peaceful industry to the national defence have not arrested the plough, the shuttle, or the ship. The axe has enlarged the borders of our settlements, and the mines, as well of iron and coal, as of the precious metals, have yielded even more abundantly than heretofore. Population has steadily increased, notwithstanding the waste that has been made in the camp, the siege aud the battle-field, and the country rejoicing in the consciousness of augmented strength and vigour is permitted to expect continuance of years with large increase of freedom,

No human counsel hath devised, nor hath any mortal hand worked out these great things. They are the gracious gifts of the Most High God, who, while dealing with us in anger for our sins, hath nevertheless remembered mercy.

It has seemed to me fit and proper that they should be solemnly, reverently, and gratefully acknowledged as with one heart and voice by the whole American people; I do, therefore, invite my fellow-citizens in every part of the United States, and also those who are at sea, and those who are sojourning in foreign lands, to set apart and observe the last Thursday of November next as a Day of Thanksgiving and Prayer to our beneficient Father who dwelleth in the heavens. And I recommend to them that, while offering up the ascriptions justly due to Him for such singular deliverances and blessings, they do also, with humble penitence for our national perverseness and disobedience, commend to His tender care all those who have become widows, orphans, mourners, or sufferers, in the lamentable civil strife in which we are unavoidably engaged, and fervently implore the interposition of the Almighty hand to heal the wounds of the nation, and to restore it, as soon as may be consistent with the Divine purposes, to the full enjoyment of peace, harmony, tranquillity and union.

In testimony whereof, I have hereunto set my hand, and caused the Seal of the United States to be affixed.

Done at the City of Washington, this third day of October, in the year of our Lord one thousand eight hundred and sixty-three, and of the independence of the United States the eighty-eighth.

ABRAHAM LINCOLN.

By the President, WILLIAM H. SEWARD,
Secretary of State.

In accordance with the above Proclamation, the loyal Americans in London and their guests attended a THANKSGIVING DINNER, at St. James's Hall, Regent Street, at three o'clock, p.m., on Thursday the 26th of November, 1863, given under the direction of the following:

Committee.

HON. R. J. WALKER, Washington, D.C.
CHARLES L. WILSON, ESQ., Illionis.
P. MC. D. COLLINS, ESQ., California.
DR. W. R. BALLARD, New York.
CAPTAIN E. G. TINKER, Conn.
HON. F. H. MORSE, Maine.
B. MORAN, ESQ. Pennsylvania.
SEWALL WARNER, ESQ. Mass.
R. HUNTING, ESQ. New York.
HENRY STARR, ESQ., Mass.
GERARD RALSTON, ESQ., Pennsylvania.
G. W. BELDING, ESQ., New York.
A. J. VALENTINE, ESQ. Maine.
B. F. BROWN, ESQ., Mass.
W. E BRODERICK, ESQ., Maryland.

The following were the order of Exercises:—1st. Reading of the President's Proclamation for Thanksgiving, by Richard Hunting, Esq. 2nd. Prayer by Rev. Sella Martin. 3rd. Hymn written for the occasion—TUNE, *Auld Lang Syne.*

We meet, the Sons of Freedom's Sires
  Unchanged, where'er we roam,
While gather round their household fires
  The happy bands of home;
And while across the far blue wave
  Their prayers go up to God,
We pledge the faith our fathers gave,—
  The land by Freemen trod!

The heroes of our Native Land
  Their sacred trust still hold,
The freedom from a mighty band
  Wrenched by the men of old.
That lesson to the broad earth given
  We pledge beyond the sea,—
The land from dark oppression riven,
  A blessing on the free!

DINNER.

MENU.

Potages.

A la Condè. Brunvillier. Bisque aux Écrevisses.

Poissons.

Turbot, Sauce Hollandaise.

Cabillaud, Sauce aux Huitres.

Turbans de Filets de Merlans au Gratin.

Éperlans frits.

Entrées.

Petites Bouchées garni de Coq de Bruyère.

Fricassée de Poulet à la Washington.

Côtelettes de Lièvre aux Truffes.

Ris de Veau piqué à l'Oseille.

Pâté chaud de Poulardes aux Champignons.

Quenelles de Gibier à la Lincoln.

Grosses Pièces.

Dindons rôtis farci aux Truffes.

Poulardes braisé à la Prairie.

Oisons rôtis, Sauce aux Pommes.

Selle de Mouton. Quartier de Bœuf.

SECOND SERVICE.

Rôts.

Faisans. Perdreaux. Canards sauvages.

Entremets.

Gelée à la Macédoine. Crême d'Amérique.

Gelée à la Victoria. Suédoise d'Orange.

Crême de Maizena à la Glen Cove.

Abricôt à la Régence. Méringues Suisses à la Chantilly.

Gâteaux à la Napolitaine. Pâtisserie assortie.

Pumpkin Pie à l'Américaine. Mince Pie à l'Anglaise.

Pouding à la Diplomatique. Pouding glacé à la St. James.

Dessert.

The Hon. Robt. J. Walker, President, assisted by the Hon. Freeman H. Morse, the United States' Consul at London, and Gerard Ralston, Esq., of Pennsylvania, the Consul General of Liberia at London.

On the right of the Chair were seated the Hon. Charles Francis Adams, the United States' Minister, and Charles L. Wilson, Esq., and Benj. Moran, Esq., Secretaries of Legation; and on the left, Geo. Thompson, Esq., J. Snow, Esq., Editor of the "Observer;" P. M'D. Collins, Esq., Consul of the United States at Amour River, &c. &c.

Amongst those present were Hon. Charles Francis Adams, United States' Minister; Charles L. Wilson and Benj. Moran, Secretaries of Legation; Hon. Freeman H. Morse, U. S. Consul; Miss Morse, Hon. Robert J. Walker and Mrs. Walker, Miss Walker, Robert J. Walker, Jun., Captain Mayne Reed and Mrs. Reed, Miss Weir, Mr. and the two Misses Rose; Richard Hunting and Mrs. Hunting, New York; Dr. W. R. Ballard and Mrs. Ballard, ditto; Geo. W. Belding and Mrs. Belding, ditto; E. C. Hall and Lady, ditto; Wellington Lee, ditto; C. S. Porter and Mrs. Porter; Mr. Taylor and Mrs. Taylor; P. M'D. Collins, California; Sewell Warner and Mrs. Warner, Miss M. Warner, Mass.; B. F. Brown and Mrs. Brown, ditto; Mr. Henry B. Adams; B. F. Fuller, ditto; J. G. Avery, ditto; E. W. Fox and Mrs. Fox; Z. K. Pangborn, ditto; F. C. Cross, ditto; Capt. J. C. Hoadley, ditto; Henry Starr and Mrs. Starr, Pa.; Gerard Ralston, ditto; A. L. Holley, Conn.; N. A. Lyman, ditto; Charles Cheney and Mrs. Cheney; A. G. Shaver, ditto; W. J. Valentine, Maine; J. Emmons and lady, ditto; G. W. Belding and Mrs. Belding, Vermont; E. H. Hopkins, ditto; Charles P. Button, ditto; Charles Churchill and lady, New Jersey; C. H. McCormick, Chicago; James T. Griffin, ditto; W. E. Broderick and Mrs. Broderick, Maryland; Alonzo Kimball, New Hampshire; Geo. R. Cathcart, South Carolina; Albert Steers, Wisconsin; Washington Wilkes and lady; Joshua Nunn and Mrs. Nunn; Peter Sinclair; Edward McDermott and Mrs. McDermott;

&c. &c. Several English Ladies and Gentlemen were also present.

Upon the removal of the cloth, the Hon. ROBERT J. WALKER, as Chairman, introduced the Toasts prepared for the occasion, as follows:—

1. The President of the United States.
His Excellency Mr. Adams.

2. Her Majesty the Queen.
Introduced with Remarks by Mr. Walker.

3. The Day. Devoted to thanking God for our victories in the cause of LIBERTY and UNION.
George Thompson, Esq.

4. The Union. From the Atlantic to the Pacific, from the Lakes to the Gulf, from the Source to the Mouth of the Mississippi, for ever one and inseparable.
Z. K. Pangborn.

5. The Emancipation Proclamation,— Slavery's Epitaph; written by the finger of God on the heart of the American President. *Hon. Freeman H. Morse.*

6. The Army and Navy,—Immortal champions of freedom, who bleed that our country may live.
Capt. Mayne Reid.

7. WASHINGTON, The Man without a Peer. We follow his farewell advice—NEVER TO SURRENDER THE UNION.
Capt. J. C. Hoadley.

8. The Press. The Tyrant's foe, the People's friend,—where it is free, despotism must perish.
J. Snow and Washington Wilkes.

9. The Ladies. Our Sweethearts, Wives, Mothers, Daughters, Sisters, Friends. Their holy influence will break all chains but those which bind our hearts to them.

The Hon. R. J. Walker, as Chairman, then said:—Ladies and Gentlemen, by the request of my countrymen, I shall preface the toasts prepared for the occasion by a few introductory remarks. This day has been set apart by the President of the United States for thanksgiving to Almighty God for all the blessings which He has vouchsafed to us as a people. Among these are abundant crops, great prosperity in all our industrial pursuits, a vast addition, even during the war, to our material wealth, and augmented immigration to our shores from Europe. Our finances have been conducted with great ability and success by the Secretary of the Treasury, Mr. Chase, who has also succeeded in giving us, for the first time in our history, a uniform national currency, which, as a bond of union, and as an addition to our wealth and resources, is nearly equal to all the expenses of the great contest (loud cheers for Mr. Chase). During the present year, nearly 400,000,000 dollars of the Six per cent. Stock of the United States has been taken at home, at or above par; whilst within the last few months, European capitalists, unsolicited by us, are making large investments in the securities of the Union. But, above all, we have to thank God for those victories in the field which are bringing this great contest to a successful conclusion. This rebellion, is, indeed, the most stupendous in history. It absorbs the attention, and affects the political institutions and material interests of the world. The armies engaged exceed those of Napoleon. Death never had such a carnival, and each week consumes millions of treasure. Great is the sacrifice, but the cause is peerless and sublime (cheers). If God has placed us in the van of the great contest for the rights and liberties of man—if He has assigned us the post of danger and of suffering, it is that of unfading glory and imperishable renown (loud cheers). The question with us, which is so misunderstood here, is that of national unity (hear, hear), which is the vital element of our existence; and any settlement which does not secure this, with the entire integrity of the Union and freedom throughout all its borders, will be treason to our country and to mankind (loud cheers). To acknowledge the absurd and anarchical doctrine of secession, as is demanded of us here, to abdicate the power of self-preservation, and permit the Union to be dissolved, is ruin, disgrace, and suicide. There is but one alternative; we must and will fight it out to the last (loud and prolonged applause). If need be, all who can bear arms must take to the field, and leave to those who cannot the pursuits of industry (hear, hear). If we count not the cost of this contest in men or money, it is because all loyal Americans believe, that the value of our Union cannot be estimated (hear, hear). If martyrs from every State, from England, and from nearly every nation of Christendom have fallen in our defence, never, in humble faith we trust, has any blood since that of Calvary, been shed in a cause so holy (cheers).

Most of the rebellions which have disturbed or overthrown Governments, have been caused by oppression on their part. Such rebellions have been the rising of the oppressed against the oppressor; but this rebellion was caused exclusively by slavery (cheers). To extend and perpetuate and nationalise slavery, to demand of the American Congress the direct and explicit recognition of the right of property in man, to cover the whole vast territory of the Union with chattel servitude, to keep open the interstate slave trade between the border and the Cotton States, to give the institution absolute mastery over the Government and people, to carry it into every new State by fraud and violence and forgery, as was exemplified in Kansas, and then, as a final result, to force it upon every free State of the Union,—these were the objects conceived by those who are engaged in this foul conspiracy to dissolve the American Union (cheers). I have said that the American Union never will be dissolved (loud and continued cheers). This was the advice of the peerless Washington, the father of his country, in his farewell address, and this was the course of the immortal Andrew Jackson, when he suppressed the Carolina rebellion of 1833, by coercion and a Force Bill. The American Union is the great citadel of self-government, entrusted to our charge by Providence; and we must defend it against all assailants, until our last man has fallen. This is the cause of labour and humanity, and the toiling and disfranchised masses of the world feel that their fate is involved in the result of our struggle. In England especially, this feeling on the part of the working classes has been manifested in more than one hundred meetings, and the resolutions in favour of the Union, passed by the operatives of Manchester, who were the great sufferers from this contest, indicate a sublimity of feeling, and a devotion to principle on the part of these noble martyrs, which exalts and dignifies the character of man (cheers). The working classes of England, of France, and of Germany, who are all with us, in case of foreign intervention, must have constituted the armies that would have been taken to our shores to make war upon the American people. The men who are for us would have been transported across the ocean to fight against us in the cause of slavery and for the degradation of labour. Can there be any doubt as to the result of such a conflict? It is now quite certain that this rebellion will receive no foreign aid; but if any European despot or usurper had thus intervened, and sent his myrmidons to our shores, the result, though it might have been prolonged, would have been equally certain—he would have lost his crown and destroyed his dynasty (cheers); our whole country would have been a camp; we should have risen to the magnitude of the contest, and all who could bear arms would have taken the field. We know, as Americans, that our national unity is the essential condition of our existence. Without it we should be disintegrated into sections, states, counties, and cities; and ruin and anarchy would reign supreme (cheers). No, the Lakes can never be separated from the Gulf, the Atlantic from the Pacific; the source from the mouth of the Mississippi, nor the sons of New England from the homes of their kindred in the great West (cheers). But, above all, the entire valley of the Mississippi was ordained by God as the residence of a united people. Over every acre of its soil, and over every drop of its waters, must for ever float the banner of Union (loud applause), and all its rivers as they roll on together to the Gulf proclaim that "what God has joined together man shall never put asunder" (loud cheers). The nation's life blood courses this vast arterial system, and to sever it is death. No line of latitude or longitude shall ever separate the mouth from the centre or sources of the Mississippi. All the waters of the imperial river, from their mountain springs and crystal fountains, shall ever flow in commingling currents to the Gulf, uniting, evermore, in one undivided whole, the blessed homes of a free and happy people. This great valley is one vast plain without an intervening mountain, and can never be separated by any line but that of blood, to be followed surely by military despotism. No; separation by any line is death; disunion is suicide. Slavery having made war upon the Union, the result is not doubtful. Slavery will die (cheers). Slavery having selected a traitor's position, will meet a traitor's doom (loud cheers).

The Union will still live. It is written by the finger of God, on the scroll of destiny, that "neither principalities nor powers" shall affect its overthrow, nor shall "the gates of hell prevail against it." But what as to the results? It is said that we have accomplished nothing; and this is re-echoed every morning by the pro-slavery press of England. We have done nothing! Why, we have conquered and now occupy two-thirds of the entire territory of the South, an area far larger (while overcoming a greater resisting force) than that traversed by the armies of Cæsar or Alexander. The whole of the Mississippi river, from its source to its mouth, with all its thirty thousand miles of tributaries, is exclusively ours (cheers). So is the great Chesapeake Bay. Slavery is not only abolished in the Federal district, containing the capital of the Union, but in all our vast territorial domain, comprising more than eight hundred millions of acres, and nearly half the size of all Europe. The four slave-holding States of Delaware, Maryland, Kentucky, and Missouri, are devotedly loyal, and thoroughly sustaining the Union. And how as to Virginia? Why, all the counties of Virginia east of the Chesapeake are ours; all that vast portion of eastern Virginia, north of the Rappahannock, is ours also. But still more, all that great territory of Virginia, from the mountains to the Ohio, is ours also; and not only ours, but, by the overwhelming voice of her people, has formed a State Government. By their own votes they have abolished slavery, and have been admitted as one of the Free States of the American Union (loud cheers). And where is the great giant state of the west—Missouri? She is not only ours, but, by an overwhelming majority of the popular vote, carried into effect by her constitutional convention, has provided for the abolition of slavery, and enrols herself soon as one of the Free States of the American Union (cheers). And now, as to Maryland. The last steamer brings us the news of the recent elections in Maryland, which have not only sustained the Union, but have sent an overwhelming majority to Congress and to the State Legislature in favour of immediate emancipation, and Delaware adopts the same policy (loud applause). Tennessee is also ours. From the Mississippi to the Cumberland and Tennessee rivers, from Knoxville, in the mountains of the East, to Nashville, the capital, in the centre; and Memphis, the commercial metropolis, in the West, Tennessee is wholly ours. So is Arkansas. So is Louisiana, including the great city of New Orleans. So is North Alabama. So is Western Texas. So is two-thirds of the State of Mississippi; and now the Union troops hold Chattanooga, the great impregnable fortress of North-Western Georgia. From Chattanooga, which may be regarded as the great geographical central pivot point of the rebellion, the armies of the Republic will march down through the heart of Georgia, and join our troops upon the seaboard of that state, and thus terminate the rebellion (loud cheers).

Into Georgia and the Carolinas, nearly half a million of slaves have been driven by their masters in advance of the Union army. From Virginia, from Kentucky, Missouri, Arkansas, Louisiana, Mississippi, Tennessee, and North Alabama, thousands of their slaves have been driven and huddled together in the two Carolinas and Georgia; because, if they had been left where they were, they would have joined the Northern armies. They preferred to be freemen rather than slaves; they preferred to be men and women rather than chattels; they preferred freedom to chains and bondage; and just so soon as that Union army advances into the Carolinas and Georgia, will the slaves rush to the standard of freedom, and fight as they have fought with undaunted courage for liberty and the Union (loud applause).

But how is it with the South? Why, months ago, they had called out, *en masse*, all who were capable of bearing arms. They have raised their last army. And how as to money? Why, they are in a state of absolute bankruptcy. Their money, all they have, that which they call money, according to their own estimation, as fixed and taken by themselves, one dollar of gold purchases sixteen dollars of Confederate paper, which must soon cease to circulate at any rate. The price of flour is now 100 dollars a barrel, and other articles in like proportion. No revenue is collected, or can be. The army and the Government are supported exclusively by force, by seizing the crops of farmers and planters, and using them for the benefit of the so-called Confederate Government. Starvation is staring them in the face. The collapse is imminent, and, so far as we may venture to predict any future event, nothing can be more certain than that before the closing of the coming year the rebellion will be brought entirely to a close (hear, hear). We must recollect, also, that there is not a single State of the South, in which a large majority of the population (including the blacks) is not now, and always has been, devoted to the Union. Why, in the State of South Carolina alone, the blacks, who are devoted to the Union, exceed the whites more than 100,000 in number. The recent elections have all gone for the Union by overwhelming majorities, and volunteering for the army progresses with renewed vigour. For all these blessings the President of the United States invites us to render thanks to Almighty God. Our cause is that of humanity, of civilisation, of Christianity. We write upon our banners, from the inspired words of Holy Writ, "God has made of one blood all the nations of the earth." We acknowledge all as brothers; we invite them to partake with us alike in the grand inheritance of freedom; and we repeat the Divine sentiment from the sermon on the Mount, "Do unto others as you would have them do unto you" (loud cheers). Nor let it be supposed that we, as Americans, are entirely selfish in this matter. We believe that this union is the most sacred trust ever confided by Almighty God to man. We believe that this American Union is the best, the brightest, the last experiment of self-government, and as it shall be sustained and perpetuated, or broken and dissolved, the light of liberty shall beam upon the hopes of mankind, or be for ever extinguished, amid the scoffs of exulting tyrants, and the groans of a world in bondage (loud applause). All nations and ages will soon acknowledge that, in this contest, we have made greater sacrifices of blood and treasure in the cause of human freedom than was ever before recorded in history. We will have suppressed the most gigantic and the most wicked rebellion, a task that could have been accomplished by no other Government. We have succeeded, because our institutions rest on the broad basis of the affections, the interests, and the power of the people. No other nation could bring a million of volunteers to the field (loud cheers), and millions more would come if necessary. As a result of this war, we will extinguish slavery, we will perpetuate and consolidate the Union, we will prove that man is capable of self-government, and secure the ultimate ascendancy of free institutions throughout the world. This, therefore, is a day in which all humanity may unite with us in the hymn of praise, and the toiling millions of the earth join with us in fervent thanksgiving to Almighty God for the approaching redemption of our race from slavery and oppression (loud and long continued cheering and applause).

Thanking you, Ladies and Gentlemen, for the

kind indulgence with which you have been pleased to receive these remarks, I will now proceed to the toasts which have been prepared for the occasion. Ladies and Gentlemen, the first toast will be "The President of the United States," under whose proclamation we are this day convened. Before asking you to drink to that toast, I would say that we are honoured by the presence this evening of his Excellency the American Minister, Mr. Adams, who will reply to this sentiment (prolonged applause). This is a name for a century, and during three generations most honourably and conspicuously connected with the cause of our country and of human liberty. The grandfather and father of our American Minister, were each elevated to the Presidency of the United States by the votes of the American people. The first, the illustrious John Adams, moved, in 1776, the declaration of American independence, and supported that motion by an immortal and most eloquent address. He was the successor of the peerless Washington as President of the United State. The second, John Quincy Adams, eminent for courage, for integrity, for opposition to slavery, for devotion to the cause of liberty, for learning, science, eloquence, diplomacy, and statesmanship, was the successor of President Munroe. His son, our honoured guest, inheriting the great qualities and noble principles of an illustrious ancestry, will respond to the first toast, "The President of the United States." The toast was drunk amid the most enthusiastic applause. Three cheers for the President, called for by Mr. Walker, were given most enthusiastically.

Mr. ADAMS, the American Minister, in acknowledging the toast, said: I thank you for the honour you have done me by calling upon me to respond to the toast of the President of the United States. Of late years we have rather got out of the habit of giving any great amount of laudation to the President of the United States. There may have been causes for that which you will all understand; but I will say that with respect to our good Chief Magistrate, he has not had himself any such great amount as would be likely to turn his head (laughter)—not half so much, Mr. Chairman, as you have been kind enough to shower upon me this evening. On the contrary, it has become the practice of our people generally to hold the President responsible for any mistake that is committed by anybody, and every misfortune that happens at any time. There is hardly a single act that he does against which somebody is not found to carp. Even with respect to this proclamation, asking us to have a thanksgiving-day, I have seen it somewhere remarked, that it was a most extraordinary thing that when there seemed to be nothing but calamity in the United States, when there was an immense loss of life going on, great destruction of property, and painful distress in all classes, the President should take this occasion to call upon his fellow citizens to give thanks to God. It seemed to indicate either great moral obtuseness, or else a savage, vindictive feeling of joy over the distress of the people whom he was trying to subject. Now, Mr. Chairman, it is to this point that I propose to address the few remarks I mean to make to you this evening. I am perfectly willing to concede that this is a time of great calamity. I believe that the great majority, indeed almost all of our people ir America, feel that it is a calamity which they would gladly have avoided if they could; but that they have been obliged to view it as much a necessary evil as if it had been an earthquake or an inunda tion. It was an affliction which they could not avoid. Under these circumstances, all that they could do was to apply themselves as quickly as possible to the perfection of a remedy and a restoration. This could only be done through perseverance in the war (hear, hear). But we are asked, what is the precise blessing for which we are at present to give God thanks? In order to get something like a correct idea of this matter, it will be necessary for me to recall to your minds, as briefly as possible, the course of events since the time when the President came into office. I scarcely need say to you, what I believe is perfectly well known to every one, that that gentleman came to his post with less of practical experience in Government than any individual had done since the foundation of the Government (cheers). He came into office at a time of the greatest difficulty and danger which had occurred since the establishment of that office (cheers). He, as you will all recollect, found himself occupying a position in which all the portions of the edifice of Government seemed crumbling around him. Why, it was exceedingly doubtful, whether the President would be able to arrive at the place where he could assume the performance of his duties. It was only by a little contrivance that he succeeded in defeating the plot which had been formed, for the seizure of his person, thus to disable the country from arriving at the constitutional organisation of the Executive Department (cheers). He came to Washington, and was qualified as President. But President of what? He looked around him on all the branches of the departments of the Executive Government, and everything seemed to be shaking about them. He looked to the organisation upon which he was to depend for action, and he found that wherever he touched, it was unsound to trust. So ingeniously had the poison of rebellion been disseminated through all the ramifications of the Government, that treachery was cropping out every where (cheers). He had to begin by a thorough scrutiny of men, from those occupying the uppermost seats down to almost the lowest place. There was a necessity for a searching reform, by which the lurking not less than the overt treason and treachery were to be eliminated from the executive machinery (cheers). That work has now been done (cheers). The Government in its position at Washington is now safe, and is served faithfully (cheers). Is not this something to be thankful for? (cheers). Is not this something for which we have a right to echo the President's appeal to us to meet together, and to be thankful for upon this occasion? (cheers). But that was not by any means the worst point. The President looked upon the foreign department of his Government, and when he cast his eyes abroad there was to be found scarcely an individual in the foreign service who sympathised with him in his feelings or his difficulties. Nay, more, there was, with a few honourable exceptions, scarcely a person who was not practically disseminating distrust of the Power under which he was serving (cheers). Not a few persons produced a considerable effect in almost every country of Europe in creating that sentiment which became prevalent, that the complete subversion of the old system was at hand and that a new one was inevitable. I have a little anecdote in connection with this subject to tell you. Very shortly after the election of Mr. Lincoln he did me the honour to designate me as the individual to come out and represent the country at this Court. I came out as soon as I could. I got here in about two months after the inauguration of the President. On my arrival the first news which met me was, that three "distinguished commissioners," as the newspapers called them, had come out from the rebel authorities, and were at that time in London. I had the pleasure of learning also that these commissioners had confidently announced among their friends, that before I should reach London the Government and capital of Washington would be in their hands; consequently I should stand no chance of being recognised by the British Government as the representative of the United States (cheers and laughter). This is simply a specimen of the mode in which that class of persons laboured throughout Europe, and not without effect. And it has taken all the time from that day to this to inspire the different Governments of Europe with a tolerable share of confidence in our intentions to remain the Government of the United States (cheers). Now, Mr. Chairman, I think we have got so far, that I begin to feel as if I could assure you that they have seen reason to modify their views of the condition of that Goverment (cheers). If after three years this change has taken place, I ask, have we not something to thank God for? Is it not a fit occasion to meet and rejoice in this restoration? But let me go a step further. When the President looked upon the Treasury, he found that so ingeniously had the individuals laboured in the preceding Administration, many high in office were conspiring to destroy the United States, to undermine the credit of the country, that it was with great difficulty some of the moneyed men could be persuaded to come forward to loan the Government a small sum of money to enable it to go on, until the time of taking his post. There probably never was a time in its whole history, when the national credit had been so much shaken; and that by the machinations of those who had been its secret enemies. The President had to reorganise credit by re-establishing the foundations of it in the integrity of the administration of the Treasury. He did so. What has been the result? From that degree of feebleness when confidence in a government promise seemed to be shaken almost beyond repair, the people have gradually increased in faith, until they now daily rush in swarms, voluntarily to offer their money to the Government in exchange for the obligations which they are anxious to obtain (cheers). Is not that something to be thankful for? Let me go a step further. When this war broke out, the President looked around to see where was his military organisation upon which he had to rely for the support of his coercive measures. He found here too, that so vigorously had treason worked itself through all the affiliations of the military organisation, that there was not one man out of three who could be trusted. He found one set who were, and who ultimately declared themselves traitors. He found another set who were not traitors, but so timid and lukewarm, as scarcely to know whether they would, or would not support the Government. He found still another set who had been in service so long, and had arrived at such an age that, however excellent their disposition and capacity were, they could not well be relied upon in the field on account of physical disability. That was the state of the organisation which he had got to begin a gigantic war with. I do not believe that in the whole history of the world a greater undertaking was ever assumed by an individual who had no experience in such matters. He had to reorganise an army on a scale of half a million of men upon the narrow basis which was thus left to him to operate upon (cheers). At the outset, as you all know, he met with difficulties of all kinds. He had to try numbers, and a great many failed. But look at the organisation as it exists now, and compare it with what it was at the beginning, and you will see that by patience, and perseverance and fidelity to his duty, he has got you an army which will carry you through (loud cheers). There are no men now in the army whom you are obliged to mistrust (hear, hear). There are no men who you suspect may betray all your movements to the Rebels. Is not this a result for which we are ready now to give thanks? (applause). Let us turn for a moment from that side of the picture to the other side—the navy. The navy was of most essential importance to the Government at the beginning of the war. When the President looked after his navy, he found that some ships had to be destroyed to save them from treacherous abandonment, and the rest had been sent away as far over the globe as they could go. He had to restore the whole system almost from its foundation. He had to go through the same process as that he had applied to the army, to build ships, to reorganise the bureaux; in short to place the navy on a footing that it had never stood before. It has taken two short years, and a little more, to do all this, and we have now a navy both in numbers and power which will make the United States, you may depend on it, respected upon every sea in any part of the globe (loud cheers). And is not this something to be thankful for? Thus, on a review of all the different departments of the Executive Government, you will see that the destiny of this President, who had no experience when he began, was to reorganise, rebuild, and restore the whole system from its foundation. But this is not all. There was one question which had baffled all attempts ever to reach a solution to it, and which, I, for one, will frankly admit, I looked on as one almost impossible to dispose of with success. I need not say that I allude to the great question of the condition of the Slaves. Much as we all had discussed it for years, we had never had presented to us from any source a practicable mode of dealing with it. When it came simply to Emancipation, the people throughout the United States were utterly incredulous that there could be devised any plan of effecting it which would not lead to bloodshed and ruin throughout the whole region in which they dwelt. It was the great argument against doing anything at all. It was said to be impossible to hope for any issue that would not involve the destruction of all classes within its reach. Now the great and crowning act of the administration of this President is, that in two distinct measures he has opened a way to a practical result which we all supposed could not be found (cheers). The Proclamation, and the enlistment of negroes as soldiers, are the two great instruments by which emancipation, without revolution, will be carried out (cheers). And here we are now, at the end of two years and a half, having made slow, but regular, progress in this movement until it has taken shape distinctly before us so that we can forsee the ultimate issue. Have we not in all this something to be thankful for? And have we not a right to meet together at the call of our President, and, looking back to our difficulties to bless God that they are diminished to the extent we now see them? (loud cheers).

But you are all aware that one of the great difficulties incident to this change has been the fear that the people would not sanction it; and when the President first enunciated his propositions they were denounced at once as the weakest and wickedest of measures. There were even indications, at one time, that the opposition would go so far as seriously to impair the energy of the Government in executing the policy. Last year, at this time, there was an expression of popular sentiment which looked adversely; but another year has since passed. The system has in the interval had a chance of being carried out to its practical development, and lo, and behold, the great body of people, having watched the result, have joined together as with one voice, almost from one end of the country to the other, rallied in favour of sustaining that policy (applause). And is not this something to be thankful for? Let us, then, recapitulate what is our present position, and what it was when this inexperienced President first took office. *Then* the Government was almost disintegrated. *Now* it is solid, able to act through honest agents, faithful men, working with vigour and effect whenever and however it pleases (cheers). Then the people were staggered in their confidence in the country and the President. Now the President has all the departments of his Government faithful to him, and to the constitution. The people have rallied round the Government, and maintained the policy of the President. They have money, they have men, and they have ideas which they mean to establish as the only true and successful conclusion of the struggle. Is not this something to be thankful for? (cheers). We stand now firmly, having every reliance that the Government is able, and the people willing, to go through this trial triumphantly (cheers.) And all this change has been effected through the agency of a President, who came into power with less practical political experience than any one man preceding him (hear, hear). And how has this been done? Has it been by any superior genius on the part of the President?

Not at all. The President has shown ability and capacity, but not above that of most of his predecessors. What is the reason, then, why he has succeeded in all these results? I will tell you the reason. He has succeeded because he has, from the beginning to the end, impressed upon the people the conviction of his honesty and fidelity to one great purpose. (Loud cheers.) I therefore say, Mr. Chairman, in conclusion, that for these reasons I have to thank you for having enjoyed the opportunity of expressing these sentiments as an echo to the toast of the health of the President of the United States. (His Excellency resumed his seat amidst the greatest applause.)

THE CHAIRMAN (Mr. Walker).—Ladies and Gentlemen, the next toast is one to which I trust every friend of constitutional freedom, every loyal American, every admirer of the great virtues of the woman, and the excellence of the Sovereign will most heartily respond, especially those of us who have been in this country for some time, and who know how strong and deep have been the personal feelings of the Queen, and of her lamented Consort, the good Prince Albert, against slavery, and in favour of the American Union, will join in the next toast, "Her Majesty the Queen."

(The toast was responded to by prolonged cheering.)

A VOICE.—Three cheers more for the Queen.

(Loud cheering.)

The Chairman—(Mr. Walker).—Ladies and Gentlemen, please fill up for the third toast. But before giving that toast, I have the pleasure to announce to you that beside me, who has kindly consented to respond to the sentiment, is a gentleman who has represented the largest constituency of England in the British Parliament, and with distinguished ability. He is a friend of England and of America, and he regards the alliance of the great Anglo-Saxon race, speaking the same language, descended from the same glorious ancestry, having the same common law and literature, and, as he believes, the same destiny—he considers that the true alliance for the benefit of England and America, and of the human race, is that of the mother and daughter (cheers). Ladies and Gentlemen, there was a time when there was a great contest in England as regards the suppression of the African Slave Trade. The wealth, the trade, the power, the great and governing classes of England, at that date, were in favour of the African Slave Trade. But there rose up great champions of humanity and of the rights of man, without regard to country or colour, and after a long and doubtful contest, Clarkson and Wilberforce were triumphant, and the African Slave Trade was suppressed, so far as England was concerned, by the British Parliament. These were the heroes of the early part of this century, connected with that great question. But there has since arisen a greater question, not merely the suppression of the African Slave Trade, but the extinction of slavery itself, in the United States, in England, in the West Indies, and throughout the world (cheers). But by far the most important of all is the extinguishment of slavery in our own country, for if it falls there, slavery will perish throughout every other portion of the habitable globe (loud cheers). Now, then, whilst Clarkson and Wilberforce were the heroes of the suppression of the African Slave Trade, I announce an opinion to which every loyal American and every well informed Englishman will respond, that George Thompson, the Member whom the Tower Hamlets sent to Parliament, is the hero of this century for the extinguishment of slavery itself (loud applause). It is now more than a quarter of a century since this illustrious friend of the human race came to our shores, leading a forlorn hope in favour of the abolition of American slavery, where he spoke against it at the risk of his life. Now, if he were to return to America in the same cause, he would be received with plaudits, from the Lakes to the Gulf, from the Atlantic to the Pacific, from Boston, where he first landed, to New Orleans (loud cheers). I have to request that you will drink this next toast, with all the honours, and our friend Mr. Thompson will then respond. "The day — Devoted to thanking God for our victories in the cause of Liberty and Union" (cheers).

Mr. George Thompson.—[Who on rising was received with loud and continued cheering.]—Mr. Chairman, Ladies, and Gentlemen, I shall occupy but a very few moments of the attention of this assembly, because I shall presently be due in another place, where I shall have a duty to perform, in an humble attempt to explain to a few of my countrymen one of the aspects of that great question in which you all take so deep an interest—the present condition and future destinies of America. But before I go to discharge that duty, allow me to express the pleasure which I feel in uniting with you on this occasion. While I have been sitting here my thoughts have not been circumscribed by the walls which are around us, but I have been present in spirit in those multitudinous gatherings of your countrymen and countrywomen all over the world, who, like yourselves, are on this evening assembled together to offer up their fervent and deep-felt acknowledgment to Divine Providence for His guardian care over your country, the success with which He has crowned the efforts of its friends, and the prospects with which He now cheers you of an ultimate victory, and a future career separate and apart altogether from what has been at once your reproach and your disaster, the Institution of Slavery, so long protected amongst you. I wish that some gentleman more worthy to appear as the representative of England had occupied my place to-night. One of those men with whom I have been associated in times past in great public movements, and who have recently added fresh lustre to their names, and laid still deeper foundations for general and universal gratitude by so nobly identifying themselves with your cause, contrary, I am sorry to say, to the opinions and feelings of many with whom they ordinarily mix. But, Sir, if I want rank, and influence, and position to recommend me, I may at least claim credit for having been amongst the earliest, as I have been certainly amongst the most sincere and earnest friends and advocates of Union and Emancipation in America. And, permit me to say, Ladies and Gentlemen, that ardent as my feelings have always been in favour of the extinction of slavery in your country, I have not the less appreciated your exertions for the maintenance of your great and noble Union, nor have I the less, but rather the more on that account appreciated your terrible difficulties; made full allowance for what some have deemed slow progress, and have been disposed to give credit to those great men in your country who have set party predilections and long cherished prejudices aside, won a noble victory over them, and have during this great struggle identified themselves, in many cases in spite of past prejudices, so closely with the great cause of emancipation in which I am so particularly engaged. Gentlemen, I think I need scarcely furnish to you to-night any notice for thankfulness, in addition to those which have been so ably and so happily brought before you by your Chairman and by his Excellency, your Minister at the Court of my Sovereign. They have, I think, said enough to inspire in all your hearts feelings of the most glowing gratitude to that Being who is the God of nations, and who has appeared to strengthen you, to give you fortitude and resolution, and to bless you in the midst of your struggles with such abundance in regard to the material things of this world. I have been thinking how, notwithstanding the many reasons for sorrow, arising from the melancholy bereavements which have been occasioned by the war, while you have been, on the one hand, rejoicing in so much that is good, how different has been the condition of those your arrogant and proud enemies who a few years ago aimed to subjugate you, and to give laws to the world. While you are thanking God in the terms of the President's proclamation for teeming fields and healthful skies, for increase of population, far above any of the losses that you have sustained in the battle-field—while you are rejoicing in the harmony that prevails among you as a people in their undaunted resolution to persevere in the great work in which they are engaged, and while employment and plenty, even affluence abound; on the other hand, a fearful and striking and instructive retribution has fallen on those who are your opponents. I was reading to-day that in the city of Richmond, parties going to market to buy beef, carry their money in the basket, and put their beef into their pocket-books, and that pound for pound beef has a much higher value than the currency of the Confederate States (cheers). I find also that at Charleston the commonest necessaries of life, such as flour, firewood, sugar, butter, tea and coffee, are up at almost fabulous prices; and that even when the money is forthcoming, the butter is not always to be found. You have cause therefore to be thankful, and I hope when you shall assemble another year you will not only have reason to be thankful, but permission to say with my Lord John Russell, let us "rest and be thankful" (cheers). At present, however, there does not appear to be any opportunity for pause or rest; but there is, as his Excellency has stated, a glorious prospect in future. But, Sir, before I sit down, I would ask you, who are Americans, the men and women of America, the mothers and the daughters of America, while you are rejoicing on your own account, also to rejoice upon ours? When this war broke out, I did entertain the most grave and painful apprehensions of the consequences that would ensue to England from the stoppage of the supply of the raw material of our great cotton manufacture. When I have contemplated years and years ago such an event, for I have always deemed it not only possible but probable, I have never been able to look at it except in connection with whatever was disastrous, paralysing, and calamitous to our own country; and there is no doubt that there were those of the South in America who thought they had it in their power to bring upon us all these disasters by withholding from us what was so essential to the maintenance of our great manufacture, for we know, and volumes might be accumulated to prove it, that the South did boast that they held the destinies of this country in their hands, and not only could they control through sympathisers in the North and profligate politicians, the opinions of the Northern people, but they could, if they failed in coaxing, succeed in coercing England, not only into a recognition of their independence, when they should separate themselves from the North, but into active co-operation with them in the event of the North attempting to recover the portion of territory taken from them. Well, Sir, the crisis came, and we have for the last two years and a half been passing through that crisis. They did stop our supply of cotton; they did debar us from receiving that cotton upon which the welfare directly or indirectly of some five millions of our population has been wont to depend. We have been from compulsion constrained to remain for two and a half years almost wholly independent of American cotton. But, Mr. Chairman, I, as an Englishman, ask you, while you are sending up to Heaven your thanksgivings on behalf of the mercies and blessings vouchsafed to your country, to mingle with them thanksgivings on our behalf, that that which was apprehended to be one of the greatest calamities that could befal us, has turned out promotive of the best interests of our country, and as a means of more widely than ever developing not only the resources of our own dependencies, but the resources of other countries, which are now giving us that which the Southern States have for the present withheld from us (hear, hear). Sir, I do not know anything more likely to co-operate with the wise measures of President Lincoln, and the efforts of the friends of Emancipation in America, than this grand discovery, now no longer a matter of conjecture or theoretical demonstration, but a matter of actual practical accomplishment, that we can, if it must be so, do without that which heretofore has been furnished to us by the proprietors of plantations in the Southern States, through the agency of the uncompensated labour of their slaves. I think, Sir, that this will have the effect, seeing that we shall no longer be under any absolute necessity of looking to the Southern States for our supply of slave-grown cotton, of more completely dispossessing the minds of the people of the South of any idea that they can recover that predominance which they have hitherto enjoyed; and which will lead them up to the conclusion that policy, as well as justice and humanity, require that they should adopt another, a wider, a sounder, and more humane system; and if they are still to continue to be the growers of our great staple, cotton, they must condescend to grow it as other men grow it in other parts of the world, by free, voluntary, and compensated labour (hear,

hear). From the very best calculations that have been made, and no gentleman is better informed on that subject than the veteran statesman who sits in the chair before you to-night; I say that the very best calculations that have yet been made agree, at all events, in the opinion that we shall, during the coming year 1864, receive from various parts of the world, the Southern States included, a snpply fully equal to the employment of our population in the manufacturing districts for four days and a half per week. There are those, and they are very enlightened men, and well informed on this branch of the question, who believe that it will be found exceedingly difficult on the conclusion of the war to furnish anything like an adequate supply of cotton from the South—except it come as the produce of free labour to our ports (hear, hear). Now, Sir, I am no friend to that doctrine which teaches that we should be all for ourselves nationally, as well as individually. I think we should live for others as well as for ourselves. I am quite willing that we should continue, as we have done for the last century, to receive a large portion of our supply of cotton from the United States, but I am desirous that hereafter it should come to us, not as it has come associated with a system than which none can be either more unjust, or more inhuman, but that it should come to us as the produce of free labour, under the direction of men who are at once the friends of their country and the friends of mankind (cheers). While you have won many great victories in the field, I think you have also won many greater victories still in the conquests you have achieved over those many prejudices and party ties which in years that are gone prevented you from being so earnestly as it was wished you might have been the friends of Emancipation. Contrasting, as I do in my mind, what is the *status* which the negro, or the descendant from the negro, occupies in your country at this moment with the position which he occupied some few years ago, I cannot but congratulate him and congratulate you on the change which has taken place in his condition, brought about, I am willing to believe, and do believe, not more by the exigeneies of this war, than by the cultivation and development of a better and kindlier and juster feeling towards the man himself. It was to me, a remarkable sign of the times, that before we descended from yonder gallery into this room to partake of this banquet, and after the President's Proclamation had been read, that a gentleman, long a resident and senator from Mississippi, reared in the midst of slavery in the United States, should, as the president of this meeting, call on a gentleman of colour, an American, and but a few years ago a slave, to ask, upon our meeting together to-day, the benediction of Almighty God (loud cheers). Sir, I see the future destiny of America typified in that incident. Never again will the negro in America, the men who led the forlorn hope at Fort Hudson, the men who perished with the brave Colonel Shaw before Fort Wagner—I say never will the men who by their colour are linked with men like these, the twenty-five coloured regiments which I undertand from your chairman have already been enrolled in the State of Louisiana alone—never will those in your country who stand identified by colour and by race, by condition and by suffering with such men, be looked on as they have been in any part of the United States of America; and I believe the day will come when, as we have seen to-night, an enlightened statesman of the South, and a coloured man, lately a slave in North Carolina, are joined together in communion and fellowship. So in the United States, while men shall consult their tastes and their associates, we shall see a mutual recognition of the rights of man as man, and a free and generous acknowledgment of the right, even of the humblest to enjoy the immunities of citizenship and equality. Gentlemen, I thank you for the honour done me by being called on to respond to this toast—"The day," a day which I shall ever remember in connection with an assembly like this, in which not only have I seen a coloured man put in a position in which I never saw him before, but I have seen myself placed in a position very unusual to me, to be received so kindly by an audience like this, to whom I am personally a stranger, and for the sake of opinions and efforts which, at one time, were not considered very praiseworthy by the people of America, is to me another cheering sign of the times. Believe me, Gentlemen, that it is a source of inexpressible gladness to me that sentiments that twenty-five years ago were unpopular and exposed me to some small amount of odium, are to-day, I was going to say, as popular, and even more so, in the United States than they are now in my own country. I have always done justice to the American's love of liberty. I have always, as I think, justly estimated the great difficulties in which you were placed; the prejudices in which you were brought up, the dangers to which you thought your country might be exposed by a premature handling of this great and perilous Institution; and I have always been sensible of the Constitutional restrictions placed upon the actions of public men, and therefore I have not expected more than I knew men were competent to accomplish. But, on the other hand, so far from not having seen that accomplished, which I hoped and believed would be, all my largest expectations have been more than realized by the progress of events in the United States. Now that you are left to yourselves—now that even those who two years and a half ago preceded His Excellency your Minister at our Court, prognosticated even that he would not arrive, or, arriving, would find no nation to represent—seeing that those gentlemen and birds of the same feather have taken wing to their own roosts, and have given up in despair the cause which they thought was to prevail and conquer in Europe—now that they have gone back carrying evil tidings to their compatriots, and assuring them that no help is to be looked for, even from England—not even from France herself—I feel confident that the time is short that will intervene between the present and the moment when you will see your lost territory reunited to that which already you possess—your Constitution re-established—your laws not so much enforced as obeyed with willingness and with cheerfulness — your peaceful avocations also restored, and men withdrawn from the field of battle again busy in pursuing the peaceful arts of life—that you will find yourselves at the end of this great struggle far greater, far wiser, far happier, far more honourable, and far more stable than you were before it. For you, as I predicted twenty-nine years ago, in the last address I delivered before I was compelled to leave the country, for you there remained this second Revolution. You are going through it. It was necessary; it was to come. Every man saw it would come. Every man was desirous of putting off the evil day as far as he could. No man could predict precisely when the rupture would take place, but a rupture was certain at some period near or more distant. That rupture has come. It found your country in the state described. You have outlived all the difficulties, all the weakness, all the discord, all the embarrassments which beset you at the commencement. You now are strong—strong not only in the righteousness of your cause, but strong even in the respect of the nations of the world—stronger still in the good opinion of the discriminating few, the unselfish few, the truly generous few—the men who love your institutions, and who could wish that some of them were almost, if not altogether, as you are, Sovereigns of your own country (hear, hear). In their opinion, most of all, you stand high, and I have no doubt the time will come when events having falsified all the predictions of your enemies, and Heaven having smiled upon your exertions and rewarded your fortitude, you shall see your country reunited, and not only reunited, but its borders extended, its population augmented, its resources more greatly developed and purged of this hindrance, at once to your honour and your usefulness, which has so long existed in your midst, and altogether a free people, you shall, in communion with the lovers of freedom throughout the world, run a great and glorious career. Sir, once again I thank this assembly for their kind attention, and beg leave to submit the toast for their adoption (loud applause).

The Chairman.—I call for three cheers for George Thompson, the Anti-Slavery hero of this country (loud cheers).

The Chairman.—Now, Ladies and Gentlemen, fill up for the next toast, which will be responded to by Major Pangborn. It is sufficient to say that he comes from Boston, the cradle of American liberty—that he travels daily the field upon which Warren bled, and walks under the shadow of the monument at Bunker Hill. That toast is, "The Union—from "the Atlantic to the Pacific, from the Lakes to the "Gulf, from the source to the mouth of the Missis-"sippi, for ever one and inseparable" (loud cheers).

MAJOR PANGBORN: Mr. Chairman, Ladies and Gentlemen: I scarcely expected that here in England, more than three thousand miles from camp and field, I should be subjected to such a summary conscription; yet, Sir, after having regularly drafted another for service, you have allowed him to escape, and have laid the conscripting hand suddenly upon me. I submit, however, and shall only claim to be regarded as a substitute; thereby gaining this advantage; that, as a substitute is only required to serve for so long a time as he contracts, I shall make my term of service on this occasion as brief as possible; and besides, to make the contrast as sharp as may be, as it would have been far more agreeable to you and myself had the gentleman to whom was assigned the duty of responding to this sentiment been present, and in that case you would have had a *Wintering* season, I will make my action as summary as possible (laughter and cheers). The sentiment, to which you have done me the honour of asking me to respond, is not new to any American; yet, Sir, in its truest and best sense, it is one which never can become trite or old. "The Union for ever, one and inseparable," is a sentiment that finds a ready response in every American heart, at home or abroad, whether that heart be in the man or the child: it is instilled into our bosoms in childhood, and remains with us from the cradle to the grave; it needs no elucidation, and can scarcely receive embellishment, even from the tongue of eloquence. Here to-night, we, sojourners in a foreign land, unite our voices with those of our friends across the sea, who are keeping this national festival, in singing, with all sincerity and enthusiasm, "The Union, one and inseparable, now and for ever" (loud cheers). Why do we say this, and what right have we to thus insist on the maintenance of this sentiment, when we comprehend the struggle and the sacrifice which its triumphant assertion must involve? You all, doubtless, remember, as I do, the occasions in the past when we were wont to gather in the thanksgiving anniversary beneath the paternal roof and around the family fireside. Do you not also recall the feelings that chastened the rejoicings, and in a manner saddened the delights of the house, as we anxiously looked to see what links of the golden chain that bound the family circle had been severed since last we met? Not seldom have the tears that coursed adown the mother's cheek or bedewed the children's eyes, spoken touchingly, in the midst of the hilarity, of the "vacant chair," and the loved and lost," "who would join no more in the family thanksgiving. But, there is one possible incident of this anniversary more sad than this. Imagine the man from home, returning after years of absence to find, not one, but all his kindred gone; and more than this, as he stands upon the hill that overlooked the valley where he was born, he finds that even his homestead has passed away, and the place, that once knew it, shall know it no more for ever. Would he desire again to revisit the scene, and would not the anticipated joy of his thanksgiving be turned to an unutterable sorrow? (cheers). Well, my friends, regarding ourselves now, not merely as members of separate families, but as the children of one common country, this is precisely the position we should occupy, were the Union to be destroyed. If we could consent, by any act or word of ours, to practically deny the sentiment of the integrity and the perpetuity of the Union, we should, with our own hands, have assisted to pull down our own national rooftree, and we should never again celebrate a national thanksgiving, or have a habitation and a name among the nations. Can we consent to this? Here is just the point of greatest importance in the consideration of the struggle in which we as a nation are now involved. Ours is no contest of mere rival factions; no effort for ambitious conquest; no attempt at increased dominion, nor do any of the motives that ordinarily give rise to warfare underly this stupendous combat. It is neither more nor less than a struggle for a nation's life (cheers). We are contending for national existence, against traitors and rebels, who aim at nothing less than a national assassination. Are we not then justified in persisting in our determination to maintain the Union, and in doing this we must subdue the rebellion? (Loud cheers.) Those, who would rightly measure the enormity of the crime, must estimate the magnitude of the consequences that would ensue were the rebellion to succeed. The death of an individual is of comparatively small importance. You or I may be struck down—it is but a single unit withdrawn from the sum of human existence—the wave passes over it, and no ripple marks the place where it went down. Not so when a nation dies. Language is inadequate to portray the wreck and ruin that follow upon the destruction of a powerful, prosperous, and happy nationality. The wounds may cicatrize and partially be healed, but the evil consequences that inevitably ensue, mark the pathway of history for generations, with signs as ineffaceable as the track of the fiery lava flood (loud applause). And, therefore, I say again, to prevent this immeasurable calamity, we must preserve the Union; and our only antagonists in the contest, are those who have inaugurated and are sustaining a rebellion, which, for atrocity, has no parallel in human history, and no prototype, unless it be in the imaginative words of the great poet, who tells how Lucifer rebelled against the rightful authority of the Almighty, and "drew after him the third part of the stars of Heaven" (cheers). Again, our national honour demands of us that we maintain the Union. We are committed to this issue. With the individual when honour is sacrificed all is lost; and if I had better retire from association with civilized men, or even yield up existence, when I have sacrificed my personal honour, how much greater is the obligation upon us when aggregated as communities and nations, to see to it that our national honour is never stained or surrendered (applause). I will not enlarge upon this point; it is too obvious to need any amplification, as there is no nation on earth that would not now justly hold us in contempt and shower scorn upon us, if we should make terms with rebels in arms, or even discuss with them the question of the indissolubility of the Union (cheers). The Hon. Gentleman who presides here to-night has so ably and eloquently stated the reasons why we cannot, as a nation, for geographical and commercial considerations, consent to a division of the Union, that I will not dwell upon that theme. I fully concur with him, and with the sentiments to which I am responding, that "from the Atlantic to the Pacific, from the Lakes to the Gulf, from the source to the mouth of the Mississippi," the Union must be one and inseparable. We cannot afford to have either a divided nationality, or a country with a soil recognising conflicting jurisdictions. Our interlacing system of lakes and rivers, our continuous mountain ranges, whose towering peaks stand as answering sentinels to one another from Katahdin's brow to the snowy Sierra Nevada's crest, all tell us that the God of nature has given us one land for our inheritrnce. The Mississippi, with all its mighty tributary streams, must roll its waters to the Gulf, owning the protection and acknowledging the sway of but one national flag ; and the citizen of Boston and San Francisco, of New Orleans and New York, must enjoy equal privileges in each and all, and own allegiance to one national Government (loud cheers). But there are other considerations than those that spring from motives of patriotism or self-interest. The claims of humanity have an important place in the pending contest in our country, and lend weight to our resolution. It is but candour to admit that, in the commencement of our civil war, few even of our statesmen foresaw or believed that it would lead directly and speedily to the abolition of human slavery. Now, even the dullest of visions can see, through the smoke and rift of battle, that the rainbow of hope is not set for us alone. It portends the liberation of the long-enslaved race. All men see now that slavery is doomed—it must die the death. The problem is solved for which not even the wisest have found a solution. The sword has cut the Gordian knot. Nor can our erring brethren of the rebel States complain of us, if they have by their own act unwittingly contributed to this result. The arrogant slave-holder rebelled, hoping to make human bondage perpetual, and the rebellion has throttled slavery (cheers). The Haman of the slaveocracy is hanged to-day, in the sight of the civilised world, upon the gallows he built for the despised Mordecai of Emancipation. Shall we not give thanks for this? (Cheers.) The glaring inconsistency of which we have been guilty, in proclaiming the inalienable right of all men, without regard to colour, race, or creed, "to life, liberty, and the pursuit of happiness," while, at the same time, we were fastening the chains upon our bondmen, has made us too long the by-word of a mocking world. How could we intercede with the despots and tyrants of other lands on behalf of their oppressed victims, while this foul blot stained our national escutcheon? I remember the burning words of one of the noblest of American poets, penned long years ago, and applicable now:—

> "Go, ask the Czar of Russia's line,
> To loose his grasp on Poland's throat;
> Or beg the lord of Mahmoud's line,
> To free the struggling Sulliote.
>
> Will not the scorching answer come
> From turbaned Turk and fiery Russ,
> 'Go, loose your fettered slaves at home,
> Then turn and ask the like of us?'"

Shall we not rejoice in the near prospect that opens to us now, in anticipation of that hour, when we can stand up and in the face of the civilised world say, "Behold, our reproach is taken away?" Some poet has pictured, in the future, that a grand temple shall rise wherein all nations shall celebrate the final disenthralment of all the races from the dominion of error and tyrannic rule: and when that hour shall strike, no anthem of rejoicing will be welcomed with a more loud acclaim than that which commemorates the emancipation of the long-suffering sons of Afric's sunny clime, as, mingling with other choral songs, it echoes through the long colonnade and dies away upon the gilded architrave (loud applause). One word more, Mr. Chairman, and I have done. The Union will be preserved and made perpetual, because the loyal people will it so. It is the springing hope, the firm faith, and the unalterable determination of the government and people of the United States that gives me the confident assurance of our final victory. That determination is as immoveable as the foundations of our granite hills, and that hope and that faith as exhaustless as the sources of our mighty streams. The army, the navy, and the whole people alike sympathise in these views and feelings. Let me say that our soldiers fight from patriotic motives—no aspersion could be more unjust than that they are mercenary: no men ever went forth to battle with more unselfish promptings, none ever were more resolute in their purpose than the soldiers of the Union. Ask them why they fight; and they will answer you in the words of the appeal made by one of their own gallant comrades:—

"Stand by the flag—on land and ocean billow,
By it your fathers stood, unmoved and true;
Living, defended—dying, from their pillow,
With their last blessing passed it on to you.

"Stand by the flag—all doubt and treason scorning,
Believe with courage true and faith sublime,
That it will float, until the eternal morning
Pales in its glories all the lights of time."

(Loud cheers.)

And if you go to the citizens not in "the tented field," you will find in them the same abiding faith in the triumph of the right and the stability of the Union. They know that the dawning of the day of victory is sure to come. It is as true in public affairs, in national convulsions, as in the realm of nature, that—

"The night is mother of the day,
The winter of the spring;
And even upon old decay
The greenest mosses cling."

"Behind the cloud the starlight lurks,
Through showers the sunbeams fall,
Let 'patience have her perfect work,'
For God is over all."

So, in this faith and hope, we here to-night, whether homeward bound, or loiterers still upon a foreign shore, may look forward to many returns of this our anniversary; and rest assured, that when this ruthless storm of civil war, that burst upon our defenceless nation's head is overpast—as overpast it surely will be,—we shall all descry the rainbow, promise of perpetual peace, spanning a continent; and while its eastern arch shall spring from where the Atlantic surges answer back the sighing of the pines of the Aroostook and sing the requiem of the Puritans by Plymouth Rock, its western bow, with undimmed brilliancy, shall sink in the unvexed wave by the golden gate of the Pacific Sea (tremendous cheering).

THE CHAIRMAN (Mr. Walker).—Ladies, and Gentlemen, I am about to announce as the next toast, the great central sentiment which marks this contest, Emancipation. Next to the redemption of man, emancipation is that grand idea which most affects his present and future destiny. Emancipation which is to be the sure result of the present contest. It will change four millions of chattels into four millions of men and women, and will extend to them the rights to which all human beings are justly entitled under the providence of God (cheers). To respond to this great sentiment which is made a reality by this contest, we have selected one of the sons of New England, where liberty was first rocked in her cradle, and where would be the last mourners over her grave. Our worthy and excellent American Consul, at London, the Honorable Freeman H. Morse, will respond to the next toast—"The Emancipation Proclamation—Slavery's epitaph, written by the finger of God on the heart of the American President."

Mr. Morse rose amid great applause—and said—Mr. President, Ladies and Gentlemen: Of the many favours for which Americans have cause to turn towards their Maker with gratitude and thanksgiving, perhaps the greatest of all is the bright prospect of the early removal of that great injustice to an unoffending race of men, which has been the sole cause of long and bitter contention between North and South (applause), and which has at last ended in a gigantic civil war.

Of the many strange events brought into high relief by the struggle now going on in America perhaps there is none so impressive, and likely to prove so great in results, as the fact alluded to in the sentiment just announced. Civil war, the very means resorted to by the propagandists of slavery to enlarge, make more secure and enduring one of the greatest of national evils and crimes, human slavery, appears to be, for some inscrutable reason, the chosen instrument to overthrow that stupendous wrong, and to give liberty, free homes, and happiness to oppressed millions, making a great nation united, prosperous, and free indeed (great applause). Truly the ways of Providence are mysterious and past finding out. Slavery in the United States was once so weak in political, economical and social influence; and was so condemned by the moral sense of the American people, North and South, that but few volunteered in its defence, while nearly all shrunk from it, as from a thing, the touch of which was injustice and moral contamination. From such a feeble, undefended and despised thing it wound itself into the economic, social and political condition of the Southern people. It increased in strength, and to them became the most cherished and sacred of all their interests, and finally the all-powerful and dominant power in the nation. In the earlier years of the republic, the brave, the wise and good of the land, turned from slavery with pain and sadness, yet strong in faith that the day of its doom was not far in the future (cheers).

Years passed on, and men began to coin gold, to enjoy luxurious ease and to gain personal and political power, all wrung from the torn sinews and agonized hearts of the poor bondmen, when lo! whole States spring to its defence as if engaged in a holy cause.

Men calling themselves Statesmen, merchants, lawyers, planters, slave traders and slave drivers, even the poor houseless and homeless lazzaroni of the South, who have been made but little better than wandering gypsies under the iron rule of slavery, all sung its praises and cherished it as some something of more than mortal origin. Even those claiming to be the ministers of the Most High God, defended it as an institution divinely ordained, and upon which men and States could not rightfully lay their sacrilegious hands. From the day the slaveholders began to make slavery profitable to themselves by the production of cotton, sugar, and rice, they determined to make it a permanent and powerful institution. Henceforward, their public measures nearly all tended to one end, such an increase of sectional power as would give expansion, strength and permanency to human bondage. Perhaps there is not so strong an example in all history of the devotion of an entire class, or caste of men to a single idea and object, and that object so unjust, and so crowded with unmixed evil. For a period of years, running back over the third of a century, the firm embodiment of African Slavery into American institutions, and making it the controlling power in the Government, or the creation of a great, independent, slave-holding empire, has been the dominant and dearly cherished idea of Southern statesmen. For this detestable end they laboured, and persevered, and dissembled, and deceived the honest hearted and patriotic of their own section, as men have rarely laboured and presevered and dissembled before (applause). For this end they brought about a war with Mexico, and acquired territory over which they expected to spread human bondage. For this end they "filibustered" in Cuba and in Central America. For this end they have sought perseveringly to carry slavery into our national Territories, that new Slave States might the more readily gain admittance to the Union. For this end they established a parliamentary rule, excluding from Congress all petitions on the subject of slavery, while at the same time they claimed the right, without authority of law, to carry slavery under State law, into the national Territories, and to have these Territories admitted into the Union as Slave States (applause). It was for this they promulgated the heresy of State rights and nullification, by which they sought to uphold the South Carolina rebellion of 1832. To accomplish this end, always in view, they succeeded in securing *five* out of the nine judges on our Supreme Bench, that thereafter our Constitution, on all questions touching slavery, such as the Dred Scott case, might be constructed according to Southern opinion. For this end alone, the cold-blooded and cruel Fugitive Slave law of 1850, of which the Confederate Commissioner to England, Mr. Mason, was the author, was devised and forced from Northern fears of dissolution, into a law. It was for this they procured a repeal of the Missouri Compromise law, that they might carry slavery north of 36° 30 into Kansas; and they tried to establish it there by force, and by frauds the most stupendous and infamous that ever blackened the records of crime. Of the truth of this charge, Mr. President, no man is a better witness than yourself, being Governor of Kansas at the time, and no man did more to expose the frauds by which they attempted to impose slavery upon that young State, made strong and brave by suffering, than yourself (applause). For this they wrung from the Supreme Court the notorious Dred Scott decision, which set aside and overthrew as far as it could, the uniform decisions of all branches of the Government, legislative, executive and judicial, covering the whole period of our national existence from 1776 to 1857. Always persevering, they succeeded, by constant threats of destroying the Union, in intimidating the great Conservative party of the free States, and in making its policy vacillating and yielding. This constant dread of the future, made the party itself but too ready and anxious to compromise away its principles, in order to avoid dangers which could easily have been crushed in the bud, had the slaveholders and disunionists been boldly met, and before they obtained control over the Government, sternly rebuked. While they thus destroyed the power and influence of one of the great political parties of the free States, they succeeded in corrupting and debauching the other by the tempting bait of political power, and the "spoils of Office." Finally, so arrogant and imperious had they become, that they modestly demanded to have our fundamental law, the constitution of the United States, so amended as to recognise and establish therein the idea of property in man, and to guarantee the defence and protection of slavery, like other property, by the whole nation. They then proposed to engraft slavery into the national constitution, and to throw around it the protection of the laws and the shield of the whole republic, instead of leaving it where it was, under the weaker and more limited protection of the local State laws of the individual States, tolerating it.

The slave-holding States clearly beheld the moral sense of mankind rising up and protesting against the barbarism of slavery. They saw that nearly all the Powers of Europe had thrown off the disgrace, and that even Russia, so long called "the model despotism," was giving freedom to millions of serfs, and that public sentiment in America was fast rising to the just and grand idea of universal freedom; they therefore resolved on some bold and decisive measure to prolong the life of slavery, and give to it additional security. They saw too, the utter hopelessness of inducing the citizens of the free States to participate in their crime, and to consent to such a change in the constitution and laws of the republic as would make us a nation of Slave-holders, and Slave-traders (applause). I declare it, Mr. President, as my deliberate conviction, that there never was a people who shared so largely in the blessings of a good, generous, and just government, and yet felt its burdens so lightly. But they appreciated it not. They saw slowly-advancing but sure disaster gathering over their dearly cherished object, and they resolved to save it, even though at the risk of a nation's life. They hung in deceitful dalliance round the "Peace Congress," and feigned earnestness and anxiety in the Peace Committee of the House of Representatives, while in reality they were plotting secession, treason and rebellion in their secret midnight conclaves at Washington, under the very eye of their friend Buchanan (applause). The whole North was anxious, painfully anxious, to avoid a rupture, and to restore harmony between discordant States. For this purpose a Committee of one from each of the thirty-three States was raised in the House of Representatives, and instructed to take into consideration "the perilous condition of the country;" and, if possible, to unite on and report to the House, measures for the restoration of peace and concord. But, Sir, the disunionists had long before made up their minds to accept nothing, and to break up the Union. Their whole efforts in that Committee, called the "Committee of Thirty-three," because it was composed of one member from each State, was to force from the North new guarantees for slavery, such as would for ever disgrace the nation (applause). The Committee was willing to stand by the Constitution in every particular, as it had come from the founders of the Republic, and to execute it as it had been construed by the legal tribunals. This, our legal obligations as citizens of a common country, under a national constitution, bound us to do. But we could go no further. We could not take the downward step demanded of us; we could not, without relapsing into semi-barbarism, repudiate the principles upon which our government was founded, and vote ourselves a nation of slaveholders.

Slavery in the United States is a local institution, and exists only by the authority of the local municipal laws of the States tolerating it. The laws of one State are perfectly dead and have no force whatever in another State, or in a Territory. A law establishing or regulating slavery in one State, neither establishes it, prevents it, or tolerates it anywhere out of that State. Yet the Slave States claimed and demanded the right to carry slavery into the national Territories, those embryo States not of sufficient growth and strength to be admitted into the Union as States, and therefore remaining under the jurisdiction, care and protection of the national government. There being no law regulating or permitting slavery in the Territories, and slaves not being held under the Constitution of the United States, or under the common law, as property, by what right did they expect to establish their auction blocks in the national Territories? By none other than the right of the strongest, or by the consent of a whole nation, extorted from its dread of discord and its fear of a threatened dissolution of the Union. The North declined to turn back from its career of civilization and liberty to become the degraded instrument of spreading more widely the "barbarism of slavery," and riveting more firmly the fetters of the bondman. This refusal, perhaps, somewhat accelerated the revolt which the slaveholders had long before determined on, and for which they had been so long preparing. Thus we see, Sir, that the slaveholders' rebellion was caused entirely and solely by their determination to give a wider range and a greater security and stability to their cruel system of human bondage. Our system of State and national government is such that the United States have no legal right to emancipate slaves within the limits of any State in time of peace. Nor have they, perhaps, a right to do so in *loyal* States in time of war, unless there should be a strong public necessity for such a measure. But in States which are in rebellion against the government, and which are doing all they can to destroy it, the right of emancipation does exist under the war power. The President and his advisers, finding the slaves to be an arm of great strength to the rebellion; that they fed its armies, dug its trenches, reared its fortifications, performed useful labour of all kinds, even fighting in the ranks as soldiers, thought the time had come to weaken the rebellion by offering freedom to all slaves in rebel territory. By this measure the President expected to weaken the rebellion, aid in restoring the Union, and at the same time to do justice to a long oppressed race, and make a nation free in fact as well as in name. The United States profess to be the freest of all enlightened nations. They started in their career with the grand declaration that all men are created equal in the eye of the law, and are "endowed by their Creator with certain inalienable rights," and yet they have permitted *four million* human beings to be held in the most abject bondage within their limits, held and controlled by the most inhuman and barbarous laws that ever disgraced any age or people. Why do not the principles of the Declaration apply to our long-suffering bondmen? The *right* to freedom is not the gift of kings or emperors, of parliaments or congresses, but it comes from that ever wise and just God who created both black and white, intelligent and accountable beings (great applause). To steal a human being, to rob him of this heavenly gift, and appropriate him and his issue, mind and body, to our use, is a crime that never did, and never will go unpunished. Sooner or later, a just retribution will overtake individuals and nations in some form. America's time has come, and she is reaping the bitter fruit of her great transgression. The nations which have been sent to premature graves by the deadly influence of slavery, the future peace and prosperity of a great nation and her millions of bond-men, are all pleading with us, not to let what seems to be God's appointed time, go by without making an earnest effort to root the whole system of slavery out of every foot of our soil (applause). The series of measures adopted by Congress with a view to this most desirable result, are all that could be expected or perhaps desired. Then followed the grandest measure of all, the Emancipation Proclamation, of the 22nd of September, 1862, which gave, as we believe, the death-blow to slavery, and made the name of Abraham Lincoln immortal applause). This Proclamation declared all persons held as slaves in States or parts of States, which should be in rebellion against the United States, on the 1st of January, 1863, to be, with their descendents for ever, free; and it pledged the civil and military arms of the government to the maintenance of their freedom. This bold and just measure rather startled old timid Conservatives and venomous copper-heads from their propriety. The first did not want to be disturbed, and could not realize that they were passing through a great moral and political revolution. The latter had so long administered the government, on their pro-slavery party platform, instead of by the Constitution and laws, that they had naturally come to believe the country could not be governed, for their interests, by any other rule. This class of men, with many in the border Slave States, raised the cry of abolitionism (as though that were still a word of power), of servile insurrection, the sacred rights of property, radicalism and revolution, to alarm the country, intimidate the President and induce him to withdraw the Proclamation. But the country would not be alarmed, and our brave chief stood firm and would take no step backward (loud applause). On the contrary he pressed on to the fulfilment of his appointed work, and on the first day of January, 1863, a day hereafter to be ever remembered in the history of liberty, the final Proclamation was issued, and the glorious work of giving liberty to the bondmen in America commenced in sober earnest. It is something to be sincerely thankful for, Mr. President, that slavery in America, the greatest barrier to universal emancipation, will soon be for ever removed. Our country is the most powerful and enlightened of all the nations that tolerated slavery, prior to the first day of the present year. When this foul reproach upon our honour, love of justice, and our good name is wiped away, then without the blush of shame mantling to our cheeks, we can take our place among the free nations of the earth, to urge on the work of overthrowing slavery, until a bond-man shall no where be found within the limits of civilized States. The abolition of slavery in America will also have a very favourable influence on the civilization of Africa. For nearly four centuries that country has been the prey of nations calling themselves civilized. Tribe has been set against tribe, and the country kept in a state of constant civil war for hundreds of years, that slaves might be obtained for the markets of Christendom. For the last few years that market has been reduced almost entirely to Cuba and the Slave States of America. What a position, what an association! Would to Heaven we could have seen ourselves as others saw us. When slavery in America falls, as fall it soon will, the system in Cuba, and wherever it may still linger in the Western Continent, will not long survive the shock, and there will be rejoicing in Africa, and peace and civilization at last, for that long persecuted race.

In our own country too, emancipation will be a blessing in any point of view, especially considered morally, socially and politically. Instead of the large plantation of hundreds and sometimes thousands of acres, where a single man sits enthroned a despot, controlling the happiness and lives of hundreds of human beings destined to immortality like himself; instead of a superficial cultivation that soon exhausts the soil and forces its abandonment, instead of a few isolated families scattered over an extended territory, with the auction block where human flesh is bought and sold, with the whipping post and scourge, the armed overseers and negro drivers, the slave catchers and their bloodhounds, emblems all of a slaveholding civilization, we shall see scattered everywhere the thrift, energy, prosperity and intelligence of a free people, relying upon their own exertion for success (applause). Instead of the general idleness of the native white population, the simple industrial pursuits to which the slaves are confined, the poverty, ignorance and semi-barbarism which so largely prevail in a country where nature has lavished her richest gifts, churches and school-houses will dot her valleys and hill sides, and a free, industrious, intelligent, and law-abiding population, will take the place of the human machines which move, toil, suffer, and often die, at the pleasure of their owners. Instead of those vast solitary plantations, where tyranny reigns and bondmen toil for others gain, independent farmers will work with free hands their own soil, and make it always productive. Slavery removed, immigrants from the free States, and from Europe will make that favoured land their home, and carry with them all industrial pursuits. The removal of slavery and the breaking up of a powerful slaveholding aristocracy, will in my judgment so increase the value of land, draw out the natural resources of the country, and create such a homogeneousness of pursuits, such a harmony of interests all over the country, as to make the United States stronger and more united and inseparable than ever (loud applause).

I firmly believe too, Mr. President, that in less than twenty years from this date the United States, taken as a whole, will be far richer than if there had been no civil war, and slavery had gone on its career of tyranny and misrule.

The first day of January 1863 will form an epoch in human history, an era in human progress, at which future historians of civilization will linger with special pleasure, as the chosen time from which to date a great advance in the life and exaltation of a whole race of the human family.

To this race it will ever be a holiday, the annual

dawn of which will be ushered in with joy and rejoicing, and a grateful remembrance of the far-seeing and good author of the Emancipation Proclamation. His name will be associated with that Proclamation, and go with it to the future, blessed and beloved, as long as liberty and justice shall be revered among men (loud applause).

The CHAIRMAN (Mr. Walker).—Ladies and Gentlemen, I must ask you for three cheers for the Hon. Freeman H. Morse, the American Consul to London (loud and continued cheering).

THE CHAIRMAN (Mr. Walker).—Ladies and Gentlemen, I will call your attention to the next toast, which is "The Army and Navy—immortal champions of freedom, who bleed that our country may live." It was our Army and Navy, under the lead of Washington, through a seven years' war, that established the American Union. It is that Army and Navy which is now carrying the same flag triumphantly throughout the rebel States, and which will soon float that banner over every acre of the soil, and over every drop of the waters of the South (loud cheers). We have now here a gallant and distinguished representative of that flag, who has carried it forward to victory in many a bloody battle-field, Captain Mayne Reid, who will respond to this toast (loud cheers).

CAPT. MAYNE REID.—Mr. Chairman, Ladies and

Gentlemen, the toast for which I have the honour to stand sponsor needs no support from me. It is fortunate that it is so, else I might have declined the duty upon the score of incapacity. I have one advantage, however, which is not always the privilege of a public speaker. I understand my subject. I know the Army and the Navy of the United States, perhaps not so well as their enemies know them (laughter). But I know them well, and the world begins to know them too (cheers). I feel myself in a proud position, standing as I do in the presence of this assemblage of American patriots, graced as it is by some of America's fairest daughters (applause). Who would not feel flattered at being, even for a brief moment, the cynosure of such eyes? I do; not the less that I am half an American in nationality and wholly one in heart, and yet in this presence I feel something of shame—shame that my sword has not gone with my soul into that struggle between God and the devil upon the other side of the Atlantic which is now progressing (loud cheers). I can plead but one apology, which by some may be considered a poor one, and would scarcely win me even the compassion of the ladies, that my duty to my fellow-women has outweighed that which I owe to my fellow-men. I shall speak no more of myself but of my subject, and that is war. I am no advocate for war, though I am far from being imbued with that holy, or rather with that hypocritical horror of it that has so lately sprung up in the bosoms of so many Englishmen. I shall hail with joy that happy millennium when the sword becomes transformed into the sickle. When that time comes, I shall be found one among the foremost of the apostles of peace; but that time cannot come so long as there are men on the earth who will not cease to do evil and learn to do well. Till that time, war will not only be a stern necessity, but a sacred duty, ascending at times even to holiness. Give but a noble cause, and the warrior becomes ennobled.

> "Give that and welcome war to brace
> Her drums, and rend heaven's reeking space;
> The colours plant face to face,
> The charging cheer,
> Though death's pale horse lead on the chase,
> Shall still be dear."

And what nobler cause than that in which the Army and Navy of the United States are now contending? (cheers). Where shall we seek for a holier and a nobler cause? Shall we seek for it in history, in religion, in romance? We may look for it but we shall not find it. What is this cause? It is the North against the South, of Federal against Confederate. Sink those silly words. They are but the emblems of a faction, a mere faction,—a big faction it is true; but still an almost imperceptible fraction of that assemblage of souls and bodies to be affected by the issue of this struggle. But the strife is not even American—it is not confined within the limits of a continent or a hemisphere, it belongs to the whole universal world; for I repeat again, it is the cause of God against the enemy of mankind. If it prevail I look forward to the time, and that time ere long, when the down-trodden helots of earth shall taste that sweet cup which has been so long withheld from their lips, the cup of liberty. If it be the will of God it should falter and fail, and that the hour of man's regeneration has not yet arrived, then will the despot plant his heel more firmly, and grasp with his hand more tightly, the neck of his unfortunate victim; not only will the black bondsman of Africa retain his chains and his slavery, but the white bondsmen of Europe—aye, of England—tax his toil in his eternal degradation. The throes of this great struggle are already felt to the remotest corners of the earth, but what are those throes when compared with its results? Not since the fiend fell from Paradise has there been such a strife so eventful of consequences to the whole human race. Surely God has not designed such a destiny for the children of freedom. Surely he will not abandon the soldiers whom he has chosen to fight on his side. No, I cannot believe it. The Army and Navy, which I have here the honour to represent, will crush the rebellion, because it is causeless and accursed (loud cheers). Accursed! the only rebellion in history that has earned this epithet. America has obtained the credit of producing new and strange phenomena, and here is one of the newest and strangest of all—

a rebellion without a cause. In all my readings I can find no rebellion, revolution, or emeute that cannot plead the justification of a cause. Some injury to be redressed—in most instances a desire to obtain human rights. But here is a rebellion that has no injury to redress, and has not got any right to acquire, but, on the contrary, has no cause, no creed, unless we accept that infamous one it has unblushingly avowed in the face of the world, the perpetuation of human wrongs (applause). Such a creed in the middle of the nineteenth century, they have dared to put forth in the face of all mankind—in the second half of a century which boasts of its civilization. Death to the champions of such a cause! Shame and confusion to its abettors! Ah, its abettors! I have been wandering far away over the world of mind and matter, but that idea brings me home. You Americans wonder that it has found abettors, and above all in England. England, so long wedded to a detestation of slavery. Some of you have, perhaps, found the explanation with that cuteness for which your nation is proverbial. You have no doubt been able to see to the bottom of our shallow and hypocritical cant. You perhaps know why that twenty millions was spent in the purchase of the West India negro, loudly proclaimed to the four corners of the earth. Why, one of your clever countrywomen was fêted here—not so much for her literary talents, as for her advocacy of abolitionism.

If you do not know that, I shall tell you, for it was to brew the bad blood which has since sprung up between you; and now that the hell broth has come to a boil, the twenty million expenditure is repented, and the authoress receives the cold shoulder. Perhaps you will ask for another reason. You will think that you have discovered it in our jealousy of your Republic. There you will be mistaken. It is not from jealousy of your Republic, but from a pure hatred of your Republic and of every other on the face of the earth that we had this hostility which is called neutrality. How could it be otherwise? The English child is generally trained to detest the word "Republic," from the time that he is able to lisp it. He is taught hostility towards it, he is taught to hate it, he is taught to hate it in his church and his school, he finds it in his Common Prayer, and meets with it in his primer and spelling book. The clergyman of his parish and his subservient satellite, the schoolmaster, if they teach him nothing else—and but little else do they teach him—take care emphatically to embue his mind with this hatred of the Republic. How then can you expect most Englishmen to do otherwise than hate the Republic? Just now, your unhappy struggle has furnished his instructors with what they believe to be an unanswerable argument. They point to that struggle, and cry, "all," "all," and loudly proclaim, through unprincipled speakers and truculent scribblers, the failure of Republican Institutions. Happy words for their witlings. Were they not stricken with Cimmerian blindness, they would see as I do in this failure of Republican Institutions their greatest triumph and success. They would recognize in this struggle of twin giants, a power that united would have challenged the whole monarchical world in arms. They will see it yet. The scales will drop from their eyes, perhaps when it is too late. The sentries who should have warned them have not been asleep, only untrue to their trust. It is perfectly absurd to suppose that the half dozen lordlings, who, under the pseudonym of statesmen, preside over the destinies of England, can scarcely be ignorant of the terrible legacy that they are leaving to England's people. They may not live to see it administered, though it will some day yet be distributed in tears. What care they! Statesmen, forsooth! rather let us call them state-craftsmen, jugglers in the philosophy of social science, standers behind the chairs of conspiring sovereigns, expounders of fossilized formularies, which have so long held the whole of the human race in thraldom—these are the things presented to us under the appellation of statesmen. And the first bottle-holder of the *troupe*, he who erst promised to pass himself off for the guardian of liberty—an eagle seated upon a rock, and watching over its destinies—he, too, has proved himself but a spurious bird—not even a peacock, with all his vanity, but a poor turkey, with bedraggled plumes, which, please God, I shall one day pluck out, leaving him in all the nakedness of his infamy. What cares he for the legacy he is leaving to England! What cares he for the tears which are to follow at its administration! Nothing—even if there should be enough of weeping to supply water for an ocean. *Après moi le deluge* was the motto of his prototype. *Après moi le deluge et enfer,* seems to be the guiding star of his servile imitator. But I weary you with the subject. I am myself sick of it; but I cannot close my lips until I have purified them with a higher and holier theme. The army and navy of the United States—the immortal champions of freedom who have bled that their country may live. Alas! too many of them have already bled, and too many of them must still bleed —I had almost said, die. But no; they will not die. 'Tis not death to fall in the fight of freedom. They only will die who fight against her—murder-sullied in the sight of heaven! Our soldiers and sailors who may fall in this eventful struggle will not die. They will live in the memories of their comrades who survive, of their friends who sent them forth, of the nation who will be proud of their deeds; and, if fewest in number, not less foremost in thought, in the hearts of the patriotic assemblage that here encircles me. Who need lament the death of a hero to whom the grave is already robbed of half its gloom? So sang the greatest of your own poets; not that pretty prattler, whose feeble warblings so well suit the silly sentimentality of the age, but a bird of bolder flight and nobler song—Fitz-Green Halleck. Hear how one of your own poets apostrophizes when it fell upon a soldier of freedom:—

> " But to the hero, when his sword
> Has won the battle for the free,
> Thy voice sounds like a prophet's word,
> And in its bolder tones are heard
> The thoughts of millions yet to be.
> Come when this task of fame is wrought;
> Come in his laurel-leaf, blood-bought;
> Come in his crowning hour; and then,
> Thy sunken eye's unearthly light,
> To him is welcome as the sight
> Of sky and stars to prisoned men;
> Thy grasp is welcome as the hand
> Of brothers in a foreign land;
> Thy summons welcome as the cry,
> That told the Indian Isles were nigh,
> To the world-seeking Genoese,
> When the land wind, from fields of balm,
> And orange groves, and trees of palm,
> Blew o'er the Haytian seas."

No, soldier and sailor of America, should you fall in this fight, do not fear that your country will forget you—

> " For thee her poet's lyre is wreathed,
> Her marble wrought, her music breathed.
> For thee she rings her birthday bells,
> For thee her babes first lisping tells,
> For thee her evening prayer is said,
> By palace, couch, and cottage bed.

Her soldier closing with the foe,
Gives for thy sake a deadlier blow.
Her plighted maiden when she fears
For him, the pride of her young years,
Thinks of thy fate, and checks her tears.
And e'en the mother of thy boys—
Though in her eye and faded cheek
I read the grief she may not speak,
The memory of her buried joys—
Will by the pilgrim-circled hearth,
Talk of thy doom without a sigh;
For throughout Freedom's age and Fame's,
Some of the few, the immortal names
That were not born to die."

[Loud cheers.]

THE CHAIRMAN [Mr. Walker].—Ladies and Gentlemen, I will give you the next toast, embodying a name to which the whole civilized world will respond, and which will be re-echoed in Heaven—"Washington, the man without a Peer. We follow his farewell advice—NEVER TO SURRENDER THE UNION." We have present Captain J. C. Hoadley, a brave and distinguished officer of the Army of the United States, who will respond to this toast. Words or monuments can add no eulogy to Washington. His sublime and stainless history is written in the freedom of his country and mankind. I will simply announce the toast, and recommend his last advice—"NEVER TO SURRENDER THE UNION" [loud cheers].

CAPTAIN HOADLEY.—Mr. Chairman, Ladies and

Gentlemen, I should be no less oppressed by the duty you have assigned to me than I am confused by the partiality of your introduction if I supposed I could be expected to say anything which could add to the sentiments of love and veneration in which you all hold the name of the father of our country. Most of you have heard no doubt Mr. Everett's elegant eulogy; all of you hold enshrined in your hearts the image of Washington. You all know how far that image transcends; you all know how much the halo which enshrines it outshines the sun of even his golden sentences. I shall therefore not be silent. One single trait I may, however, call to mind, since, if I remember right, it was passed by in silence by Mr. Everett, who may well be pardoned for omitting a single trait, and indeed many traits, in an hour's review of a character so rich. The point to which I allude was the emancipation of his slaves by Washington. In the maturity of his judgment, in the fulness of his fame, in the richness of his character, when the shadows of time were drawing less powerfully upon his mind, and the solemn results of eternity began to assert their power, Washington, with strict justice, with a strict reference to all the rights of others so far as it lay in his power, emancipated every bondsman which the law said he owned. He thus placed the weight of his great name and the power of his vast influence on the side of emancipation. And for this, we at this hour know how to reverence him. On a single other point I will venture to say a word, and that is an instance of the symmetry of his character, which like that of the Belviderean Apollo, comes out and reveals new beauties wherever it is unveiled and wherever seen. In the important discussions which have just taken place before the august court within the precincts of Westminster Hall, the name of Washington has been brought into familiar acquaintance with the jurists and jurisprudence of England, and there is no American but must have been proud and happy to see the honourable position which Washington is seen to have taken so early on the important questions which are to be settled by this suit, whose echoes will reach far beyond the echoes of the walls within which it was conducted. Very early, almost without precedent, before it had ever been discovered that neutrals had rights, stemming the current of the irritation against England, that the revolutionary war had left, resisting the more generous impulses which drew him and the nation towards the late generous ally of his struggling country, he laid down a system of policy so just, so wise, and because it was so wise and just, a system so politic, that it has steered us safely through all the wars of the world since our country's existence—has carried us through more than half a century of war, perhaps sometimes not actual war, but that latent war which is the busy preparation of future war which inexperienced statesmen call peace, through more than half a century of perpetual war, without ever having led us, or permitted us to commit any acts which any nation could complain of—which has enabled us to maintain an actual neutrality, and to do right and justice to all the world without any injustice or constraint on the liberties of our own citizens. But the second portion of the toast claims my attention, and, indeed, in thinking of Washington, we must naturally think of his chief work, the American Union, of which he was one of the chief authors. And what a work it is! The Government which has given us peace for three generations, over half the world, which has only been known by its blessings, and which would have given us peace for ever, but for infernal treason which broke the spell. But it is said that the Union is destroyed. We are perpetually told that it is gone—dead—dead as the Heptarchy. But if the Heptarchy died in the embraces of the Union, would you have us erect a Heptarchy—nay a quintuple Heptarchy—on the ashes of our Union? If you would, you will not see it. That is not our destiny. We shall not permit it. It is true that the organs of public opinion in England, which I have followed pretty constantly during the few weeks that I have been residing here, after having gained our attention and probably opened our hearts to the reception of their generous sentiments by the overtures of calumny, misrepresentation, and ridicule, now reason with us very plausibly to show how much better off we should be, if we only, like the South, were to erect ourselves into a sovereign power with a military oligarchy on our frontiers. It was said of old that when the Roman Empire passed away, there was an end of liberty; so now it may be said that if the Empire and the Union were to perish, the liberty of the world would be gone. There is something a little suspicious in the smoothness of this counsel; it is a little too like the tones of the good wife who calls to her ducks, "dilly, dilly, dilly, come and be killed." The American Union in war is better than Europe in peace. But it is said, it is done—divided—the country is gone. It is a war of boundaries, and you must settle the question of boundaries, otherwise the war will never end. But suppose it should not end! Suppose we fight this century out! Suppose the twentieth century should dawn, and the war still be raging! I venture to say, if the peace of Europe remains unbroken from this hour to that, that the nineteenth century will have given us more institutions, more of peace, more of liberty, more of prosperity, less of devastations and evil, than the institutions of Europe will give to Europe. But it is said the country is gone, the country is divided; you must make your line. Mr. Chairman, I have thought this advice important enough to attempt to follow it. Having traversed my country in every direction, having swept down its magnificent rivers and crept up them, and travelled over the railways in all directions, having been in all the States, save a few of the Atlantic seaboard, I took Colton's excellent map to see if I could find a boundary. Not confining myself to the Potomac or the Ohio, which did not answer the conditions, I tried every thing that would serve as a boundary—I took the line of alluvial hills on some sluggish stream, and I even resorted to railway tracks, indeed to anything that might serve as a demarcation between the countries. I thought at first that the best mode would be to shut my eyes and tear the map in two. But I have discovered a boundary, and wonderful to say it is a boundary which we can accept, and a boundary which the traitors must in the last resort make; but which we may admit without disgrace to our country. I have found a boundary which, if inevitable, must be accepted. It is the surface of God's free earth from sun to sun, and from the Lakes to the Gulf. We will give the traitors all below, down to the central fires; but by the leave and permission of Heaven, the people of the United States will have all above up to the Empire of the Eternal Throne. In conclusion, I beg to offer a sentiment which I will preface with a single remark. The name I am about to offer you is a name loved in America as the name of the only Englishman in place and power who seemed to hesitate to plunge with headlong fury, almost with glee, into a war with us in the moment of our dire extremity. The name of the man whose voice was raised to soften the utterance of an unwelcome, unpalatable despatch, so that it might be accepted by a proud and high-spirited people without humiliation. I offer you the memory of "His Royal Highness, the late Prince Consort." The Americans will always cherish with gratitude and admiration the name of "Albert the Good." (Loud and continued cheering.)

Here Mr. WALKER said he knew by personal intercourse with Prince Albert in 1851 and 1852, that this able and excellent man was a great friend and admirer of our country. Inheriting these kind feelings of both his illustrious parents, the Prince of Wales repeatedly expressed similar sentiments during his recent visit to America. It would be wicked and absurd to deny that these facts have produced a profound impression in our country in favour of England.

THE CHAIRMAN, (Mr. Walker).—I am about to present a toast which is never received in America except with the deepest feeling, because it announces a power which is above that of artillery, above that of President or Cabinets, more potent than all other political influences—it is "The Press." We have selected to respond to that toast one of the distinguished editors of this great city, one on whose head rests not the *snow* of many winters, but one who is endeared to every friend of liberty and of the Union by the distinguished part which he has taken in this great contest. When others turned back he was firm, when the great political machinery which is supposed to control the vast Government of England—when the still more magic power of gold was brought to bear against us, the Press, which he controls, the "Observer," together with the ever glorious "News" and "Star," in our darkest hour, in the very midst of our greatest disasters, when our friends turned back and rebellion seemed to have achieved a victory, he stood firm. He was courageous and undazzled; to him every true American patriot owes an immeasurable debt of gratitude. That friend, whose head is not yet frosted by the snow of many winters, is Mr. Snow, the Editor of the Observer. To this toast he has kindly consented to respond. That toast is this, "The Press, The Tyrants' foe, the People's friend—where it is free, despotism must perish." (Loud applause.)

Mr. Snow:—Mr. Chairman, Ladies and Gentlemen: I have very little to say of the Press. We have a free Press in this country; you have a free Press in your country, and we both make use of it. I am sorry to say that a great deal is said by the Press of both countries that had better be left unsaid; for my own part, I can only say, that proud and pleased as I am to be amongst so many Americans here, I never knew an American in my life until the commencement of your struggle. When your contest commenced, I said to myself, it will be a calamity to mankind if this great Republic is broken up, and I took such steps as I deemed advisable on the occasion. With regard to what your Chairman, Mr. Walker, has said about gold, I know nothing, and therefore I have nothing to say on that subject. I thank you all for your courtesy and consideration in drinking my health, and I am very much obliged to you.

Mr. WASHINGTON WILKS, being called on in complimentary remarks by the Chair, said, Mr. Chairman, Ladies, and Gentlemen, I thank you for the honour and pleasure of being one of your guests to-night. I had hoped to have spent this thanksgiving day in your country, to have been perchance in New England, and have partaken there of that hospitality which has become familiar to me through your literature. I hoped to have had the opportunity, in the close of this year, to have said something in America touching the feelings of England towards your great country in its present struggle. I was told I could do better service if I remained, and so I have given up for this year that pleasant hope. But I am glad to meet you here to-night. I have waited through the five hours of your feasting in order to have an opportunity of responding to the toast of "The Press," which has just been given. Perhaps I might expect that as a right as well as accept it as a privilege, for I make bold to say that if there be any journalist in England to whom the credit of really continuous self-service on this question belongs, it is even to so humble a person as myself (cheers). I believe I have written upon this question, in various papers, fully 500 articles since the election of Mr. Lincoln, or the beginning of this war. I have made more than 200 speeches. I am sure that every article and every speech might have been made or written by one of yourselves as well as by me (cheers). When journalists who now are honoured by the approbation of Americans, were writing against you week by week, I day by day was battling in your cause. Gentlemen, do not misunderstand the English press in this matter. There is a portion of the English press that is essentially sectional. There is a portion essentially venal. There is a portion essentially popular. The sectional press may be aristocratic in one case, and may be mercantile in another case, because it is very likely to be pro-American in your struggle. The venal press has been sometimes against you, and sometimes for you, and I take its support or opposition to be of about like value. The popular press I take to be that which advocates precisely for the people of England, the rights which men enjoy, as men, in your own country (applause). That press represents just those men who have always been accused of trying to Americanise English Institutions. Now, Sir, that was the only portion of the English press from whom you had any right at all to expect sympathy in this struggle. I say deliberately, you had no right to expect from the aristocratic press of England sympathy in this struggle. If it had been for you, so much the worse for you; the chances are that the people would not have been with you, and you ought to have them with you. If the venal press was against you or for you, it all depended upon whether you bought it. But if the popular press—the press which has advocated the application to England of precisely those principles which are embodied in American institutions, and which, consequently, has always been abused as American, democratic, and revolutionary; if they had not been with you, then I take leave to say, you ought to have enquired whether or not you might not yourselves be wrong. But I am confident that that Press as a body, and the men whom it represents—the men who speak its language on the platform—have been with you from the very beginning of this struggle, and will be with you to the very end of it. It is no good at all to mince this matter—it is of no use for the American people across the Atlantic in their own country to be abused, as I fear they are much abused, by continual representations that the people of England, nearly one and all, are against them, and that it is simply exceptional men who plead for them. That is not so. I would not consent to be honoured with an invitation to an American Banquet in England, or welcomed by Americans in America, as an exceptional Englishman, I claim to be a representative Englishman. It is the men who are against you, who are the exceptional men the men who are with you are the representative men. The men who are against you are the men who stand in high places, belonging to the aristocracy of birth, or the aristocracy of wealth. You cannot name one man distinguished in the aristocracy of intellect and letters who has gone against you. Such men as our Stuart Mills, and men of that stamp, our very chieftains of intellect and of eloquence—are the men who have gone for you as by the instinct and by the law of their being. I take you to witness that all the popular chieftains of England—the natural exponents of English thought and feeling, not only men like Cobden and Bright, but inferior men, influential in their various spheres, have as certainly gone with you, and as naturally as the stars in their orbits have accomplished their purpose and destined path. It could not be otherwise. You are struggling for precisely the things that we are struggling for. You are struggling to establish popular sovereignty when threatened by aristocratic rebellion. We are struggling to establish popular sovereignty against an aristocratic supremacy. (Loud Applause.) You are sustaining a just government against a wicked rebellion—we are leading a great rebellion, though only a moral one, against unjust and unrighteous institutions. With you, the battle is to defend what your fathers bequeathed to you—with us, the battle is to attain that which we want to hand down to our children. We want nothing that you have not already got—we care not much whether our commonwealth be ruled by a monarch or a president. England is no monarchy—England is a free commonwealth, as is yours, and we also want to make our commonwealth as perfectly free as yours. As you have no one Christian sect rearing its mighty head above the rest, aad looking down in contempt and arrogance on all outside her, so we want to have no ecclesiastical aristocracy domineering above the Christian commonalty. As you have no class of nobles burning to rule, but choose your senate from your wisest and your best, so we choose to have no territorial lords ruling Parliament by virtue of their acres and their pedigrees. As you have the one blot on your escutcheon, the evil being your heir-loom, a degraded and abject class whom you are endeavouring to raise—we have an abject degraded pauper class whom we are striving to emancipate from the bondage of destitution and ignorance and vice. Thus, then, you see your cause is just our cause. The men who are against you, are the men who are against us; and I protest, from the knowledge of English affairs—at least as long as my life has been—that there is not one man, who has spoken against the American Union and its struggle, whom we English Radicals do not regard as our opponent, our stumbling block, and our disgrace (hear, hear). Now, as I ought to have been gone long since, I need offer no excuse for stopping here, and certainly I will not further encroach upon your time. To attempt a speech upon the Press, at this hour, would be simply ridiculous, moreover, that is not to-night my function, I simply thank you again, Mr. Chairman, for the invitation to attend here, and for giving me the chance of saying these few words. I have only to express my hearty hope that whatever battles we may have to fight, whatever the intensity of the struggle you may have to sustain on your side of the water, however severe the struggle may be with us in the same cause, that by this time next year, when Thanksgiving Day comes round again, be it in London or in your own Boston, that I may have the happiness to meet with Englishmen and Americans rejoicing that God has blessed his people with fruitful fields and crowded storehouses, rejoicing in the progress of industry, and the profits of commerce; rejoicing in the re-election of Abraham Lincoln as President, and rejoicing, above all, that that Republic, delivered from the trouble of intestine rebellion, and foreign enmity, has escaped from all her perils, and arisen safe and glorious to the smile of God's benediction (loud and prolonged applause).

THE CHAIRMAN (Mr. Walker).—Now, Ladies and Gentlemen, I am called upon to announce the last toast. This is a toast which finds a response in all our hearts, and to which no one is able, in our opinion, to make an adequate answer. It is, therefore, the toast to which we will all—all respond—it is "The Ladies—our sweethearts, wives, mothers daughters, sisters, friends. Their holy influence will break all chains but those which bind our hearts to them." Three cheers for "the Ladies" (loud cheers).

A VOICE.—Three cheers for the old folks at home.

MR. G. W. BELDING.—Ladies and Gentlemen, before we part to night, I think our thanks are justly due to the eloquent gentleman who has so ably presided here. I propose to you the health and long life of the Honourable Robert J. Walker. I will propose that you receive that sentiment with three cheers on his behalf. (Loud cheers.)

MR. GIRARD RALSTON called for one cheer more for Mr. Walker, which was given enthusiastically, the ladies waving their handkerchiefs.

MR. WILSON.—I beg leave to second the motion of thanks to our Chairman for his great kindness, and great ability in presiding upon this occasion.

We are under the deepest obligations to him. We venerate him for his services to the Union. We love him for his affection to our country, and I hope that you will give him your hearty thanks for his kindness in presiding upon this occasion. (Loud and continued cheering.)

Mr. Chairman.—Ladies and Gentlemen, I thank you all my countrymen, but infinitely more my country-women, for the indulgent kindness with which you have received the few words which have been announced to you in favour of my poor and humble services. I can only say to you, I have no sentiment, no wish, no faith—beyond that embraced in the success of the American Union. In that I feel all that is dear to man, but especially all that is dear to woman is included. Whilst our men have contributed much to maintain the American Union, although they have offered up their lives upon the battle-field—have suffered in rebel dungeons—have endured all that man can suffer in such a struggle as this, I feel that without the aid, the smiles, and encouragement of the ladies, we could have done nothing. If, therefore, as we all believe, the American Union shall be preserved for the benefit of our country, and mankind, more, infinitely more—far beyond anything that pen can write, or tongue can speak, will be due to the loyal ladies of America. It is they who urged us on to conquer or die for our country. It is they whose inspiration cheered us on to victory, rallied the faltering column, or sustained us in defeat. Without their aid we could never have had a million of volunteers for this contest. It is they who solaced the captive, nursed the wounded soldier; they who smoothed the pillow of death, and received the last sigh of the departing spirit, as it rose to the bosom of its God. Then, as a farewell toast, with all my heart, with all the thoughts it can breathe, and all the sentiments it can utter, I give "The Ladies of America." God bless them! (Prolonged applause.)

AMERICAN

FINANCES AND RESOURCES.

LETTER

No. I.

OF

HON. ROBERT J. WALKER, M.A.

COUNSELLOR AT LAW IN THE SUPREME COURT OF THE UNITED STATES,
LATE LAW REP. MI., SENATOR OF THE UNITED STATES,
SECRETARY OF THE TREASURY, COMMISSIONER TO CHINA,
GOVERNOR OF KANSAS, ETC., ETC.

LONDON:
WILLIAM RIDGWAY, 169, PICCADILLY, W.
1863.

AMERICAN FINANCES AND RESOURCES.

LETTER No. I.

London, 10, *Half Moon Street, Piccadilly.*
August 5, 1863.

THE question has been often asked me, here and on the Continent, *how has your Secretary of the Treasury (Mr. Chase) so marvellously sustained American credit during this rebellion, and when will your finances collapse?* This question I have frequently answered in conversations with European statesmen and bankers, and the discussion has closed generally in decided approval of Mr. Chase's financial policy, and great confidence in the wonderful resources of the United States.

Thus encouraged, I have concluded to discuss the question in a series of letters, explaining Mr. Chase's system, and stating the reasons of its remarkable success. The interest in such a topic is not confined to the United States, nor to the present period, but extends to all times and nations. Indeed, finance, as a science, belongs to the world. It is a principal branch of the doctrine of "the wealth of nations," discussed, during the last century, with so much ability by Adam Smith. Although many great principles were then settled, yet political economy is emphatically progressive, especially the important branches of credit, currency, taxation, and revenue.

Mr. Chase's success has been complete under the most appalling difficulties. The preceding administration, by their treasonable course, and anti-coercion heresies, had almost paralyzed the Government. They had increased the rate of interest on Federal loans from six to nearly twelve per cent per annum. Their Vice-President (Mr. Breckenridge), their Finance Minister (Mr. Cobb), their Secretary of War (Mr. Floyd), their Secretary of the Interior (Mr. Thompson), are now in the traitor army. Even the President (Mr. Buchanan), with an evident purpose of aiding the South to dissolve the Union, had announced in his messages the absurd political paradox, that *a State has no right to secede, but that the Government has no right to prevent its secession.* It was a conspiracy of traitors, at the head of which stood the President, secretly pledged, at Ostend and Cincinnati, to the South (as the price of their support), to aid them to control or destroy the republic. Thus was it that, in time of profound peace, when our United States six per cents. commanded a few weeks before a large premium, and our debt was less than $65,000,000, that Mr. Buchanan's Secretary of the Treasury (Mr. Cobb) was borrowing money at an interest of nearly twelve per cent. per annum. Most fortunately that accursed administration was drawing to a close, or the temporary overthrow of the Government would have been effected. Never did any minister of finance undertake a task apparently so hopeless as that so fully accomplished by Mr. Chase in reviving the public credit. A single fact will illustrate the extraordinary result. At the close of the fiscal year ending 1st July, 1860, our public debt was only $64,769,703, and Secretary Cobb was borrowing money at twelve per cent. per annum. On the first of July, 1863, in the midst of a stupendous rebellion, our debt was $1,097,274,000, and Mr. Chase had reduced the average rate of interest to 3·89 per cent. per annum, whilst the highest rate was 7·30 for a comparatively small sum to be paid off next year. This is a financial achievement without a parallel in the history of the world. If I speak on this subject with some enthusiasm, it is in no egotistical spirit, for Mr. Chase's system differs in many respects widely from that adopted by me as Minister of Finance during the Mexican war, and which raised United States *five per cents.* to a premium. But my system was based on specie or its real and convertible equivalent, and would not have answered the present emergency, which, by our enormous expenditure, necessarily forced a partial and temporary suspension of specie payments upon our banks and Government. Mr. Chase's system is exclusively his own, and, in many of its aspects, is without a precedent in history. When first proposed by him it had very few friends, and was forced upon a reluctant Congress by the great emergency, presenting the alternative of its adoption or financial ruin. Indeed, upon a test vote in Congress in February last, it had failed, when the premium on gold rose immediately over twenty per cent. This caused a reconsideration, when the bills were passed and the premium on gold was immediately reduced more than the previous rise, exhibiting the extraordinary difference in a few days of twenty-three per cent., in the absence of any intermediate Federal victories in the field.

Such are the facts. Let me now proceed to detail the causes of these remarkable results. The first element in the success of any Minister of Finance is the just confidence of the country in his ability, integrity, candour, courage and patriotism. He may find it necessary, in some great emergency, like our rebellion, to diverge somewhat from the *via trita* of the past, and enter upon paths not lighted by the lamp of experience. He must never, however, abandon great principles, which are as unchangeable as the laws developed by the physical sciences. When Mr. Chase, in his first annual Treasury Report of the 9th of December, 1861, recommended his system of United States banks, organized by Congress throughout the country, furnishing a circulation based upon private means and credit, but secured also by an adequate amount of Federal stock, held by the Government as security for its redemption, it was very unpopular, and encountered most violent opposition. The State banks, and all the great interests connected with them, were arrayed against the proposed system. When we reflect that many of these banks (especially in the great State of New York) were based on State stocks, and in many States that the banks yielded large revenues to the local government;—when we see, by our Census Tables of 1860 (p. 193), that these banks numbered 1642, with a capital paid up of $421,890,095, loans $691,495,580, and a circulation and deposits, including specie, of $544,469,134,—we may realize in part the tremendous power arrayed against the Secretary. This opposition was so formidable, that neither in the public press nor in Congress did this recommendation of Mr. Chase receive any considerable support. Speaking of the *currency* issued by the State banks, and of the substitute proposed by Mr. Chase, he presented the following views in his first annual report before referred to, of December, 1861:—

"The whole of this circulation constitutes a loan without "interest from the people to the banks, costing them nothing "except the expense of issue and redemption and the interest on "the specie kept on hand for the latter purpose; and it deserves "consideration whether sound policy does not require that the "advantages of this loan be transferred in part at least, from the "banks, representing only the interests of the stockholders, to "the government, representing the aggregate interests of the "whole people.

"It has been well questioned by the most eminent statesmen "whether a currency of bank notes, issued by local institutions "under State laws, is not, in fact, prohibited by the national "Constitution. Such emissions certainly fall within the spirit, "if not within the letter, of the constitutional prohibition of the "emission of bills of credit by the States, and of the making by "them of anything except gold and silver coin a legal tender in "payment of debts.

"However this may be, it is too clear to be reasonably disputed "that Congress, under its constitutional powers to lay taxes, to "regulate commerce, and to regulate the value of coin, possesses "ample authority to control the credit circulation which enters so "largely into the transactions of commerce and affects in so many "ways the value of coin.

"In the judgment of the Secretary the time has arrived when "Congress should exercise this authority. The value of the "existing bank note circulation depends on the laws of thirty-"four States and the character of some sixteen hundred private "corporations. It is usually furnished in greatest proportions by "institutions of least actual capital. Circulation, commonly, is "in the inverse ratio of solvency. Well-founded institutions, of "large and solid capital, have, in general, comparatively little "circulation; while weak corporations almost invariably seek to "sustain themselves by obtaining from the people the largest "possible credit in this form. Under such a system, or rather "lack of system, great fluctuations, and heavy losses in discounts "and exchanges, are inevitable; and not unfrequently, through "failures of the issuing institutions, considerable portions of the "circulation become suddenly worthless in the hands of the "people. The recent experience of several States in the valley "of the Mississippi painfully illustrates the justice of these "observations; and enforces by the most cogent practical argu-"ments the duty of protecting commerce and industry against "the recurrence of such disorders.

"The Secretary thinks it possible to combine with this protec-"tion a provision for circulation, safe to the community and "convenient for the government.

"Two plans for effecting this object are suggested. The first "contemplates the gradual withdrawal from circulation of the "notes of private corporations and for the issue, in their stead "of United States notes, payable in coin on demand, in amounts "sufficient for the useful ends of a representative currency. The "second contemplates the preparation and delivery, to institutions "and associations, of notes prepared for circulation under national "direction, and to be secured as to prompt convertibility into "coin by the pledge of United States bonds and other needful "regulations.

"The first of these plans was partially adopted at the last "session of Congress in the provision authorizing the Secretary "to issue United States notes, payable in coin, to an amount not "exceeding fifty millions of dollars. That provision may be so "extended as to reach the average circulation of the country, "while a moderate tax, gradually augmented, on bank notes, will "relieve the national from the competition of local circulation. "It has been already suggested that the substitution of a national "for a state currency, upon this plan, would be equivalent to a "loan to the government without interest, except on the fund to "be kept in coin, and without expense, except the cost of prepara-"tion, issue, and redemption; while the people would gain the "additional advantage of a uniform currency, and relief from a "considerable burden in the form of interest on debt. These "advantages are, doubtless, considerable; and if a scheme can be "devised by which such a circulation will be certainly and strictly "confined to the real needs of the people, and kept constantly "equivalent to specie by prompt and certain redemption in coin, "it will hardly fail of legislative sanction.

"The plan, however, is not without serious inconveniences and "hazards. The temptation, especially great in times of pressure "and danger, to issue notes without adequate provision for "redemption; the ever-present liability to be called on for "redemption beyond means, however carefully provided and "managed; the hazards of panics, precipitating demands for "coin, concentrated on a few points and a single fund; the risk "of a depreciated, depreciating, and finally worthless paper

" money; the immeasurable evils of dishonoured public faith and " national bankruptcy; all these are possible consequences of the " adoption of a system of government circulation. It may be " said, and perhaps truly, that they are less deplorable than those " of an irredeemable bank circulation. Without entering into " that comparison, the Secretary contents himself with observing " that, in his judgment, these possible disasters so far outweigh " the probable benefits of the plan that he feels himself constrained " to forbear recommending its adoption.

" The second plan suggested remains for examination. Its " principal features are, (1st) a circulation of notes bearing a " common impression and authenticated by a common authority; " (2d) the redemption of these notes by the associations and " institutions to which they may be delivered for issue; and (3d) " the security of that redemption by the pledge of United States " stocks, and an adequate provision of specie.

" In this plan the people, in their ordinary business, would " find the advantages of uniformity in currency; of uniformity in " security; of effectual safeguard, if effectual safeguard is possible, " against depreciation; and of protection from losses in discounts " and exchanges; while in the operations of the government the " people would find the further advantage of a large demand for " government securities, of increased facilities for obtaining the " loans required by the war, and of some alleviation of the burdens " on industry through a diminution in the rate of interest, or a " participation in the profit of circulation, without risking the " perils of a great money monopoly.

" A further and important advantage to the people may be " reasonably expected in the increased security of the Union, " springing from the common interest in its preservation, created " by the distribution of its stocks to associations throughout the " country, as the basis of their circulation.

" The Secretary entertains the opinion that if a credit circula- " tion in any form be desirable, it is most desirable in this. The " notes thus issued and secured would, in his judgment, form the " safest currency which this country has ever enjoyed; while their "receivability for all government dues, except customs, would "make them, wherever payable, of equal value, as a currency, in "every part of the Union. The large amount of specie now in "the United States, reaching a total of not less than two hun-"dred and seventy-five millions of dollars, will easily support "payments of duties in coin, while these payments and ordinary "demands will aid in retaining this specie in the country as a "solid basis both of circulation and loans.

"The whole circulation of the country, except a limited amount "of foreign coin, would, after the lapse of two or three years, "bear the impress of the nation whether in coin or notes; while "the amount of the latter, always easily ascertainable, and, of "course, always generally known, would not be likely to be "increased beyond the real wants of business.

"He expresses an opinion in favour of this plan with the "greater confidence, because it has the advantage of recommenda-"tion from experience. It is not an untried theory. In the "State of New York and in one or more of the other States it "has been subjected, in its most essential parts, to the test of "experiment, and has been found practicable and useful. The "probabilities of success will not be diminished but increased by "its adoption under national sanction and for the whole country.

"It only remains to add that the plan is recommended by one "other consideration, which, in the judgment of the Secretary, is "entitled to much influence. It avoids almost, if not altogether, "the evils of a great and sudden change in the currency by "offering inducements to solvent existing institutions to withdraw "the circulation issued under State authority, and substitute that "provided by the authority of the Union. Thus, through the "voluntary action of the existing institutions, aided by wise "legislation, the great transition from a currency heterogeneous, "unequal, and unsafe, to one uniform, equal, and safe, may be "speedily and almost imperceptibly accomplished.

"If the Secretary has omitted the discussion of the question "of the constitutional power of Congress to put this plan into "operation, it is because no argument is necessary to establish "the proposition that the power to regulate commerce and the "value of coin includes the power to regulate the currency of the "country, or the collateral proposition that the power to effect "the end includes the power to adopt the necessary and expedient "means.

"The Secretary entertains the hope that the plan now sub- "mitted, if adopted with the limitations and safeguards which "the experience and wisdom of Senators and Representatives "will, doubtless, suggest, may impart such value and stability to "government securities that it will not be difficult to obtain the "additional loans required for the service of the current and the "succeeding year at fair and reasonable rates; especially if the "public credit be supported by sufficient and certain provision "for the payment of interest and ultimate redemption of the "principal."

Congress adjourned after a session of eight months, and failed to adopt Mr. Chase's recommendation. Indeed, it had then but few advocates in Congress or the country. Events rolled on, and our debt, as anticipated by Mr. Chase, became of vast dimensions. In his report of December, 1861, the public debt on the 30th June, 1862 (the close of the fiscal year), was estimated by the Secretary at \$517,372,800; and it was \$514,211,371, or more than \$3,000,000 less than the estimate. In his report of December 4, 1862, our debt, on the 30th June, 1863, was estimated by Mr. Chase at \$1,122,297,403, and it was \$1,097,274,000, being \$25,023,403 less than the estimate. The *average* rate of interest on this debt was 3·89, being \$41,927,980, of which \$30,141,080 was payable in gold, and \$11,786,900 payable in Federal currency.

It will thus be seen that the whole truth, as to our heavy debt, was always distinctly stated in advance by Mr. Chase, and that the debt has not now quite reached his estimate. Long before the date of the second annual report of the Secretary, the banks had suspended specie payments, and the Secretary renewed his former recommendation on that subject in these words:—

" While the Secretary thus repeats the preference he has here-
" tofore expressed for a United States note circulation, even when
" issued direct by the government, and dependent on the action
" of the government for regulation and final redemption, over the
" note circulation of the numerous and variously organized and
" variously responsible banks now existing in the country; and
" while he now sets forth, more fully than heretofore, the grounds
" of that preference, he still adheres to the opinion expressed in
" his last report, that a circulation furnished by the government,
" but issued by banking associations, organized under a general
" act of Congress, is to be preferred to either. Such a circula-
" tion, uniform in general characteristics, and amply secured as
" to prompt convertibility by national bonds deposited in the
" treasury, by the associations receiving it, would unite, in his
" judgment, more elements of soundness and utility than can be
" combined in any other.

" A circulation composed exclusively of notes issued directly by
" the government, or of such notes and coin, is recommended
" mainly by two considerations:—the first derived from the faci-
" lity with which it may be provided in emergencies, and the
" second, from its cheapness.

" The principal objections to such a circulation as a permanent
" system are, 1st, the facility of excessive expansion when expen-
" ditures exceed revenue; 2d, the danger of lavish and corrupt
" expenditure, stimulated by facility of expansion; 3d, the dan-
" ger of fraud in management and supervision; 4th, the impossi-

" bility of providing it in sufficient amounts for the wants of the " people whenever expenditures are reduced to equality with " revenue or below it.

" These objections are all serious. The last requires some " elucidation. It will be easily understood, however, if it be " considered that a government issuing a credit circulation cannot " supply, in any given period, an amount of currency greater than " the excess of its disbursements over its receipts. To that " amount, it may create a debt in small notes, and these notes " may be used as currency. This is precisely the way in which " the existing currency of United States notes is supplied. That " portion of the expenditure not met by revenue or loans has " been met by the issue of these notes. Debt in this form has " been substituted for various debts in other forms. Whenever, " therefore, the country shall be restored to a healthy normal " condition, and receipts exceed expenditures, the supply of " United States notes will be arrested, and must progressively " diminish. Whatever demand may be made for their redemption " in coin must hasten this diminution; and there can be no re- " issue; for reissue, under the conditions, necessarily implies dis- " bursement, and the revenue, upon the supposition, supplies " more than is needed for that purpose. There is, then, no mode " in which a currency in United States notes can be permanently " maintained, except by loans of them, when not required for " disbursement, on deposits of coin, or pledge of securities, or in " some other way. This would convert the treasury into a " government bank, with all its hazards and mischiefs.

" If these reasonings be sound, little room can remain for doubt " that the evils certain to arise from such a scheme of currency, " if adopted as a permanent system, greatly overbalance the tem- " porary though not inconsiderable advantages offered by it.

" It remains to be considered what results may be reasonably " expected from an act authorizing the organization of banking " associations, such as the Secretary proposed in his last report.

" The central idea of the proposed measure is the establish- " ment of one sound, uniform circulation, of equal value through-

"out the country, upon the foundation of national credit com-"bined with private capital.

"Such a currency, it is believed, can be secured through bank-"ing associations organized under national legislation.

"It is proposed that these associations be entirely voluntary. "Any persons, desirous of employing real capital in sufficient "amounts, can, if the plan be adopted, unite together under pro-"per articles, and, having contributed the requisite capital, can "invest such part of it, not less than a fixed minimum, in United "States bonds, and, having deposited these bonds with the "proper officer of the United States, can receive United States "notes in such denominations as may be desired, and employ "them as money in discounts and exchanges. The stock-"holders of any existing banks can, in like manner, organize "under the act, and transfer, by such degrees as may be found "convenient, the capital of the old to the use of the new associa-"tions. The notes thus put into circulation will be payable, "until resumption, in United States notes, and, after resumption, "in specie, by the association which issues them, on demand; "and if not so paid will be redeemable at the treasury of the "United States from the proceeds of the bonds pledged in "security. In the practical working of the plan, if sanctioned "by Congress, redemption at one or more of the great commer-"cial centres, will probably be provided for by all the associations "which circulate the notes, and, in case any association shall fail "in such redemption, the treasurer of the United States will pro-"bably, under discretionary authority, pay the notes, and cancel "the public debt held as security.

"It seems difficult to conceive of a note circulation which will "combine higher local and general credit than this. After a few "years no other circulation would be used, nor could the issues "of the national circulation be easily increased beyond the legiti-"mate demands of business. Every dollar of circulation would "represent real capital, actually invested in national stocks, and "the total amount issued could always be easily and quickly "ascertained from the books of the treasury. These circum-

"stances, if they might not wholly remove the temptation to ex- "cessive issues, would certainly reduce it to the lowest point, "while the form of the notes, the uniformity of devices, the sig- "natures of national officers, and the imprint of the national seal "authenticating the declaration borne on each that it is secured "by bonds which represent the faith and capital of the whole "country, could not fail to make every note as good in any part "of the world as the best known and best esteemed national "securities.

"The Secretary has already mentioned the support to public "credit which may be expected from the proposed associations. "The importance of this point may excuse some additional ob- "servations.

"The organization proposed, if sanctioned by Congress, would "require, within a very few years, for deposit as security for cir- "culation, bonds of the United States to an amount not less than "$250,000,000. It may well be expected, indeed, since the "circulation, by uniformity in credit and value, and capacity of "quick and cheap transportation, will be likely to be used more "extensively than any hitherto issued, that the demand for bonds "will overpass this limit. Should Congress see fit to restrict the "privilege of deposit to the bonds known as five-twenties, autho- "rized by the act of last session, the demand would promptly "absorb all of that description already issued and make large "room for more. A steady market for the bonds would thus be "established and the negociation of them greatly facilitated.

"But it is not in immediate results that the value of this "support would be only or chiefly seen. There are always "holders who desire to sell securities of whatever kind. If "buyers are few or uncertain, the market value must decline. "But the plan proposed would create a constant demand, equal- "ling and often exceeding the supply. Thus a steady uni- "formity in price would be maintained, and generally at a rate "somewhat above those of bonds of equal credit but not avail- "able to banking associations. It is not easy to appreciate "the full benefits of such conditions to a government obliged to "borrow.

"Another advantage to be derived from such associations "would be found in the convenient agencies which they would "furnish for the deposit of public moneys.

"The Secretary does not propose to interfere with the indepen-"dent treasury. It may be advantageously retained, with the "assistant treasurers already established in the most important "cities, where the customs may be collected as now, in coin or "treasury notes issued directly by the government, but not fur-"nished to banking associations.

"But whatever the advantages of such arrangements in the "commercial cities in relation to customs, it seems clear that the "secured national circulation furnished to the banking associations "should be received everywhere for all other dues than customs, "and that these associations will constitute the best and safest "depositaries of the revenues derived from such receipts. The "convenience and utility to the government of their employment "in this capacity, and often, also, as agents for payments and as "distributors of stamps, need no demonstration. The necessity "for some other depositaries than surveyors of ports, receivers, "postmasters, and other officers, of whose responsibility and "fitness, in many cases, nothing satisfactory can be known, is "acknowledged by the provision for selection by the Secretary "contained in the internal revenue act; and it seems very clear "that the public interest will be secured far more certainly by the "organization and employment of associations organized as pro-"posed than by any official selection.

"Another and very important advantage of the proposed plan "has already been adverted to. It will reconcile, as far as "practicable, the interests of existing institutions with those of "the whole people.

"All changes, however important, should be introduced with "caution, and proceeded in with careful regard to every affected "interest. Rash innovation is not less dangerous than stupified "inaction. The time has come when a circulation of United "States notes, in some form, must be employed. The people "demand uniformity in currency, and claim, at least, part of the "benefit of debt without interest, made into money, hitherto enjoyed "exclusively by the banks. These demands are just and must be "respected. But there need be no sudden change; there need "be no hurtful interference with existing interests. As yet the "United States note circulation hardly fills the vacuum caused by "the temporary withdrawal of coin; it does not, perhaps, fully "meet the demand for increased circulation created by the "increased number, variety, and activity of payments in money. "There is opportunity, therefore, for the wise and beneficial "regulation of its substitution for other circulation. The mode "of substitution, also, may be judiciously adapted to actual "circumstances. The plan suggested consults both purposes. "It contemplates gradual withdrawal of bank note circulation, "and proposes a United States note circulation, furnished to "banking associations, in the advantages of which they may "participate in full proportion to the care and responsibility "assumed and the services performed by them. The promptitude "and zeal with which many of the existing institutions came to "the financial support of the government in the dark days which "followed the outbreak of the rebellion is not forgotten. They "ventured largely, and boldly, and patriotically on the side of the "Union and the constitutional supremacy of the nation over "States and citizens. It does not at all detract from the merit of "the act that the losses, which they feared but unhesitatingly "risked, were transmuted into unexpected gains. It is a solid "recommendation of the suggested plan that it offers the "opportunity to these and kindred institutions to reorganize, "continue their business under the proposed act, and with little "loss and much advantage, participate in maintaining the new "and uniform national currency.

"The proposed plan is recommended, finally, by the firm "anchorage it will supply to the union of the States. Every "banking association whose bonds are deposited in the treasury "of the Union; every individual who holds a dollar of the "circulation secured by such deposit; every merchant, every "manufacturer, every farmer, every mechanic, interested in trans-

"actions dependent for success on the credit of that circulation, "will feel as an injury every attempt to rend the national unity, "with the permanence and stability of which all their interests "are so closely and vitally connected. Had the system been "possible, and had it actually existed two years ago, can it be "doubted that the national interests and sentiments enlisted by it "for the Union would have so strengthened the motives for adhe- "sion derived from other sources that the wild treason of secession "would have been impossible?

"The Secretary does not yield to the phantasy that taxation is "a blessing and debt a benefit; but it is the duty of public men "to extract good from evil whenever it is possible. The burdens "of taxation may be lightened and even made productive of "incidental benefits by wise, and aggravated and made intolerable "by unwise, legislation. In like manner debt, by no means "desirable in itself, may, when circumstances compel nations to "incur its obligations, be made by discreet use less burdensome, "and even instrumental in the promotion of public and private "security and welfare.

"The rebellion has brought a great debt upon us. It is pro- "posed to use a part of it in such a way that the sense of its "burden may be lost in the experience of incidental advantages. "The issue of United States notes is such a use; but if exclusive, "is hazardous and temporary. The security by national bonds of "similar notes furnished to banking associations is such a use, "and is comparatively safe and permanent; and with this use "may be connected, for the present, and occasionally, as circum- "stances may require, hereafter, the use of the ordinary United "States notes in limited amounts.

"No very early day will probably witness the reduction of the "public debt to the amount required as a basis for secured "circulation. Should no future wars arrest reduction and again "demand expenditures beyond revenue, that day will, however, at "length come. When it shall arrive the debt may be retained on "low interest at that amount, or some other security for circula- "tion may be devised, or, possibly, the vast supplies of our rich "mines may render all circulation unadvisable except gold and "the absolute representatives and equivalents, dollar for dollar, of "gold in the treasury or on safe deposit elsewhere. But these "considerations may be for another generation.

"The Secretary forbears extended argument on the constitu- "tionality of the suggested system. It is proposed as an auxiliary "to the power to borrow money; as an agency of the power to "collect and disburse taxes; and as an exercise of the power to "regulate commerce, and of the power to regulate the value of "coin. Of the two first sources of power nothing need be said. "The argument relating to them was long since exhausted and is "well known. Of the other two there is not room, nor does it "seem needful to say much. If Congress can prescribe the "structure, equipment, and management of vessels to navigate "rivers flowing between or through different States as a regula- "tion of commerce, Congress may assuredly determine what cur- "rency shall be employed in the interchange of their commodi- "ties, which is the very essence of commerce. Statesmen who "have agreed in little else have concurred in the opinion that the "power to regulate coin is, in substance and effect, a power to "regulate currency, and that the framers of the Constitution so "intended. It may well enough be admitted that while Congress "confines its regulation to weight, fineness, shape, and device, "banks and individuals may issue notes for currency in competi- "tion with coin. But it is difficult to conceive by what process "of logic the unquestioned power to regulate coin can be sepa- "rated from the power to maintain or restore its circulation, by "excluding from currency all private or corporate substitutes "which affect its value, whenever Congress shall see fit to exer- "cise that power for that pnrpose.

"The recommendations, now submitted, of the limited issue of "United States notes as a wise expedient for the present time, "and as an occasional expedient for future times, and of the or- "ganization of banking associations to supply circulation secured "by national bonds and convertible always into United States "notes, and after resumption of specie payments, into coin, are "prompted by no favour to excessive issues of any description of "credit money.

"On the contrary, it is the Secretary's firm belief that by no "other path can the resumption of specie payments be so surely "reached and so certainly maintained. United States notes re- "ceivable for bonds bearing a secure specie interest are next best "to notes convertible into coin. The circulation of banking as- "sociations organized under a general act of Congress, secured by "such bonds, can be most surely and safely maintained at the "point of certain convertibility into coin. If, temporarily, these "associations redeem their issues with United States notes, re- "sumption of specie payments will not thereby be delayed or "endangered, but hastened and secured; for, just as soon as vic- "tory shall restore peace, the ample revenue, already secured by "wise legislation, will enable the government, through advan- "tageous purchases of specie, to replace at once large amounts, "and, at no distant day, the whole, of this circulation by coin, "without detriment to any interest, but, on the contrary, with "great and manifest benefit to all interests.

"The Secretary recommends, therefore, no mere paper money "scheme, but, on the contrary, a series of measures looking to a "safe and gradual return to gold and silver as the only perma- "nent basis, standard, and measure of values recognized by the "Constitution—between which and an irredeemable paper cur- "rency, as he believes, the choice is now to be made."

Congress, however, was still unwilling to adopt the recommendations of the Secretary, until the necessity was demonstrated by the course of events. On reference to the laws, which are printed in the Appendix, it will be found, that the great features of the system of the Secretary were as follows:—

1. A loan to the Government upon its bonds reimbursable in twenty years, but redeemable after

five years, at the option of the nation, the interest being six per cent. payable semi-annually in *coin*, as is also the principal.

2. The issue of U. S. legal tender notes, receivable for all dues to the nation except customs, and fundable in this U. S. 5.20 six per cent. stock.

3. The authorization of the banks recommended in his report, whose circulation would be secured not only by private capital, but by adequate deposits of U. S. stock with the Government.

4. To maintain, in the meantime, as near to specie as practicable, this Federal Currency,—1st, by making it receivable in all dues to the Government except for customs; 2nd, by the privilege of funding it in United States stock; 3rd, by enhancing the benefit of this privilege, not only by making the stock, both principal and interest, payable in specie, but by making it gradually the ultimate basis of our whole bank circulation, which as shown by the Census Tables before referred to, (including deposits) nearly doubles every decade.

5. By imposing such a tax on the circulation of the State banks, as together with state or municipal taxes, would induce them to transfer their capital to the new banks proposed by the Secretary.

6. To relieve the *new banks* from all state or municipal taxation.

7. In lieu thereof, to impose a moderate Federal tax on all bank circulation, as a bonus to be paid cheerfully by these banks for the great privilege of

furnishing ultimately the whole paper currency of the country, and the other advantages secured by these bills.

This tax, as proposed by the Secretary, was one per cent. semi-annually, which *in effect* would have reduced the interest on our principal loans from six to four per cent. per annum, so far as those loans were made the basis of bank circulation. Congress, however, fixed this tax at about one half, thus making the interest on such loans equivalent in fact to five per cent. per annum, so far as such loans, at the option of the holder, are made the basis of banking and of bank circulation. This is a privilege which gives great additional value to these loans, for the right to issue the bank paper circulation of the country free from state or municipal taxes, is worth far more than one-half per cent. semi-annually, to be paid on such circulation. That this privilege is worth more than the Federal tax, is proved by the fact, that many banks are already being organized under this system, and by the further fact, that more than $200,000,000 of legal tenders have already been funded in this stock, and the process continues at the rate of from one to two millions of dollars a day. It will be observed, that the holders of such bonds can keep them, *if they please*, disconnected with all banks, receiving the principal at maturity, as well as the semi-annual interest, in gold, free from all taxes.

This system has been attended with complete

success, and, notwithstanding the increase of our debt, the premium on gold, for our Federal currency, fundable in this stock, has fallen from 73 per cent. in February last, before the adoption of Mr. Chase's system, to 27 per cent. at present; and before the 30th of June next, it is not doubted that this premium must disappear. No loyal American doubts the complete suppression of the rebellion before that date, in which event, our Federal currency will rise at once to the par of gold. In the meantime, however, gold is at a premium of 27 per cent., which is the least profit (independent of future advance above par) so soon to be realized by those purchasing this currency now, and waiting its appreciation, or investing it in our U. S. 5.20 six per cent. stock.

But, besides the financial benefits to the Government of Mr. Chase's system, its other advantages are great indeed. It will ultimately displace our whole state bank system and circulation, and give us a *national currency*, based on ample private capital and Federal stocks, a currency of *uniform* value throughout the country, and always certainly convertible on demand into coin. Besides, by displacing the state bank circulation, the whole bank note currency of the Union will be based on the stocks of the Government, and give to every citizen who holds the bonds or the currency, (which will embrace the whole community in every State) a direct interest in the maintenance of the Union.

The annual losses which our people sustain under

the separate State bank system, in the rate of exchange, is enormous, whilst the constant and ever-recurring insolvency of so many of these institutions, accompanied by eight general bank suspensions of specie payment, have from time to time spread ruin and devastation throughout the country. I believe that, in a period of twenty years, the saving to the people of the United States, by the substitution of the new system, would reach a sum very nearly approaching the total amount of our public debt, and in time largely exceeding it. As a question, then, of national wealth, as well as national unity, I believe the gain to the country in time by the adoption of the new system, will far exceed the cost of the war. It was the State bank system in the rebel States that furnished to Secession mainly the sinews of war. These banks are now generally insolvent, but, if the banking system now proposed had been in existence, and the circulating medium in all the States had been an uniform national currency based entirely on the stocks of the United States, the rebellion could never have occurred. Every bank and all its stockholders, and all the holders of the stock and notes of all the banks, embracing our whole paper currency, would have been united to the Government by an interest so direct and universal, that rebellion would have been impossible. Hamilton and Madison, Story and Marshall, and the Supreme Court of the United States, have declared that to the Federal Government belongs the "entire regulation of the currency of the country." That power they have now exercised in the adoption of the system recommended by the Secretary. Our whole currency, in coin as well as paper, will soon, now, all be national, which is the most important measure for the security and perpetuity of the Union, and the welfare of the people, ever adopted by Congress. It is to Congress that the Constitution grants the exclusive power "to regulate commerce with foreign nations and among the States;" and a sound uniform currency, in coin, or convertible on demand into coin, is one of the most essential instrumentalities connected with trade and exchanges.

Having given in the Appendix the three great Acts of Congress carrying into effect the system of the Secretary, marked 1, 2, 3, I shall, after these preliminary remarks, proceed with the discussion of the subject in my next letter.

R. J. WALKER.

APPENDIX.

NATIONAL CURRENCY ACT.

No. I.

AN ACT

TO PROVIDE A NATIONAL CURRENCY, SECURED BY A PLEDGE OF UNITED STATES STOCKS, AND TO PROVIDE FOR THE CIRCULATION AND REDEMPTION THEREOF.

Be it enacted by the Senate and House of Representatives of the United States of America in Congress assembled, That there shall be established in the Treasury Department a separate bureau, which shall be charged with the execution of this and all other laws that may be passed by Congress respecting the issue and regulation of a national currency secured by United States bonds. The chief officer of the said bureau shall be denominated the Comptroller of the Currency, and shall be under the general direction of the Secretary of the Treasury. He shall be appointed by the President, on the nomination of the Secretary of the Treasury, by and with the advice and consent of the Senate, and shall hold his office for the term of five years unless sooner removed by the President, by and with the advice and consent of the Senate; he shall receive an annual salary of five thousand dollars; he shall have a competent deputy, appointed by the Secretary, whose salary shall be two thousand five hundred dollars, and who shall possess the power and perform the duties attached by law to the office of Comptroller during a vacancy in such office and during his absence or inability; he shall employ, from time to time, the necessary clerks to discharge such duties as he shall direct, which clerks shall be appointed and classified by the Secretary of the Treasury in the manner now provided by law. Within fifteen days from the time of notice of his appointment the Comptroller shall take and subscribe the oath of office prescribed by the Constitution and laws of the United States; and he shall give to the United States a bond in the penalty of one hundred thousand dollars, with not less than two responsible freeholders as sureties, to be approved by the Secretary of the Treasury, conditioned for the faithful discharge of the duties of his office. The Deputy Comptroller so appointed shall also take the oath of office prescribed by the Constitution and laws of the United States, and shall give a like bond in the penalty of fifty thousand dollars. The

Currency Bureau established.

Comptroller of the Currency.

Deputy Comptroller.

Clerks.

Oath and bond of Comptroller.

Oath and bond of Deputy.

Interest forbidden.

Comptroller and Deputy Comptroller shall not, either directly or indirectly, be interested in any association issuing national currency under the provisions of this act.

Seal of bureau.

SEC. 2. *And be it further enacted*, That the Comptroller of the Currency, with the approval of the Secretary of the Treasury, shall devise a seal, with suitable inscriptions, for his office, a description of which, with a certificate of approval by the Secretary of the Treasury, shall be filed in the office of the Secretary of State with an impression thereof, which shall thereupon become the seal of office of the Comptroller of the Currency, and the same may be renewed when necessary.

Sealed instruments evidence

Every certificate, assignment, and conveyance executed by the Comptroller, in pursuance of any authority conferred on him by law, and sealed with his seal of office, shall be received in evidence in all places and courts whatsoever; and all copies of papers in the office of the Comptroller, certified by him and authenticated by the said seal, shall in all cases be evidence equally and in like manner as the original.

Impression of seal.

An impression of such seal directly on the paper shall be as valid as if made on wax or wafer.

Office for the bureau in the treasury.

SEC. 3. *And be it further enacted*, That there shall be assigned to the Comptroller of the Currency by the Secretary of Treasury suitable rooms in the Treasury building for conducting the business of the Currency Bureau, in which shall be safe and secure fire proof vaults, in which it shall be the duty of the Comptroller to deposit and safely keep all the plates and other valuable things belonging to his department; and the Comptroller shall from time to time furnish the necessary furniture, stationery, fuel, lights, and other proper conveniences for the transaction of the said business.

U. S. bonds defined.

SEC. 4. *And be it further enacted*, That the term "United States bonds," as used in this act, shall be construed to mean all coupon and registered bonds now issued, or that may hereafter be issued, on the faith of the United States by the Secretary of the Treasury in pursuance of law.

Associates not less than five.

SEC. 5. *And be it further enacted*, That associations for carrying on the business of banking may be formed by any number of persons, not less in any case than five.

Preliminary certificate required, and what to contain.

SEC. 6. *And be it further enacted*, That persons uniting to form such an association shall, under their hands and seals, make a certificate which shall specify—

Name.

First. The name assumed by such association.

Place of business.

Second. The place where its operations of discount and deposits are to be carried on; designating the State, Territory, or district, and also the particular city, town, or village.

Third. The amount of its capital stock, and the number of shares into which the same shall be divided; which capital stock shall not be less than fifty thousand dollars; and in cities whose population is over ten thousand persons, the capital stock shall not be less than one hundred thousand dollars. Capital stock.

Fourth. The names and places of residence of the shareholders, and the number of shares held by each of them. Names, &c. of shareholders.

Fifth. The time when such association shall commence.

Sixth. A declaration that said certificate is made to enable such persons to avail themselves of the advantages of this act. General declaration.

The said certificate shall be acknowledged before a judge of some court of record or a notary public, and the acknowledgment thereof, certified under the seal of such court or notary, and shall be transmitted, together with a copy of the articles of association which shall have been adopted, to the Comptroller of the Currency, who shall record and carefully preserve the same in his office. Copies of such certificate, duly certified by the Comptroller, and authenticated by his seal of office, shall be legal and sufficient evidence in all courts and places within the United States, or the jurisdiction of the government thereof, of the existence of such association, and of every other matter or thing which could be proved by the production of the original certificate. Certificate to be acknowledged and transmitted. Certified copies to be evidence.

SEC. 7. *And be it further enacted*, That at least thirty per centum of the capital stock of such association shall be paid in at the time of the commencement of its banking business, and the remainder of the capital stock of such association shall be paid in instalments of at least ten per centum each on the whole amount to which the association shall be limited, as frequently as one instalment at the end of each succeeding two months from the time of the commencement of its banking operations, until the whole of the capital stock shall be paid in. How capital stock must be paid in.

SEC. 8. *And be it further enacted*, That if any shareholder, or his assignee, shall fail to pay any instalment on the stock when the same is required by the foregoing section to be paid, the directors of such association may sell the stock held by such delinquent shareholder, at public auction, having given three weeks' previous notice thereof in a newspaper published and of general circulation in the city where the association is located, if the same be located in a city, and if not so located, then in a newspaper printed, or of general circulation, in the county where the same is located, to any person who will pay the highest price therefor, and not less than the amount then due thereon, with the expenses of advertisement and sale; and the excess, if any, shall be paid to the delinquent shareholder. Proceedings against delinquent shareholders.

If no bidder can be found who will pay for such stock the amount due thereon to the association, and the costs of advertisement and sale, the amount previously paid shall be forfeited to the association, and such stock may subsequently be sold as the directors may order.

Comptroller to be notified of amount of stock paid in.

SEC. 9. *And be it further enacted*, That whenever a certificate shall have been transmitted to the Comptroller of the Currency, as provided in this act, and the association transmitting the same shall notify the Comptroller that at least thirty per centum of its capital stock has been paid as aforesaid, and that such association has complied with all the provisions of this act required to be complied with before such association shall be authorized to commence the business of banking, and that such association is desirous of commencing such business, the Comptroller shall immediately proceed, in such manner as he shall by general rules prescribe, to examine the condition of such association; to ascertain especially the amount of money paid in on account of its capital stock; the name and place of residence of each of the directors of such association, and the amount of the capital stock of which each is the *bona fide* owner, and generally whether such association has complied with all the requirements of this act to entitle it to engage in the business of banking; and shall cause to be made, and attested by the oaths of a majority of the directors and by the president or cashier of such association, a statement of all the facts necessary to enable the Comptroller to determine whether such association is lawfully entitled to commence the business of banking under this act.

Proceedings of Comptroller upon receipt of notice.

Proceedings continued.

SEC. 10. *And be it further enacted*, That if, upon a careful examination of the facts so reported, and of any other facts which may come to the knowledge of the Comptroller, whether by means of a special commission appointed by him for the purpose of inquiring into the condition of such association, or otherwise, it shall appear that such association is lawfully entitled to commence the business of banking, the Comptroller shall give to such association a certificate under his hand and official seal, showing that such association has complied with all the provisions of this act required to be complied with before being entitled to commence the business of banking under it, and that such association is authorised to commence said business accordingly; and it shall be the duty of such association to cause said certificate to be published in some newspaper, published in the city or county where such association is located for at least sixty days next after the issuing thereof: *Provided*, That if no newspaper is published in such city or county, such certificate shall be published as the Comptroller of the Currency shall direct.

Certificate of authority to commence banking.

Publication of certificate.

SEC. 11. *And be it further enacted*, That every association formed pursuant to the provisions of this act may make and use a common seal, and shall have successsion by the name designated in its articles of association and for the period limited therein, not, however, exceeding twenty years from the passage of this act; by such name may make contracts, sue and be sued, complain and defend in any court of law or equity as fully as natural persons, and may make by-laws, approved by the Comptroller of the Currency, not inconsistent with the laws of the United States or the provisions of this act, for the election of directors, the management of its property, the regulation of its affairs, and for the transfer of its stock; and shall have power to carry on the business of banking by obtaining and issuing circulating notes in accordance with the provisions of this act; by discounting bills, notes, and other evidences of debt; by receiving deposits; by buying and selling gold and silver bullion, foreign coins, and bills of exchange; by loaning money on real and personal security in the manner specified in their articles of association for the purposes authorized by this act, and by exercising such incidental powers as shall be necessary to carry on such business; to choose one of their number as president of such association, and to appoint a cashier and such other officers and agents as their business may require; and to remove such president, cashier, officers, and agents at pleasure, and appoint others in their place; and their usual business shall be transacted in banking offices located at the places specified respectively in its certificate of association, and not elsewhere.

Corporate organization and limitation.

Banking privileges conferred.

Officers.

Place of business.

SEC. 12. *And be it further enacted*, That the shares of associations formed under this act shall be deemed personal property, and shall be transferable on the books of the association in such manner as may be prescribed in the by-laws or articles of association; and every person becoming a shareholder by such transfer shall, in proportion to his shares, succeed to all the rights and liabilities of the prior holder of such shares; and no change shall be made in the articles of association by which the rights, remedies, or security of the existing creditors of the association shall be impaired. For all debts contracted by such association for circulation, deposit, or otherwise, each shareholder shall be liable to the amount, at their par value, of the shares held by him in addition to the amount invested in such shares.

Shares personal property, and how transferred.

Rights of creditors secured.

Individual liabilities of shareholders.

SEC. 13. *And be it further enacted*, That it shall be lawful for any association formed under this act, by its articles of association, to provide for an increase of its capital from time to time as may be deemed expedient, subject to the limitations

Capital stock, how increased.

of this act; but no such increase shall be valid until the increased capital shall be paid in and notice thereof shall have been transmitted to the Comptroller of the Currency, and his certificate obtained specifying the amount of such increase of capital stock, and that the same has been duly paid to such association.

What real estate may be held.

SEC. 14. *And be it further enacted*, That it shall be lawful for any such association to purchase, hold, and convey real estate as follows:

First. Such as shall be necessary for its immediate accommodation in the transaction of its business.

Second. Such as shall be mortgaged to it in good faith by way of security for loans made by such association, or for moneys due thereto.

Third. Such as shall be conveyed to it in satisfaction of debts previously contracted in the course of its dealings.

Fourth. Such as it shall purchase at sales under judgments, decrees, or mortgages held by such association.

Such association shall not purchase or hold real estate in any other case or for any other purpose than as specified in this section.

U. S. bonds to be deposited.

SEC. 15. *And be it further enacted*, That every association, after having complied with the provisions of this act preliminary to the commencement of banking business under its provisions, shall transfer and deliver to the Treasurer of the United States any United States bonds bearing interest, to an amount not less than one third of the capital stock paid in, which bonds shall be deposited with the Treasurer of the United States, and by him safely kept in his office until the same shall be otherwise disposed of, in pursuance of the provisions of this act.

Notes for circulation.

Ninety per cent of bonds deposited.

SEC. 16. *And be it further enacted*, That upon the making of any such transfer and delivery, the association making the same shall be entitled to receive from the Comptroller of the Currency circulating notes of different denominations, in blank registered and countersigned as hereinafter provided, equal in amount to ninety per centum of the current market value of the United States bonds so transferred and delivered, but not exceeding the par value thereof, if bearing interest at the rate of six per centum, or of equivalent United States bonds bearing a less rate of interest; and at no time shall the total amount of such notes, issued to any such association, exceed the amount at such time actually paid in of its capital stock.

Limitation of notes supplied to 300,000,000 dollars.

SEC. 17. *And be it further enacted*, That the entire amount of circulating notes to be issued under this act shall not exceed three hundred millions of dollars. One hundred and fifty millions of which sum shall be apportioned to associations in the States, in the District of Columbia, and in the Territories, according to representative population, and the remainder shall be apportioned by the Secretary of the Treasury among associations formed in the several States in the District of Columbia and in the Territories, having due regard to the existing banking capital, resources, and business, of such States, District and Territories. Apportionment of notes.

SEC. 18. *And be it further enacted,* That, in order to furnish suitable notes for circulation, the Comptroller of the Currency is hereby authorized and required, under the direction of the Secretary of the Treasury, to cause plates to be engraved, in the best manner to guard against counterfeiting and fraudulent alterations, and to have printed therefrom and numbered, such quantity of circulating notes, in blank, of the denominations of five dollars, ten dollars, twenty dollars, fifty dollars, one hundred dollars, five hundred dollars, and one thousand dollars, as may be required to supply, under this act, the associations entitled to receive the same; which notes shall express upon their face that they are secured by United States bonds, deposited with the Treasurer of the United States and issued under the provisions of this act, which statement shall be attested by the written or engraved signatures of the Treasurer and Register, and by the imprint of the seal of the treasury; and shall also express upon their face the promise of the association receiving the same, to pay on demand, attested by the signatures of the president or vice-president and cashier; and the said notes shall bear such devices and such other statements, and shall be in such form, as the Secretary of the Treasury shall, by regulation, direct. Comptroller to prepare and furnish notes. Denominations defined. Signature of president and cashier.

SEC. 19. *And be it further enacted,* That the plates and special dies to be procured by the Comptroller of the Currency for the printing of such circulating notes shall remain under his control and direction, and the expenses necessarily incurred in executing the provisions of this act respecting the procuring of such notes, shall be audited and paid as contingent expenses of the Treasury Department; and for the purpose of reimbursing the same, and all other expenses incurred under this act, and in lieu of all taxes upon the circulation authorized by this act,* or upon the bonds deposited for the security of the same, such association organized under this act shall semi-annually, on the first days of January and July, after its organization, pay to the Comptroller of the Currency, in lawful money of the United States, one per centum on the amount of Care and control of plates and dies. Expenses, how paid. One per cent reserved.

* Modified by section 7 of the "Act to provide ways and means for the support of the government," approved March 3, 1863, which section is printed for convenience of reference at the end of this act. See page 33.

circulating notes received by such association, and in default thereof the Treasurer of the United States is hereby authorized to reserve and retain one per centum on the amount of said bonds so deposited, at each semi-annual payment of interest thereon; and all sums so reserved and retained shall be paid into the treasury under the direction of the Secretary, and every bank, banking association, or corporation not organized under the provisions of this act, issuing notes calculated or intended to circulate as money, shall, on the first day of July next, and regularly on the first days of January and July thereafter, make and deliver to the Comptroller of the Currency a true and accurate return of the gross amount of notes issued by it, whether in circulation, or in its vaults, or on deposit elsewhere; and in default of any such return, the bank, banking association, or corporation so failing to make return, shall pay to the United States a penalty of two per centum upon its entire capital stock, to be recovered, for the use of the United States, in any court of competent jurisdiction.

Returns of banks not organized under this act.

Penalty for default.

Associations authorized to issue these notes.

SEC. 20. *And be it further enacted*, That after any such association shall have caused its promise to pay such notes on demand to be signed by the president or vice-president and cashier thereof, in such manner as to make them obligatory promissory notes, payable on demand, at its place of business, such association is hereby authorized to issue and circulate the same as money; and the same shall be received at par in all parts of the United States in payment of taxes, excise, public lands, and all other dues to the United States, except for duties on imports; and also for all salaries and other debts and demands owing by the United States to individuals, corporations, and associations within the United States, except interest on public debt; and no such association shall issue post notes or any other notes to circulate as money than such as are authorized by the foregoing provisions of this act.

Notes to be received for all U.S. dues, except imports.

Issue of other notes forbidden.

Transfers of bonds by associations, how made.

SEC. 21. *And be it further enacted*, That all transfers of the United States bonds which shall be made by any association as security for circulating notes under the provisions of this act, shall be made to the Treasurer of the United States, with a memorandm written or printed on the certificate of such bonds, and signed by the cashier or some other officer of the association making the deposit, stating that it is held in trust for the association on whose behalf such transfer is made, and as security for the redemption and payment of the circulating notes delivered to such association; and no transfer of any such bonds by the Treasurer shall be deemed valid, or of binding force and effect, unless sanctioned by the order or request of the Comptroller of the Currency upon the Treasurer.

No transfer by Treasurer valid except.

It shall be the duty of the Comptroller of the Currency to keep in his office a book in which shall be entered the name of every association from whose accounts such transfer of bonds is made by the Treasurer, and the name of the party to whom such transfer is made, unless such transfer is made in blank, in which case the fact shall be stated in said book, and in either case the par value of the bonds so transferred shall be entered therein; and it shall be the duty of the Comptroller, immediately upon countersigning and entering the same, to advise by mail the association from whose account such transfer was made, the kind of bonds and the amount thereof so transferred.

Duties of Comptroller upon transfer.

Association to be advised by the Comptroller.

SEC. 22. *And be it further enacted*, That it shall be the duty of the Comptroller of the Currency to countersign and enter in the book, in the manner aforesaid, every transfer or assignment of any bonds held by the Treasurer presented for his signature; and the Comptroller shall have at all times during office hours access to the books of the Treasurer, for the purpose of ascertaining the correctness of the transfer or assignment presented to him to countersign; and the Treasurer shall have the like access to the book above mentioned, kept by the Comptroller, during office hours, to ascertain the correctness of the entries in the same.

Duties of Comptroller upon transfer of bonds.

SEC. 23. *And be it further enacted*, That it shall be the duty of either the president or cashier of every banking association having stocks deposited in the office of the Treasurer of the United States, once or more in each fiscal year, and at such time or times during the ordinary business hours as said officer or officers may select, to examine and compare the bonds so pledged with the books of said department, and, if found correct, to execute to the said Treasurer a certificate setting forth the different kinds and the amounts thereof, and that the same are in the possession and custody of the Treasurer at the date of such certificate. Such examination may be made by an agent of such association, duly appointed in writing for that purpose, whose certificate before mentioned shall be of like force and validity as if executed by such president or cashier.

Periodical examination of bonds deposited.

Examination by agent.

SEC. 24. *And be it further enacted*, That every association issuing circulating notes under the provisions of this act shall make a quarterly report to the Comptroller of the Currency, commencing on the first day of the quarter of the year next succeeding the organization of such association, and continuing on the first days of each succeeding quarter in every year thereafter, which report shall be verified by the oath or affirmation of the president and cashier, and all wilful false swearing in respect to such report shall be perjury, and subject to

Verified quarterly reports.

False statements perjury.

Form and contents of report.

the punishment prescribed by law for such offence. The report hereby required shall be in the form prescribed by the Comptroller, and shall contain a true statement of the condition of the association making such report, before the transaction of any business on the morning of the day specified, next preceding the date of such report, in respect of the following items and particulars, to wit: Loans and discounts, overdrafts due from banks, amount due from the directors of the association, real estate, specie, cash items, stocks, bonds, and promissory notes, bills of solvent banks, bills of suspended banks, loss and expense accounts, capital, circulation, profits, amount due to banks, amount due to individuals and corporations other than banks, amount due the Treasurer of the United States, amount due to depositors on demand, amount due not included under either of the above heads. And it shall be the duty of the Comptroller to publish full abstracts of such reports together in two newspapers, to be designated by him for that purpose—one in the city of Washington and the other in the city of New York—exhibiting the items of capital, circulation, and deposits, specie, and cash items, public securities and private securities; and the separate report of each association shall be published in a newspaper published in the place where such association is established, or, if there be no newspaper at such place, then in a newspaper published at the capital of the State, at the expense of the association making such report. In addition to the quarterly reports required by this section, every association located and doing business in the cities of Boston, Providence, New York, Philadelphia, Baltimore, Cincinnati, Chicago, St. Louis, and New Orleans, shall publish, or cause to be published, on the morning of the first Tuesday in each month, in a newspaper printed in the city in which the association making such report is located, to be designated by the Comptroller of the Currency, a statement, under the oath of the president or cashier, showing the condition of the association making such statement, on the morning of the day next preceding the date of such statement, in respect to the following items and particulars, to wit; average amount of loans and discounts, specie, deposits, and circulation.

Comptroller to publish abstracts.

Association to publish reports.

Certain associations to report monthly under oath.

Protest of notes and proceedings thereon.

SEC. 25. *And be it further enacted*, That if any such association shall, at any time fail to redeem, in the lawful money of the United States, any of its circulating notes, when payment thereof shall be lawfully demanded, during the usual hours of business, at the office of such association, the holder may cause the same to be protested, in one package, by a notary public, unless the president or cashier of the association shall offer to waive demand and notice of the protest, and shall, in pursuance of such offer, make, sign, and deliver to the party making such demand, an admission in writing, stating the time of the demand, the amount demanded, and the fact of the non-payment thereof; and such notary public, on making such protest, or upon receiving such admission, shall forthwith forward such admission or notice of protest to the Comptroller of the Currency; and after such default it shall not be lawful for the association suffering the same, to pay out any of its notes, discount any notes or bills, or otherwise prosecute the business of banking, except to receive and safely keep money belonging to it, and to deliver special deposits: *Provided, however*, That if satisfactory proof be produced to such notary public that the payment of any such notes is restrained by order of any court of competent jurisdiction, such notary public shall not protest the same; and when the holder of such notes shall cause more than one note or package to be protested, on the same day, he shall not receive pay for more than one protest.

Duties of association upon suspension.

SEC. 26. *And be it further enacted*, That on receiving notice that any such association has failed to redeem any of its circulating notes, as specified in the next preceding section, the Comptroller of the Currency, with the concurrence of the Secretary of the Treasury, may appoint a special agent, (of whose appointment immediate notice shall be given to such association,) who shall immediately proceed to ascertain whether such association has refused to pay its circulating notes, in the lawful money of the United States, when demanded as aforesaid, and report to the Comptroller the facts so ascertained; and if, from such protest or the report so made, the Comptroller shall be satisfied that such association has refused to pay its circulating notes as aforesaid, and is in default, he shall, within thirty days after he shall have received notice of such failure, declare the United States bonds and securities pledged by such association forfeited to the United States, and the same shall thereupon be forfeited accordingly; and thereupon the Comptroller shall immediately give notice is such manner as the Secretary of the Treasury shall, by general rules or otherwise, direct, to the holders of the circulating notes of such association to present them for payment at the Treasury of the United States, and the same shall be paid as presented; whereupon said Comptroller may, in his discretion, cancel an equal amount of bonds pledged by such association, equal at current market rates, not exceeding par, to the notes paid; and it shall be lawful for the Secretary of the Treasury, from time to time, to make such regulations respecting the disposition to be made of such circulating notes after presentation thereof for payment as aforesaid, and respect-

Proceedings of Comptroller upon notice of protest.

Special agent.

Notes of association paid at the treasury U. S.

ing the perpetuation of the evidence of the payment thereof, as may seem to him proper; but all such notes, on being paid, shall be cancelled; and for any deficiency in the proceeds of the bonds pledged by such association, when disposed of as hereinafter specified, to reimburse to the United States the amount so expended in paying the circulating notes of such association, the United States shall have a first and paramount lien upon all the assets of such association, and such deficiency shall be made good out of such assets in preference to any and all other claims whatsoever, except the necessary costs and expenses of administering the same.

U. S. to have prior lien upon assets.

Bonds of failing association may be sold at auction.

SEC. 27. *And be it further enacted*, That whenever the Comptroller shall become satisfied, as in the last preceding section specified, that any such association has refused to pay its circulating notes as therein mentioned, he may instead of cancelling the United States bonds pledged by such association, as provided in the next preceding section, cause so much of them as may be necessary to redeem the outstanding circulating notes of such association to be sold at public auction in the city of New York, after giving thirty days notice of such sale to such association.

Private sale of bonds.

SEC. 28. *And be it further enacted*, That the Comptroller of the Currency may, if he shall be of opinion that the interests of the United States will be best promoted thereby, sell at private sale any of the stock so transferred to him by such association, and receive therefore either money or the circulating notes of such failing association: *Provided*, That no such bonds shall be sold by private sale for less than the par, nor less than the market value thereof at the time of sale: *And provided, further*, That no sales of any such stock, either public or private, shall be complete until the transfer thereof shall have been made with the formalities prescribed in this act.

Receiver, bond and duties.

SEC. 29. *And be it further enacted*, That on becoming satisfied, as specified in this act, that any such association has refused to pay its circulating notes as therein mentioned, and is in default, the Comptroller of the Currency may forthwith appoint a receiver, and require of him such bond and security as he shall deem proper, who, under the direction of the Comptroller, shall take possession of the books, records, and assets of every description of such association, collect all debts, dues, and claims belonging to such association, and upon the order of a court of record of competent jurisdiction, may sell or compound all bad or doubtful debts, and, on a like order, sell all the real and personal property of such association, on such terms as the court shall direct and such receiver shall pay over all moneys so made to the Treasurer of the United States, and also make report to the Comptroller of the Currency of all his acts and proceedings. The Comptroller shall thereupon cause notice to be given, by advertisement in such newspapers as he may direct, for three consecutive months, calling on all persons who may have claims against such association to present the same, and to make legal proof thereof. And from time to time the Comptroller, after full provision shall have been first made for refunding to the United States any such deficiency in redeeming the notes of such association as is mentioned in this act, shall make a rateable dividend of the moneys so paid over to him by such receiver on all such claims as may have been so proved or adjudicated in a court of competent jurisdiction; and from time to time, as the proceeds of the assets of such association shall be paid over to him, he shall make further dividends, as aforesaid, on all claims previously proved or adjudicated; and the remainder of such proceeds, if any, shall be paid over to the shareholders of such association, or their legal representatives, in proportion to the stock by them respectively held: *Provided, however*, That if any such association against which proceedings have been so instituted on account of any alleged refusal to redeem its circulating notes as aforesaid, shall deny having failed to do so, such association may, at any time within ten days after such association shall have been notified of the appointment of an agent, as provided in this act, apply to the nearest circuit, or district, or territorial court of the United States, to enjoin further proceedings in the premises; and such court, after citing the Comptroller of the Currency to show cause why further proceedings should not be enjoined, and after the decision of the court or finding of a jury that such association has not refused to redeem its circulating notes, when legally presented, in the lawful money of the United States, shall make an order enjoining the Comptroller, and any receiver acting under his direction, from all further proceedings on account of such alleged refusal.

Duties of Comptroller upon report of receiver.

Disbursement of assets.

Association may enjoin proceedings.

SEC. 30. *And be it further enacted*, That the bonds transferred to the Treasurer of the United States, as hereinbefore provided, by any banking association for the security of its circulating notes, shall be held exclusively for that purpose, until such notes shall be redeemed, except as provided in this act; but the Comptroller of the Currency may give to any such banking association powers of attorney to receive and appropriate to its own use the interest on the bonds which shall have been so transferred to the Treasurer by it; but such powers shall become inoperative whenever such banking association shall fail to redeem its circulating notes as afore-

Bonds deposited to be exclusively as security.

Interest on bonds.

Return of bonds.

said. And said Comptroller may direct the return of any said bonds to the banking association which transferred the same, upon the surrender to him and the cancellation of a proportionate amount of such circulating notes: *Provided*, That ninety per centum of the current market value of the remaining bonds which shall have been transferred by the banking association offering to surrender such circulating notes shall be equal to the amount of all the circulating notes retained by such banking association: *And provided, further*, That there shall have been no failure by such association to redeem its circulating notes, and that there shall have been no other violation by such association of any of the provisions of this act for the security of the creditors of such association; nor shall the Treasurer be required to surrender such bonds in fractional sums of less than one thousand dollars. And if, at any time after said bonds shall be deposited with the Treasurer of the United States, as aforesaid, the market or cash value shall be reduced, the Comptroller of the Currency is hereby authorised to demand and receive the amount of such depreciation in other United States bonds at cash value, or in money, from the association receiving said bills, to be deposited with the Treasurer of the United States, as long as such depreciation continues.

No surrender under 1,000 dols.

Depreciation of bonds deposited.

Interest on bonds to be retained, when.

SEC. 31. *And be it further enacted*, That whenever the price of any of the bonds pledged, as aforesaid, for the redemption of the circulating notes of any such banking association shall be at the stock exchange in the city of New York for four consecutive weeks, at a rate less than that at which they shall have been estimated when so pledged, and such depreciation shall not have been made good by a deposit of other bonds or money, it shall be the duty of the Comptroller of the Currency to notify the Treasurer of the United States of such fact, and the payment of interest upon such depreciated bonds shall be suspended; and such interest shall be retained by said Treasurer until the same, when added to the current market value of the bonds so pledged, to be ascertained as before provided, shall be equal to the amount for which such bonds were pledged: *Provided*, That it shall be the duty of the Comptroller of the Currency, at the expiration of every period of three months, to cause the whole of the sums so retained, and then remaining in the treasury of the United States, to be invested in United States bonds, in the name of the Comptroller of the Currency, in trust for the respective associations by which the bonds on which such interest shall have accrued shall have been pledged. And whenever the price of such depreciated bonds at the stock exchange in New York shall rise to the price at which they

Investment of interest retained.

Transfer of proceeds of investment of interest.

were pledged, and so remain for four consecutive weeks, such investment shall be assigned to such association, and all accruing interest on such pledged bonds shall thereafter be paid to such association, on demand thereof.

SEC. 32. *And be it further enacted,* That it shall be the duty of the Comptroller of the Currency to receive worn-out or mutilated circulating notes issued by any such banking association, and to deliver in place thereof to such association other blank circulating notes to an equal amount. And such worn-out or mutilated notes, after a memorandum shall have been entered in the proper books, in accordance with such regulations as may be established by the Comptroller, as well as all circulating notes which shall have been paid or surrendered to be cancelled, shall be burned to ashes in presence of three persons, one to be appointed by the Secretary of the Treasury, one by the Comptroller of the Currency, and one by the Treasurer of the United States, under such regulations as the Secretary of the Treasury may prescribe; and in case such notes shall have been delivered to the Comptroller by an officer or agent of such association, then in the presence, also, of such officer or agent. And a certificate of such burning, signed by the parties so appointed, shall be made in the books of the Comptroller, and a duplicate thereof given to such officer or agent.

Surrender and destruction of mutilated, &c., currency.

SEC. 33. *And be it further enacted,* That it shall be unlawful for any officer acting under the provisions of this act to countersign or deliver to any such association, or to any other company or person, any circulating notes contemplated by this act, except as hereinbefore provided, and in accordance with the true intent and meaning of this act. And any officer who shall violate the provisions of this section shall be deemed guilty of a high misdemeanor, and on conviction thereof shall be punished by fine not exceeding double the amount so countersigned and delivered, and imprisonment not exceeding fifteen years, at the discretion of the court in which he shall be tried.

Punishment for delivering notes except as herein provided.

SEC. 34. *And be it further enacted,* That all fees for protesting the notes issued by any such banking association shall be paid by the person procuring the protest to be made, and such banking association shall be liable therefore; but no part of the stock pledged by such banking association, as aforesaid, shall be applied to the payment of such fees. And all expenses of any preliminary or other examinations into the condition of any association shall be paid by such association; and all expenses of any receivership shall be paid out of the assets of such association before distribution of the proceeds thereof.

Fees for protest, examination, and receiverships, how paid.

Indebtedness of stockholders restricted.

SEC. 35. *And be it further enacted,* That the stockholders, collectively, of any such association shall at no time be liable to such association, either as principal debtors or sureties, or both, to an amount greater than three-fifths of the capital stock actually paid in and remaining undiminished by losses or otherwise; nor shall the directors be so liable, except to such amount and in such a manner as shall be prescribed by the by-laws of such association, adopted by its stockholders to regulate such liabilities.

Division, assignment, and transfer of shares.

Transfers restricted, when.

SEC. 36. *And be it further enacted,* That the capital stock of any association formed under this act shall be divided into shares of one hundred dollars each, and shall be assignable on the books of the association in such manner as its by-laws shall prescribe; but no shareholder in any association under this act shall have power to sell or transfer any share held in his own right so long as he shall be liable, either as principal, debtor, surety, or otherwise, to the association for any debt which shall have become due and remain unpaid, nor in any case shall such shareholder be entitled to receive any dividend, interest, or profit on such shares so long as such liabilities shall continue; but all such dividends, interests, and profits shall be retained by the association, and applied to the discharge of such liabilities. And no stock shall be transferred without the consent of a majority of the directors while the holder thereof is thus indebted to the association.

Loans on shares forbidden.

Purchase of capital stock forbidden.

SEC. 37. *And be it further enacted,* That no banking association shall take, as security for any loan or discount, a lien upon any part of its capital stock; but the same security, both in kind and amount, shall be required of shareholders as of other persons. And no such banking association shall be the purchaser or holder of any portion of its capital stock, or of the capital stock of any other incorporated company, unless such purchase shall be necessary to prevent loss upon a debt previously contracted in good faith, or security which, at the time, was deemed adequate to insure the payment of such debt, independent of any lien upon such stock, or in case of forfeiture of stock for the non-payment of instalments due thereon; and stock so purchased or acquired shall in no case be held by such association so purchasing for a longer period of time than six months, if the same can, within that time, be sold for what the stock cost.

Elections of directors, votes of shareholders

Proxies.

SEC. 38. *And be it further enacted,* That in all elections of directors, and in deciding all questions at meetings of shareholders, each shareholder shall be entitled to one vote on each share of stock held by him. Shareholders may vote by proxies duly authorized in writing; but no officer, clerk, teller, or bookkeeper of such association shall act as proxy; and no stockholder whose liability is past due and unpaid shall be allowed to vote.

Number of directors, qualification and oath.

SEC. 39. *And be it further enacted*, That the affairs of every such association shall be managed by not less than five nor more than nine directors, one of whom shall be president of the association. Every director shall, during his whole term of service, be a citizen of the United States and a resident of the State in which such association is located. At least three-fourths of the directors shall have resided in the State in which such association is located one year next preceding their election as directors; and each director shall own, in his own right, at least one per centum of the capital stock of such association, not exceeding two hundred thousand dollars, and the half of one per centum of its capital if over two hundred thousand dollars. Each director shall take an oath that he will, so far as the duty devolves on him, diligently and honestly administer the affairs of such association, and will not knowingly violate, or willingly permit to be violated, any of the provisions of this act, and that he is the bona fide owner, in his own right, of the shares of stock standing in his name on the books of the association, and that the same is not hypothecated, or in any way pledged, as security for any loan obtained or debt owing to the association of which he is a director, which oath, subscribed by himself, and certified by the officer before whom it is taken, shall be immediately transmitted to the Comptroller of the Currency, and by him filed and preserved in his office.

Duration of office, annual election in January.

SEC. 40. *And be it further enacted*, That the directors of any such association, first elected, shall hold their places until their successors shall be elected and qualified. All subsequent elections shall be held annually, on such day in the month of January as the stockholders of said association may prescribe; and the directors so elected shall hold their places for one year, and until their successors are elected and qualified. But any director removing from the State, or ceasing to be the owner of the requisite amount of stock, shall thereby vacate his place. Any vacancy in the board shall be filled by appointment by the remaining directors. The director so appointed shall hold his place until the next annual election; and if, from any cause, an election of directors shall not be made at the time appointed, the association shall not for that cause be dissolved, but an election may be held on any subsequent day, thirty days' notice thereof having been given in a newspaper printed, or of general circulation, in the city, town, or county in which the association is located; and if no newspaper is published in such city, town, or county, such notice shall be published in a newspaper in the county adjoining.

Vacancies.

Fund to be always maintained on hand.

SEC. 41. *And be it further enacted,* That every such association shall at all times have on hand, in lawful money of the United States, an amount equal to at least twenty-five per centum of the aggregate amount of its outstanding notes of circulation and its deposits; and whenever the amount of its outstanding notes of circulation and its deposits shall exceed the above named proportion for the space of twelve days, or whenever such lawful money of the United States shall at any time fall below the amount of twenty-five per centum of its circulation and deposits, such association shall not increase its liabilities by making any new loans or discounts otherwise than by discounting or purchasing bills of exchange, payable at sight, nor make any dividend of its profits, until the required proportion between the aggregate amount of its outstanding notes of circulation and its deposits and lawful money of the United States shall be restored: *Provided, however,* That clearing-house certificates, representing specie or lawful money specially deposited for the purpose of any clearing-house association, shall be deemed to be lawful money in the possession of any association belonging to such clearing-house holding and owning such certificates, and considered to be a part of the lawful money which such association is required to have, under the foregoing provisions of this section: *Provided, further,* That any balance due to any association organized under this act in other places from any association in the cities of Boston, Providence, New York, Philadelphia, Baltimore, Cincinnati, Chicago, St. Louis, or New Orleans, in good credit, subject to be drawn for at sight and available to redeem their circulating notes and deposits, may be deemed to be a part of the lawful money which such association, in other places than the cities of Boston, Providence, New York, Philadelphia, Baltimore, Cincinnati, Chicago, St. Louis, and New Orleans, is required to have by the foregoing provisions of this section to the extent of three-fifths of the said amount of twenty-five per centum required. And it shall be competent for the Comptroller of the Currency to notify any such association whose lawful money reserve, as aforesaid, shall fall below said proportion of twenty-five per centum, to make good such reserve; and if such association shall fail for thirty days thereafter so to make good its reserve of lawful money of the United States, the Comptroller may, with the concurrence of the Secretary of the Treasury, appoint a receiver to wind up the business of such association, as provided in this act.

Clearing-house certificates.

Balances in cities equivalent to cash.

Association failing to make good the reserve may be wound up.

Limitation of indebtedness prescribed.

SEC. 42. *And be it further enacted,* That no association shall at any time be indebted, or in any way liable, to an amount exceeding the amount of its capital stock at such time actually paid in, and remaining undiminished by losses or otherwise, except on the following accounts, that is to say:—

First. On account of its notes of circulation.

Second. On account of moneys deposited with, or collected by, such association.

Third. On account of bills of exchange or drafts drawn against money actually on deposit to the credit of such association, or due thereto.

Fourth. On account of liabilities to its stockholders, for money paid in on capital stock, and dividends thereon, and reserved profits.

Pledge of notes enjoined.

SEC. 43. *And be it further enacted*, That no association shall, either directly or indirectly, pledge or hypothecate any of its notes of circulation, for the purpose of procuring money, to be paid in on its capital stock, or to be used in its banking operations, or otherwise.

Withdrawal of capital enjoined.

Loans limited to six months.

Dividends restricted.

Bad debts defined.

SEC. 44. *And be it further enacted*, That no association, or any member thereof, shall, during the time it shall continue its banking operations, withdraw, or permit to be withdrawn, either in form of dividends, loans to stockholders for a longer time than six months, or in any other manner, any portion of its capital. And if losses shall at any time have been sustained by any such association equal to or exceeding its undivided profits then on hand, no dividend shall be made; and no dividend shall ever be made by any association, while it shall continue its banking operations, to an amount greater than its net profits then on hand, deducting therefrom its losses and bad debts. And all debts due to any association, on which interest is past due and unpaid for a period of six months, unless the same shall be well secured, and shall be in process of collection, shall be considered bad debts within the meaning of this act.

Dividends, when and how made.

Semi-annual statement required.

SEC. 45. *And be it further enacted*, That the directors of every association shall, semi-annually, in the months of May and November, declare a dividend of so much of the profits of such association as they shall judge expedient; and on each dividend day the cashier shall make, and verify by his oath, a full, clear, and accurate statement of the condition of the association, as it shall be on that day after declaring the dividend; which statement shall contain—

First. The amount of the capital stock actually paid in and then remaining as the capital stock of such bank or association.

Secondly. The amount of the circulating notes of such association then in circulation.

Thirdly. The greatest amount in circulation at any time

since the making of the last previous statement, as shall have been exhibited by the weekly statements of the cashier, specifying the times when the same occurred.

Fourthly. The amount of balances and debts of every kind due to other banks and banking associations.

Fifthly. The amount due to depositors.

Sixthly. The total amount of debts and liabilities of every description, and the greatest amount since the making of the last previous statement, specifying the time when the same accrued.

Seventhly. The total amount of dividend declared on the day of making the statement.

Eighthly. The amount of lawful money of the United States belonging to the association and in its possession at the time of making the statement.

Balances in cities.

Ninthly. The amount subject to be drawn at sight, in lawful money of the United States, then remaining on deposit with any associations, banks, or bankers; specifying the amounts so on deposit in the cities of Boston, Providence, New York, Philadelphia, Baltimore, Cincinnati, Chicago, St. Louis, and New Orleans.

Tenthly. The amount then on hand of bills or notes, issued by other banks and banking associations.

Eleventhly. The amount of balances due from other banks, bankers, and banking associations, excluding deposits subject to be drawn at sight as aforesaid.

Twelfthly. The amount on hand of bills, bonds, stocks, notes, and other evidences of debts, discounted or purchased by the association, specifying particularly the amount of suspended debt, the amount considered bad, the amount considered doubtful, and the amount in suit or judgment.

Thirteenthly. The value of the real and personal property held for the convenience of the association, specifying the amount of each.

Fourteenthly. The amount of real estate taken in payment of debts due to the association.

Fifteenthly. The amount of the undivided profits of the association.

Sixteenthly. The total amount of the liability to the association by the directors thereof, collectively, specifying the gross amount of such liabilities as principal debtors, and the gross amount of indorsers or sureties.

The statement thus made shall forthwith be transmitted to the Comptroller of the Currency.

Banking privileges granted.

SEC 46. *And be it further enacted,* That every association may take, reserve, receive, and charge on any loan or discount made, or upon any note, bill of exchange, or other evidence of debt, such rate of interest or discount as is for the time the established rate of interest for delay in the payment of money, in the absence of contract between the parties, by the laws of the several States in which the associations are respectively located, and no more: *Provided, however*, That interest may be reserved or taken in advance, at the time of making the loan or discount, according to the usual rules of banking; and the knowingly taking, reserving, or charging of a rate of interest greater than that allowed by this section shall be held and adjudged a forfeiture of the debt or demand on which the same is taken, reserved, or charged; but the purchase, discount, or sale of a bill of exchange, drawn on actually existing values, and payable at another place than the place of such purchase, discount, or sale, at the current discount or premium, shall not be considered as taking, reserving, or charging interest.

Rate of interest.

Usury.

SEC. 47. *And be it further enacted*, That the total liabilities of any person, or of any company or firm (including in the liabilities of a company or firm the liabilities of the several members thereof), to any association, including liabilities as acceptor of bona fide bills of exchange, payable out of the State where the association is located, shall at no time exceed one-third; exclusive of liabilities as acceptor, one-fifth; and exclusive of liabilities on such bills of exchange, one-tenth part of the amount of the capital stock of such association actually paid in.

Liabilities of customers restricted.

SEC. 48. *And be it further enacted*, That no association shall, at any time, pay out on loans or discounts, or in purchasing drafts or bills of exchange, or in payment of deposits, nor shall it in any other mode put in circulation the notes of any bank or banking association, which notes shall not, at any such time, be receivable, at par, on deposit, and in payment of debts by the association so paying out or circulating such notes; nor shall it knowingly pay out or put in circulation any notes issued by any bank or banking association which at the time of such paying out or putting in circulation is not redeeming its circulating notes in lawful money of the United States.

Uncurrent money not to be circulated.

SEC. 49. *And be it further enacted*, That all transfer of the notes, bonds, bills of exchange, and other evidences of debt owing to any association, or of deposits to its credit; all assignments of mortgages, sureties on real estate, or of judgments or decrees in its favour; all deposits of money, bullion, or other valuable thing for its use, or for the use of any of its shareholders or creditors; and all payments of money to either, made after the commission of an act of insolvency, or in contemplation thereof, with a view to prevent the application of

Acts prejudicial to creditors in contemplation of insolvency void.

its assets in the manner prescribed by this act, or with a view to the preference of one creditor to another, except in payment of the circulating notes, shall be utterly null and void.

Malfeasance of officers and directors.

SEC. 50. *And be it further enacted,* That if the directors of any association shall knowingly violate, or knowingly permit any of the officers, agents or servants of the association to violate, any of the provisions of this act, all the rights, privileges, and franchises of the association, derived from this act, shall be thereby forfeited. Such violation shall, however, be determined and adjudged by a proper circuit, district, or territorial court of the United States, before the association shall be declared dissolved. And in cases of such violation, every director who participated in or assented to the same shall be held liable in his personal and individual capacity for all damages which the association, its shareholders, or any other person, shall have sustained in consequence of such violation.

Visitor, how and when appointed, duties of.

SEC. 51. *And be it further enacted,* That the Comptroller of the Currency, with the approbation of the Secretary of the Treasury, as often as shall be deemed necessary or proper, shall appoint a suitable person or persons to make an examination of the affairs of every banking association, which person shall not be a director or other officer in any association whose affairs he shall be appointed to examine, and who shall have power to make a thorough examination into all the affairs of the association. and, in doing so, to examine any of the officers and agents thereof on oath, and shall make a full and detailed report of the condition of the association to the Comptroller; and the association shall not be subject to any other visitorial powers than such as are authorized by this act, except such as are vested in the several courts of law and chancery. And every person appointed to make such examination shall receive for his services at the rate of five dollars for each day by him employed in such examination, and two dollars for every twenty-five miles he shall necessarily travel in the performance of his duty, which shall be paid by the association by him examined.

Compensation of.

Misdemeanor of officers.

SEC. 52. *And be it further enacted,* That every president, director, cashier, teller, clerk, or agent of any association, who shall embezzle, abstract, or wilfully misapply any of the moneys, funds, or credits of the association, or shall, without authority from the directors, issue or put in circulation any of the notes of the association, or shall, without such authority, issue or put forth any certificate of deposit, draw any order or bill of exchange, make any acceptance, assign any note, bond, draft, bill of exchange, mortgage, judgment, or decree, or shall make any false entry in any book, report, or statement of the association, with intent, in either case, to injure or defraud any other company, body politic or corporate, or any individual person, or to deceive any officer or agent appointed to examine the affairs of any such association, shall be deemed guilty of a misdemeanor, and upon conviction thereof shall be punished by imprisonment not less than five nor more than ten years.

Names, residence, &c., of shareholders.

SEC. 53. *And be it further enacted,* That the president and cashier of every such association shall cause to be kept at all times a full and correct list of the names and residences of all the shareholders in the association, in the office where its business is transacted; and such list shall be subject to the inspection of all the shareholders and creditors of the association during business hours of each day in which business may be legally transacted; and a copy of such list, verified by the oath of such president or cashier, shall, at the beginning of every year, be transmitted to the Comptroller of the Currency, commencing on the first day of the first quarter after the organization of the association.

Associations may become depositories of public moneys.

SEC. 54. *And be it further enacted,* That the Secretary of the Treasury is hereby authorized, whenever, in his judgment, the public interest will be promoted thereby, to employ any of such associations, doing business under this act, as depositaries of the public moneys, except receipts from customs.

Suits and proceedings under this act.

SEC. 55. *And be it further enacted,* That all suits and proceedings arising out of the provisions of this act, in which the United States or its officers or agents shall be parties, shall be conducted by the district attorneys of the several districts, under the direction and supervision of the Solicitor of the Treasury.

Penalties for mutilation of paper issued under this act.

SEC. 56. *And be it further enacted,* That every person who shall mutilate, cut, deface, disfigure, or perforate with holes, or shall unite or cement together, or do any other thing to any bank bill, draft, note, or other evidence of debt issued by any such association, or shall cause or procure the same to be done, with intent to render such bank bill, draft, note, or other evidence of debt unfit to be reissued by said association, shall upon conviction forfeit fifty dollars to the association who shall be injured thereby, to be recovered by action in any court having jurisdiction.

Forgery, uttering, &c., penalties for.

SEC. 57. *And be it further enacted,* That if any person shall falsely make, forge, or counterfeit, or cause or procure to be made, forged, or counterfeited, or willingly aid or assist in falsely making, forging, or counterfeiting, any note in imitation of, or purporting to be in imitation of, the circulating notes issued under the provisions of this act, or shall pass, utter, or publish, or attempt to pass, utter, or publish, any false, forged, or counterfeited note, purporting to be issued by any association doing a banking business under the provisions of this act, knowing the same to be falsely made, forged, or counterfeited, or shall falsely alter, or cause or procure to be falsely altered, or willingly aid or assist in falsely altering, any such circulating notes, issued as aforesaid, or shall pass, utter, or publish, or attempt to pass, utter, or publish as true, any falsely altered or spurious circulating note issued, or purporting to have been issued, as aforesaid, knowing the same to be falsely altered or spurious, every such person shall be deemed and adjudged guilty of felony, and being thereof convicted by due course of law, shall be sentenced to be imprisoned and kept at hard labor for a period not less than five years nor more than fifteen years, and to be fined in a sum not exceeding one thonsand dollars.

Making, engraving, &c., plates, or having them in custody, penalties for.

Sec. 58. *And be it further enacted*, That if any person shall make or engrave, or cause or procure to be made or engraved, or shall have in his custody or possession any engraved plate or block after the similitude of any plate from which any circulating notes issued as aforesaid shall have been printed, with intent to use such plate or block, or cause or suffer the same to be used, in forging or counterfeiting any of the notes issued as aforesaid, or shall have in his custody or possession any blank note or notes engraved and printed after the similitude of any notes issued as aforesaid, with intent to use such blanks, or cause or suffer the same to be used, in forging or counterfeiting any of the notes issued as aforesaid, or shall have in his custody or possession any paper adapted to the making of such notes, and similar to the paper upon which any such notes shall have been issued, with intent to use such paper, or cause or suffer the same to be used, in forging or counterfeiting any of the notes issued as aforesaid, every such person, being thereof convicted by due course of law, shall be sentenced to be imprisoned and kept to hard labor for a term not less than five nor more than fifteen years, and fined in a sum not exceeding one thousand dollars.

Having blank notes or paper adapted to banking.

Jurisdiction.

Sec. 59. *And be it further enacted*, That suits, actions, and proceedings by and against any association under this act, may be had in any circuit, district, or territorial court of the United States held within the district in which such association may be established.

Annual report of Comptroller.

Sec. 60. *And be it further enacted*, That it shall be the duty of the Comptroller of the Currency to report annually to Congress, at the commencement of its session—

First. A summary of the state and condition of every association from whom reports have been received the preceding year, at the several dates to which such reports refer, with an abstract of the whole amount of banking capital returned by them, of the whole amount of their debts and liabilities, the amount of circulating notes outstanding, and the total amount of means and resources, specifying the amount of specie held by them at the times of their several returns, and such other information in relation to said associations as, in his judgment, may be useful. Condition of associations.

Second. A statement of the associations whose business has been closed during the year, with the amount of their circulation redeemed, and the amount outstanding. Associations closed.

Third. To suggest any amendment to the laws relative to banking by which the system may be improved, and the security of the bill-holders and depositors may be increased. Amendments to law.

Fourth. To report the names and compensation of the clerks employed by him, and the whole amount of the expenses of the banking department during the year; and such report shall be made by or before the first day of December in each year, and the usual number of copies for the use of the Senate and House, and one thousand copies for the use of the department, shall be printed by the public printer and in readiness for distribution on the first meeting of Congress. Return of clerks. Copies of report.

SEC. 61. *And be it further enacted,* That any banking association or corporation lawfully in existence as a bank of circulation on the first day of January, anno Domini eighteen hundred and sixty-three, organized in any State, either under a special act of incorporation or a general banking law, may at any time within ——— years after the passage of this act become an association under the provisions of this act; that in such case the certificate of association provided for by this act shall be signed by the directors of such banking association or corporation, and in addition to the specifications required by this act shall specify that such directors are authorized by the owners of two-thirds of the capital stock of such banking association or corporation to make such certificate of association, and such certificate of association shall thereafter have the same effect, and the same proceedings shall be had thereon, as is provided for as to other associations organized under this act. And such association or corporation thereafter shall have the same powers and privileges, and shall be subject to the same duties, responsibilities, and rules, in all respects, as is prescribed in this act for other associations organized under it, and shall be held and regarded as an association under this act. Organization of other banks under this act.

SEC. 62. *And be it further enacted,* That any bank or State banks may deliver U. S. bonds and receive notes to issue.

banking association authorized by any State law to engage in the business of banking, and duly organized under such State law at the time of the passage of this act, and which shall be the holder and owner of United States bonds to the amount of fifty per centum of its capital stock, may transfer and deliver to the Treasurer of the United States such bonds, or any part thereof, in the manner provided by this act; and upon making such transfer and delivery, such bank or banking association shall be entitled to receive from the Comptroller of the Currency circulating notes, as herein provided, equal in amount to eighty per centum of the amount of the bonds so transferred and delivered.

Proceedings against State and other banks upon failure to redeem.

SEC. 63. *And be it further enacted,* That upon the failure of any such State bank or banking association to redeem any of its circulating notes issued under the provisions of the preceding section, the Comptroller of the Currency shall, when satisfied that such default has been made, and within thirty days after notice of such default, proceed to declare the bonds transferred and delivered to the Treasurer forfeited to the United States, and the same shall thereupon be forfeited accordingly; and thereupon the circulating notes which have been issued by such bank or banking association, shall be redeemed and paid at the treasury of the United States, in the same manner as other circulating notes issued under the provisions of this act are redeemed and paid.

Forfeited bonds of such banks, how treated.

SEC. 64. *And be it further enacted,* That the bonds forfeited, as provided in the last preceding section, may be cancelled to an amount equal to the circulating notes redeemed and paid, or such bonds may be sold, under the direction of the Secretary of the Treasury; and after retaining out of the proceeds a sum sufficient to pay the whole amount of circulating notes for the redemption of which such bonds are held, the surplus, if any remains, shall be paid to the bank or banking association from which such bonds were received.

Rights of Congress reserved.

SEC. 65. *Be it further enacted,* That Congress reserves the right at any time to amend, alter, or repeal this act.

Approved February 25, 1863.

No. II.

THE LOAN ACT OF 1863.

AN ACT TO PROVIDE WAYS AND MEANS FOR THE SUPPORT OF THE GOVERNMENT.

Be it enacted by the Senate and House of Representatives of the United States of America, in Congress assembled, That the Secretary of the Treasury be and he is hereby authorized to borrow from time to time, on the credit of the United States, a sum not exceeding three hundred millions of dollars for the current fiscal year, and six hundred millions for the next fiscal year, and to issue therefor coupon or registered bonds, payable at the pleasure of the government after such periods as may be fixed by the Secretary, not less than ten nor more than forty years from date, in coin, and of such denominations, not less than fifty dollars, as he may deem expedient, bearing interest at a rate not exceeding six per centum per annum, payable, on bonds not exceeding one hundred dollars, annually, and on all other bonds semi-annually, in coin; and he may in his discretion dispose of such bonds at any time, upon such terms as he may deem most advisable, for lawful money of the United States, or for any certificates of indebtedness or deposit that may at any time be unpaid, or for any of the Treasury notes heretofore issued or which may be issued under the provisions of this act. And all the bonds and Treasury notes or United States notes issued under the provisions of this act shall be exempt from taxation by or under State or municipal authority: *Provided,* That there shall be outstanding of bonds, Treasury notes and United States notes, at any time, issued under the provisions of this act, no greater amount altogether than the sum of nine hundred millions of dollars.

SEC. 2. *And be it further enacted,* That the Secretary of the Treasury be and he is hereby authorized to issue, on the credit of the United States, four hundred millions of dollars in Treasury notes, payable at the pleasure of the United States, or at such time or times, not exceeding three years from date, as may be found most beneficial to the public interest, and bearing interest at a rate not exceeding six per centum per annum, payable at periods expressed on the face of said Treasury notes; and the interest on the said Treasury notes and on certificates of indebtedness and deposit hereafter issued shall be paid in lawful money.

The Treasury notes thus issued shall be of such denomination as the Secretary may direct, not less than ten dollars, and may be disposed of on the best terms that can be obtained, or may be paid to any creditor of the United States willing to receive the same at par. And said Treasury notes may be made a legal tender to the same extent as United States notes, for their face value, excluding interest: or they may be made exchangeable under regulations prescribed by the Secretary of the Treasury by the holder thereof, at the Treasury in the city of Washington, or at the office of any Assistant Treasurer or depositary designated for that purpose, for United States notes equal in amount to the Treasury notes offered for exchange, together with the interest accrued and due thereon at the date of interest payment next preceding such exchange. And in lieu of any amount of said Treasury notes thus exchanged, or redeemed or paid at maturity, the Secretary may issue an equal amount of other Treasury notes; and the Treasury notes so exchanged, redeemed or paid, shall be cancelled and destroyed, as the Secretary may direct. In order to secure certain and prompt exchanges of United States notes for Treasury notes, when required as above provided, the Secretary shall have power to issue United States notes to the amount of one hundred and fifty millions of dollars, which may be used, if necessary, for such exchanges; but no part of the United States notes authorized by this section shall be issued for or applied to any other purposes than said exchanges; and whenever any amount shall have been so issued and applied, the same shall be replaced as soon as practicable from the sales of Treasury notes for United States notes.

Sec. 3. *And be it further enacted,* That the Secretary of the Treasury be and he is hereby authorized, if required by the exigencies of the public service, for the payment of the army and navy, and other creditors of the government, to issue, on the credit of the United States, the sum of one hundred and fifty millions of dollars of United States notes, including the amount of such notes heretofore authorized by the joint resolution approved January seventeen, eighteen hundred and sixty-three, in such form as he may deem expedient, not bearing interest, payable to bearer, and of such denominations, not less than one dollar, as he may prescribe, which notes so issued shall be lawful money and a legal tender in payment of all debts, public and private, within the United States, except for duties on imports and interest on the public debt; and any of the said notes, when returned to the Treasury, may be re-issued from time to time as the exigencies of the public service may require. And in lieu of any of said notes, or any other United States notes, returned to the Treasury, and cancelled or destroyed, there may be issued equal amounts of the United States notes, such as are authorized by this act. And so much of the act to authorize the issue of the United States notes, and for other purposes, approved February twenty-five, eighteen hundred and sixty-two, and of the act to authorize an additional issue of United States notes, and for other purposes, approved July eleven, eighteen hundred and sixty-two, as restricts the negotiation of bonds to market value, is hereby repealed. And the holders of United States notes, issued under and by virtue of said acts, shall present the same for the purpose of exchanging the same for bonds, as therein provided, on or before the first day of July, eighteen hundred and sixty-three, and thereafter the right so to exchange the same shall cease and determine.

SEC. 4. *And be it further enacted,* That in lieu of postage and revenue stamps for fractional currency, and of fractional notes, commonly called postage currency, issued or to be issued, the Secretary of the Treasury may issue fractional notes of like amounts in such form as he may deem expedient, and may provide for the engraving, preparation and issue thereof, in the Treasury Department building. And all such notes issued shall be exchangeable by the Assistant Treasurers and designated depositaries for United States notes in sums not less than three dollars, and shall be receivable for postage and revenue stamps, and also in payment of any dues to the United States less than five dollars, except duties on imports, and shall be redeemed on presentation at the Treasury of the United States in such sums and under such regulations as the Secretary of the Treasury shall prescribe: *Provided,* That the whole amount of fractional currency issued, including postage and revenue stamps issued as currency, shall not exceed fifty millions of dollars.

SEC. 5. *And be it further enacted,* That the Secretary of the Treasury is hereby authorized to receive deposits of gold coin and bullion with the Treasurer or any Assistant Treasurer of the United States, in sums not less than twenty dollars, and to issue certificates therefor in denominations of not less than twenty dollars each, corresponding with the denominations of the United States notes. The coin and bullion deposited for or representing the certificates of deposit shall be retained in the Treasury for the payment of the same on demand. And certificates representing coin in the Treasury may be issued in payment of interest on the public debt, which certificates, together with those issued for coin and bullion deposited, shall not at any time exceed twenty per centum beyond the amount of coin and bullion in the Treasury; and the certificates for coin or bullion in the Treasury shall be received at par in payment for duties on imports.

SEC. 6. *And be it further enacted,* That the coupon or registered bonds, Treasury notes and United States notes, authorized by this act, shall be in such form as the Secretary of the Treasury may direct, and shall have printed upon them such statements, showing the amount of accrued or accruing interest, the character of the notes, and the penalties or punishment for altering or counterfeiting them, as the Secretary of the Treasury may prescribe, and shall bear the written or engraved signatures of the Treasurer of the United States and the Register of the Treasury, and also, as evidence of lawful issue, the imprint of the copy of the seal of the Treasury Department, which imprint shall be made, under the direction of the Secretary, after the said notes or bonds shall be received from the engravers, and before they are issued; or the said notes and bonds shall be signed by the Treasurer of the United States, or for the Treasurer by such persons as may be specially appointed by the Secretary of the Treasury for that purpose, and shall be countersigned by the Register of the Treasury, or for the Register by such persons as the Secretary of the Treasury may specially appoint for that purpose. And all the provisions of the act, entitled "An act to authorize the issue of Treasury notes," approved the twenty-third day of December, eighteen hundred and fifty-seven, so far as they can be applied to this act, and not inconsistent therewith, are hereby revived and re-enacted.

SEC. 7. *And be it further enacted*, That all banks, associations, corporations or individuals, issuing notes or bills for circulation as currency, shall be subject to and pay a duty of one per centum each half year from and after April first, eighteen hundred and sixty-three, upon the average amount of circulation of notes or bills as currency issued beyond the amount hereinafter named; that is to say, banks, associations, corporations or individuals having a capital of not over one hundred thousand dollars, ninety per centum thereof; over one hundred thousand and not over two hundred thousand dollars, eighty per centum thereof; over two hundred thousand and not over three hundred thousand dollars, seventy per centum thereof; over three hundred thousand and not over five hundred thousand dollars, sixty per centum thereof; over five hundred thousand and not over one million of dollars, fifty per centum thereof; over one million and not over one million and a half of dollars, forty per centum thereof; over one million and a half and not over two millions of dollars, thirty per centum thereof; over two millions of dollars, twenty-five per centum thereof. In the case of banks with branches, the duty herein provided for shall be imposed upon the circulation of the notes or bills of such branches severally, and not upon the aggregate circulation of all; and the amount of capital of each branch shall be considered to be the amount allotted to or used by such branch; and all such banks, associations, corporations and individuals shall also be subject to and pay a duty of one-half of one per centum each half year from and after April first, eighteen hundred and sixty-three, upon the average amount of notes or bills not otherwise herein taxed and outstanding as currency during the six months next preceding the return hereinafter provided for; and the rates of tax or duty imposed on the circulation of associations which may be organized under the act "to provide a national currency, secured by a pledge of United States stocks, and to provide for the circulation and redemption thereof," approved February twenty-fifth, eighteen hundred and sixty-three, shall be the same as that hereby imposed on the circulation and deposits of all banks, associations, corporations or individuals, but shall be assessed and collected as required by said act; all banks, associations or corporations and individuals issuing or re-issuing notes or bills for circulation as currency after April first, eighteen hundred and sixty-three, in sums representing any fractional part of a dollar, shall be subject to and pay a duty of five per centum each half year thereafter upon the amount of such fractional notes or bills so issued. And all banks, associations, corporations and individuals receiving deposits or money subject to payment on check or draft, except savings institutions, shall be subject to a duty of one-eighth of one per centum each half year from and after April first, eighteen hundred and sixty-three, upon the average amount of such deposits beyond the average amount of their circulating notes or bills lawfully issued and outstanding as currency. And a list or return shall be made and rendered within thirty days after the first day of October, eighteen hundred and sixty-three, and each six months thereafter, to the Commissioner of Internal Revenue, which shall contain a true and faithful account of the amount of duties accrued, or which should accrue, on the full amount of the fractional note circulation, and on the average amount of all other circulation and of all such deposits for the six months next preceding. And there shall be annexed to every such list or return a declaration, under oath or affirmation, to be made in form and manner as shall be prescribed by the Commissioner of Internal Revenue, of the president, or some other proper officer of said bank, association, corporation or individual, respectively, that the same contains a true and faithful account of the duties which have accrued, or which should accrue, and not accounted for; and for any default in the delivery of such list or return, with such declaration annexed, the bank, association, corporation or individual making such default shall forfeit, as a penalty, the sum of five hundred dollars; and such bank, association, corporation or individual shall, upon rendering the list or return as aforesaid, pay to the Commissioner of Internal Revenue the amount of the duties due on such list or return, and in default thereof shall forfeit, as a penalty, the sum of five hundred dollars; and in case of neglect or refusal to make such list or return as aforesaid, or to pay the duties as aforesaid, for the space of thirty days after the time when said list should have been made or rendered, or when said duties shall have become due and payable, the assessment and collection shall be made according to the general provisions prescribed in an act, entitled "An act to provide internal revenue to support the government and to pay interest on the public debt," approved July one, eighteen hundred and sixty-two.

SEC. 8. *And be it further enacted*, That, in order to prevent and punish counterfeiting and fraudulent alterations of the bonds, notes and fractional currency, authorized to be issued by this act, all the provisions of the sixth and seventh sections of the act, entitled "An act to authorize the issue of United States notes, and for the redemption or funding thereof, and for funding the floating debt of the United States," approved February twenty-fifth, eighteen hundred and sixty-two, shall, so far as applicable, apply to the bonds, notes and fractional currency hereby authorized to be issued, in like manner as if the said sixth and seventh sections were hereby adopted as additional sections of this act. And the provisions and penalties of said sixth and seventh sections shall extend and apply to all persons who shall imitate, counterfeit, make or sell any paper such as that used, or provided to be used, for the fractional notes prepared, or to be prepared, in the Treasury Department building, and to all officials of the Treasury Department engaged in engraving and preparing the bonds, notes and fractional currency, hereby authorized to be issued, and to all official and unofficial persons in any manner employed under the provisions of this act. And the sum of six hundred thousand dollars is hereby appropriated, out of any money in the Treasury not otherwise appropriated, to enable the Secretary of the Treasury to carry this act into effect.

Approved March 3, 1863.

No. III.

Section seventh of the "Act to provide ways and means for the support of the government," approved March 3, 1863.

Sec. 7. *And be it further enacted,* That all banks, associations, corporations, or individuals, issuing notes or bills for circulation as currency, shall be subject to and pay a duty of one per centum each half year from and after April first, eighteen hundred and sixty-three, upon the average amount of circulation of notes or bills as currency issued beyond the amount hereinafter named—that is to say, banks, associations, corporations, or individuals having a capital of not over one hundred thousand dollars, ninety per centum thereof; over one hundred thousand and not over two hundred thousand dollars, eighty per centum thereof; over two hundred thousand and not over three hundred thousand dollars, seventy per centum thereof; over three hundred thousand and not over five hundred thousand dollars, sixty per centum thereof; over five hundred thousand and not over one million of dollars, fifty per centum thereof; over one million and not over one million and a half of dollars, forty per centum thereof; over one million and a half and not over two millions of dollars, thirty per centum thereof; over two millions of dollars, twenty-five per centum thereof. In the case of banks with branches, the duty herein provided for shall be imposed upon the circulation of the notes or bills of such branches severally, and not upon the aggregate circulation of all; and the amount of capital of each branch shall be considered to be the amount allotted to or used by such branch; and all such banks, associations, corporations, and individuals shall also be subject to and pay a duty of one-half of one per centum each half year from and after April first, eighteen hundred and sixty-three, upon the average amount of notes or bills not otherwise herein taxed and outstanding as currency during the six months next preceding the return hereinafter provided for; and the rates of tax or duty imposed on the circulation of associations which may be organized under the act "To provide a national currency secured by a pledge of United States stocks, and to provide for the circulation and redemption thereof," approved February twenty-fifth, eighteen hundred and sixty-three, shall be the same as that hereby imposed on the circulation and deposits of all banks, associations, corporations, or individuals, but shall be assessed and collected as required by said act. And all banks, associations, or corporations, and individuals, issuing or reissuing notes or bills for circulation as currency after April first, eighteen hundred and sixty-three, in sums representing any fractional part of a dollar, shall be subject to and pay a duty of five per centum each half year thereafter upon the amount of such fractional notes or bills so issued; and all banks, associations, corporations, and individuals receiving deposits of

Banks under the national currency act taxed one half of one per centum semi-annually, instead of one per cent. as by the original act.

money subject to payment on checks or drafts, except savings institutions, shall be subject to a duty of one-eighth of one per centum each half year from and after April first, eighteen hundred and sixty-three, upon the average amount of such deposits beyond the average amount of their circulating notes or bills lawfully issued and outstanding as currency. And a list or return shall be made and rendered within thirty days after the first day of October, eighteen hundred and sixty-three, and each six months thereafter, to the Commissioner of Internal Revenue, which shall contain a true and faithful account of the amount of duties accrued, or which should accrue on the full amount of the fractional note circulation and on the average amount of all other circulation, and of all such deposits, for the six months next preceding, And there shall be annexed to every such list or return a declaration, under oath or affirmation, to be made in form and manner as shall be prescribed by the Commissioner of Internal Revenue, of the president, or some other proper officer of said bank, association, corporation, or individual, respectively, that the same contains a true and faithful account of the duties which have accrued, or which should accrue, and not accounted for; and for any default in the delivery of such list or return with such declaration annexed, the bank, association, corporation, or individual making such default, shall forfeit, as a penalty, the sum of five hundred dollars. And such bank, association, corporation, or individual shall, upon rendering the list or return as aforesaid, pay to the Commissioner of Internal Revenue the amount of the duties due on such list or return, and in default thereof shall forfeit, as a penalty, the sum of five hundred dollars; and in case of neglect or refusal to make such list or return as aforesaid, or to pay the duties as aforesaid, for the space of thirty days after the time when said list should have been made or rendered, or when said duties shall have become due and payable, the assessment and collection shall be made according to the general provisions prescribed in an act entitled "An act to provide internal revenue to support the government and to pay interest on the public debt," approved July one, eighteen hundred and sixty-two.

INDEX

TO

AN ACT TO PROVIDE A NATIONAL CURRENCY, ETC.

B.

N.

O.

AMERICAN

FINANCES AND RESOURCES.

LETTER

No. II.

OF

HON. ROBERT J. WALKER, M.A.

COUNSELLOR AT LAW IN THE SUPREME COURT OF THE UNITED STATES,
LATE LAW REP. MI., SENATOR OF THE UNITED STATES,
SECRETARY OF THE TREASURY, COMMISSIONER TO CHINA,
GOVERNOR OF KANSAS, ETC., ETC.

LONDON:
WILLIAM RIDGWAY, 169, PICCADILLY, W.
1863.

AMERICAN FINANCES AND RESOURCES.

LETTER No. II.

London, 10, *Half Moon Street*, *Piccadilly*,
October 8, 1863.

IN view of the fact, that the people of the United Kingdom and of the United States are mainly of the same race, speak the same language, have the same literature, ancestry, and common law, with the same history for centuries, and a reciprocal commerce exceeding that of all the rest of the world, it is amazing how little is known in each country of the other. This condition of affairs is most unfavourable to the continuance of peace and goodwill between two great and kindred nations. It causes constant misapprehension by each party of the acts and motives of the other, arrests the development of friendly feeling, and retards the advance of commercial freedom. It excites almost daily rumours of impending war, disturbing the course of trade, causing large mercantile losses, and great unnecessary Government expenditures. If war has not ensued, it has led to angry controversy and bitter recrimination. It is sowing broadcast in both countries the seeds of international hatred, rendering England and America two hostile camps, frowning mutual defiance; and, if not terminating in war, must, if not arrested, end in embargoes and non-intercourse, or discriminating duties on imports and tonnage, greatly injurious to both countries. I know it has become fashionable in England and America to sneer at the fact of our common origin; but the great truth still exists, and is fraught with momentous consequences, for good or evil, to both nations, and to mankind. The United States were colonized mainly by the people of England. Ten of our original thirteen States bear English names, as do also nearly all their counties, townships, cities, and villages.

Leaving to Englishmen the task of disabusing the Americans in regard to their own country, I will endeavour to present, in a condensed form, some material and authentic facts as regards the United States for the consideration of the people of the United Kingdom. I read and hear every day here predictions of our impending bankruptcy and national dissolution, our wealth and resources depreciated; our cause, our people, our armies, and Government decried; and a war in words and in the press prosecuted against us with vindictive fury. All this hostility is fully reciprocated in America; and if the war is not confined to words and types, it will not be the fault of agitators in both countries. So far as an American can, even in part, arrest this fatal progress of misapprehension, by communicating information in regard to his own country, is the principal purpose of these essays.

In answer to the daily predictions here of our impending ruin and national bankruptcy, I shall first discuss the question of our wealth, resources, and material progress.

AREA.—The area of the United States, including lakes and rivers, is 3,250,000 square miles, being larger than all Europe. (Rep. Sec. of Interior and of Com. of Gen. Land Office, for Dec. 1860, p. 13.)

Our land surface is 3,010,370 square miles, being 1,926,636,800 acres. This area is compact and contiguous, divided into States and Territories, united by lakes, rivers, canals, and railroads. We have no colonies. Congress governs the nation by what the Constitution declares to be "*the supreme law*," whilst local regulations are prescribed and administered by the several States and Territories. We front on the two great oceans—the Atlantic and Pacific; extending from the St. Lawrence and the Lakes to the Gulf of Mexico, from near the 24th to the 49th parallel of north latitude; and in longitude, from 67° 25′ to 124° 40′ west of Greenwich. Our location on the globe as regards its land surface is central, and all within the temperate zone. No empire of contiguous territory, possesses such a variety of climate, soil, forests and prairies, fruits and fisheries, animal, vegetable, mineral, and agricultural products. We have all those of Europe, with many in addition, and a climate (on the average) more salubrious, as shown by the international census. We have a far more fertile soil and genial sun, with longer and better seasons for crops and stock; and already, in our infancy, with our vast products, feed and clothe many millions in Europe and other continents. Last year our exports to foreign countries of breadstuffs and provisions, from the loyal States alone, were of the value of $108,000,000. (Table of Com. and Nav. 1860.)

If as well cultivated as England, our country could much more than feed and clothe the whole population of the world. If as densely settled as England, our population would be more than twelve hundred millions, exceeding that of all the earth. If as densely settled as Massachusetts, (among the least fertile of all our States,) we would number 513,000,000 inhabitants.

We have seen that our area exceeds that of Europe, with a far more genial sun and fertile soil, and capable of yielding more than double the amount of agricultural products and of sustaining more than twice the number of inhabitants. We have a greater extent of mines than all Europe, especially of coal, iron, gold, silver, and quicksilver. Our Coal alone, as stated by Sir William Armstrong, (the highest British authority,) is 32 times as great as that of the United Kingdom, and our iron will bear a similar proportion.

Our maritime front is 5,120 miles; but, our whole coast line, including bays, sounds and rivers, up to the head of tide water is 33,063 miles. (Ex. doc. No. 7, pp. 75, 76, Official Report of Professor A. D. Bache, Superintendent of U. S. Coast Survey, Dec. 5th, 1848.) Our own lake shore line is 3620 miles. (Top. Rept. ib. 77.)

The shore line of the Mississippi river above tide-water and its tributaries, is 35,644, (Ib. 77); and of all our other rivers, above tide-water, is 49,857 miles, making in all 122,784 miles. Of this stupendous water mileage, more than one half is navigable by steam, employing an interior steam tonnage exceeding that of all the internal steam tonnage of the rest of the world. No country is arterialized by such a vast system of navigable streams, to have constructed which as canals of equal capacity would have cost more than ten billions of dollars, and then these canals would have been subjected to large tolls, the cost of their annual repairs would have been enormous, and the interruption by lockage, a serious obstacle. We may rest assured then, that, all Europe combined, can never have such facilities for cheap water communication as the United States. This is a mighty element in estimating the power and progress of a nation. It shows, also, why we have no such deserts as Sahara, so small a portion of our lands requiring manures or irrigation, and no general failures of crops, with so few even partial failures of any one crop.

We have more deep, capacious and safe harbours

accessible at *all tides*, than all Europe, with more than twenty capable of receiving the "Great Eastern." (Charts, U. S. Coast Survey.)

Our hydraulic power, (including Niagara,) far exceeds that of all Europe. We have more timber than all Europe, including most varieties, useful and ornamental. We have, including cotton, vastly more of the raw material for manufacturers than all Europe. With all these vast natural advantages, has man, in our country, performed his duty, in availing himself of the bounteous gifts of Providence? We are considering now the question of our material progress, in regard to which, the following official data are presented.

We have completed since 1790, 5782 miles of canals, from four to ten feet deep, and from 40 to 75 feet wide, costing $148,000,000, and mostly navigable by steam. (Census Table, 1860, No. 39.)

We have constructed since 1829, 33,698 miles of rail-road, (more than all the rest of the world,) costing $1,258,922,729. (Table 38, Census of 1860, and Addenda.)

We have in operation on the land, more miles of telegraph than all the world, a single route, from New York to San Francisco, being 3500 miles.

Our light-houses exceed in number those of any other country, and we have no light-dues, as in England.

Our coast survey, executed by Professor Bache, Superintendent of the U. S. Coast Survey, exceeds in extent and accuracy that of any other country. On this subject, we have the united opinions of British and Continental savans.

We have made since 1790, 1,505,454 linear miles of survey of the public lands of the U. States, belonging to the Government, including 460,000,000 of acres already divided into townships, each six miles squares, (23,040 acres,) subdivided into square miles, called sections, of 640 acres each, and each section further subdivided, into 16 lots of 40 acres each.

TONNAGE. The total tonnage of the United States was in—

1814,	1,368,127	tons.
June, 1851,	3,772,439	„
June, 1861,	5,539,812	„

At the same rate of increase as from 1851 to 1861, our tonnage would be

in	1871,	8,134,578	tons.
„	1881,	11,952,817	„
„	1891,	17,541,514	„
„	1901,	25,758,948	„

(*Table Com. & Nav.*)

At the close of this century our tonnage then, at this rate of increase, would far exceed that of all the rest of the world.

GOLD AND SILVER. The aggregate product of our gold and silver mines approaches now *one billion of dollars*, most of which has been converted into coin at our mint. Nearly all of this product has been obtained since the discovery of gold in

California. Less than two per cent. of the precious metals has been the product of the seceded States. This gold and silver are found now in seven States, and nine Territories; the yield is rapidly augmenting, and new discoveries constantly developed.

The Secretary of the Interior estimates the total product "next year," of our mines of precious metals, at "$100,000,000," and when our railroad to the Pacific, (traversing this region,) is completed, his estimate of the "annual yield" is "$150,000,000." The mines are declared "inexhaustible" by the highest authority, and our Nevada silver mines are now admitted to be "the richest in the world." The completion of our imperial railroad, now progressing to the Pacific, will carry an immense population to the gold and silver regions, vastly increase the number of miners, diminish the cost of mining, and decrease the price of provisions and supplies to the labourers. When we add to this, the vast and increasing product of our quicksilver mines of California, so indispensable as an amalgam in producing gold and silver, as also the great and progressive improvement in processes and machinery for working the quartz veins, it is now believed that the estimate of our Secretary of the Interior, and Commissioner of the General Land Office, will be exceeded by the result. These mines of the precious metals are nearly all on the public lands of the United States, they are the *property of the Federal Govern-*

ment, and their intrinsic value *exceeds our public debt.*

PUBLIC LANDS. The United States own an immense public domain, acquired by treaties with France, Spain, and Mexico, and by compacts with States and Indian tribes. This domain is thus described in the report of the Commissioner of the General Land Office of November 29th, 1860.

"Of the 3,250,000 of square miles which constitute the territorial extent of the Union, the public lands embrace an area of 2,265,625 square miles, or 1,450,000,000 of acres, being more than two thirds of our geographical extent, and nearly three times as large as the United States at the ratification of the definitive treaty of peace in 1783 with Great Britain. This empire domain extends from the northern line of Texas, the gulf of Mexico, reaching to the Atlantic ocean, northwesterly to the Canada line bordering upon the great lakes Erie, Huron, Michigan, and Superior, extending westward to the Pacific ocean, with Puget's Sound on the north, the Mediterranean sea of our extreme northwestern possessions.

"It includes fifteen sovereignties known as the 'Land States,' and an extent of territory sufficient for thirty-two additional, each equal to the great central land State of Ohio.

"It embraces soils capable of abundant yield of the rich productions of the tropics, of sugar, cotton, rice, tobacco, corn, and the grape, the vintage, now a staple, particularly so of California; of the great cereals, wheat and corn, in the western, northwestern, and Pacific States, and in that vast interior region from the valley of the Mississippi river to the Rocky mountains; and thence to the chain formed by the Sierra Nevada and Cascades, the eastern wall of the Pacific slope, every variety of soil is found revealing its wealth.

"Instead of dreary inarable wastes, as supposed in earlier times, the millions of buffalo, elk, deer, mountain sheep, the primitive inhabitants of the soil, fed by the hand of nature, attest its capacity for the abundant support of a dense population through the skilful toil of the agriculturist, dealing with the earth under the guidance of the science of the present age.

"Not only is the yield of food for man in this region abundant, but it holds in its bosom the precious metals of gold, silver, with cinnabar, the useful metals of iron, lead, copper, interspersed with immense belts or strata of that propulsive element coal, the source of riches and power, and now the indispensable agent not only for domestic purposes of life, but in the machine shop, the steam car, and steam vessel, quickening the advance of civilization and the permanent settlement of the country, and being the agent of active and constant intercommunication with every part of the republic."

Kansas having been admitted since the date of this report, our public domain, thus described officially, now includes the sixteen *land States*, and *all* the Territories.

Of this vast region (originally 1,450,000,000 acres), there was surveyed up to September, 1860, 441,067,915 acres, and 394,088,712 acres disposed of by sales, grants, &c., leaving, as the commissioner states, "the total area of unsold and unappropriated, of offered and unoffered lands of the public domain, 1,055,911,288 acres." This is "land surface," exclusive of lakes, bays, rivers, &c., 1,055,911,288 acres, or 1,649,861 square miles, and exceeds one half the area of the whole Union. The area of New York being 47,000 square miles, is less than a thirty-fifth part of our public domain. England *

* Our whole area is more than sixty times as large as England.

(proper) has 50,922 square miles, France 203,736, Prussia 107,921, and Germany 80,620 square miles. The area then of our public domain is more than eight times as large as France, more than fifteen times as large as Prussia, more than twenty times as large as Germany, more than thirty-two times as large as England, and larger (excluding Russia) than all Europe, containing more than 200 millions of people.

As England (proper) contained in 1861, 18,949,916 inhabitants, if our public domain were as densely settled, its population would exceed 606 millions, and it would be 260,497,561, if numbering as many to the square mile as Massachusetts. Its average fertility far exceeds that of Europe, as does also the extent of its mines, especially gold, silver, coal, and iron, with every variety of soil, climate, mineral and agricultural products.

These lands are surveyed at the expense of the Government into townships of six miles square, subdivided into sections, and these into quarter sections (160 acres), set apart for homesteads. Our system of public surveys into squares, by lines running due north and south, east and west, is so simple as to have precluded all disputes as to boundary or title. This domain reaches from the 24th to the 49th parallel, from the lakes to the gulf, and from the Atlantic to the Pacific. Its isothermes (the lines of equal mean annual temperature) strike on the north the coast of Norway midway, touch

St. Petersburg in Russia, and pass through Manchooria to the coast of Asia, about three degrees south of the mouth of the Amour river. On the south, these isothermes run through northern Africa, and nearly the centre of Egypt near Thebes, cross northern Arabia, Persia, northern Hindostan, and southern China near Canton.

Of this vast domain, less than two per cent. is cursed by slavery, which is prohibited by law in eleven of these land States, and in all the Territories.

Now, however, within our present vast domain, not only the poor, but our own industrious classes and those of Europe, may not only find a home, but a farm for each settler, substantially as a free gift by the government. Here all who would rather be owners than tenants, and wish to improve and cultivate their own soil, are invited. Here, too, all who would become equals among equals, citizens (not subjects) of a great and free country, enjoying the right of suffrage, and eligible to every office except the presidency, can come and occupy with us this great inheritance. Here liberty, equality, and fraternity reign supreme, not in theory or in name only, but in truth and reality. This is the brotherhood of man, secured and protected by our organic law. Here the Constitution and the people are the only sovereigns, and the government is administered by their elected agents, and for the benefit of the people. Those toiling elsewhere for wages that will scarcely support existence, for the education of whose children no provision is made by law, who are excluded from the right of suffrage, may come here and be voters and citizens, find a farm given as a homestead, free schools provided for their children at the public expense, and hold any office but the presidency, to which their children, born here, are eligible. What does Europe for any of its toiling millions who reject this munificent offer? He is worked and taxed there to his utmost endurance. He has the right to *work*, and *pay taxes*, but not to vote. Unschooled ignorance is his lot and that of his descendants. If a farmer, he works and improves the land of others, in constant terror of rent day, the landlord, and eviction. Indeed the annual rent of a single acre in England exceeds the price—$10 (£2. 2*s*. 8*d*.)—payable for the ownership in fee simple of the entire homestead of 160 acres, granted him here by the government. For centuries that are past, and for all time to come, there, severe toil, poverty, ignorance, the workhouse, or low wages, and disfranchisement, would seem to be his lot. Here, freedom, competence, the right of suffrage, the homestead farm, and free schools for his children.

In selecting these homestead farms the emigrant can have any temperature, from St. Petersburg to Canton. He can have a cold, a temperate, or a warm climate, and farming or gardening, grazing or vintage, varied by fishing or hunting. He can raise wheat, rye, Indian corn, oats, rice, indigo, cotton, tobacco, cane or maple sugar and molasses, sorghum, wool, peas and beans, Irish or sweet potatoes, barley, buckwheat, wine, butter, cheese, hay, clover, and all the grasses, hemp, hops, flax and flaxseed, silk, beeswax and honey, and poultry, in uncounted abundance. If he prefers a stock farm, he can raise horses, asses, and mules, camels, milch cows, working oxen and other cattle, goats, sheep and swine. In most locations, these will require neither housing nor feeding throughout the year. He can have orchards, and all the fruits and vegetables of Europe, and many in addition. He can have an Irish or German, Scotch, English, or Welsh, French, Swiss, Norwegian, or American neighbourhood. He can select the shores of oceans, lakes, or rivers; live on tide water or higher lands, valleys or mountains. He can be near a church of his own denomination; the freedom of conscience is complete; he pays no tithes, nor church tax, except voluntarily. His sons and daughters, on reaching twenty-one years of age, or sooner, if the head of a family, are each entitled to a homestead of 160 acres; if he dies, the title is secured to his widow, children, or heirs. Our flag is his, and covers him everywhere with its protection. He is our brother, and he and his children will enjoy with us the same heritage of competence and freedom. He comes where labour is king, and toil is respected and rewarded. If before, or instead of receiving his homestead, he chooses to pursue his profession, or business, to work at his trade, or for daily wages, he will find them double the European rate, and subsistence cheaper. From whatever part of Europe he may come, he will meet his countrymen here, and from them and us receive a cordial welcome. A government which gives him a farm, the right to vote, and free schools for his children, must desire his welfare.

Of this vast domain, (more than thirty-two times as large as England,) the Government of the United States grants substantially as a free gift, a *farm of 160 acres* to every settler who will occupy and cultivate the same, the title being in fee simple, and free from all rent whatsoever. The settler may be *native* or *European*, a present or future immigrant, including females as well as males, but must be at least 21 years of age, *or* the head of a family. If an immigrant, the declaration must first be made of an *intention* to become a citizen of the United States, when the grant is immediately made, without waiting for naturalization. When the children of the settler reach 21 years of age, or become the head of a family, they each receive from the Government a like donation of 160 acres. The intrinsic value of this public domain far exceeds the whole public debt of the United States.

Our national wealth, by the last census, was $16,159,616,068, and its increase during the last ten years $8,925,481,011, or 126·45 per cent. Census, 1860, p. 195. Now, if, as a consequence of the Homestead Bill, there should be occupied, improved, and cultivated, during the next ten years, 100,000 additional farms by settlers, or only 10,000 per annum, it would make an aggregate of 16,000,000 acres. If, including houses, fences, barns, and other improvements, we should value each of these farms at ten dollars an acre, it would make an aggregate of $160,000,000. But if we add the product of these farms, allowing only one-half of each (80 acres) to be cultivated, and the average annual value of the crops, stock included, to be only ten dollars per acre, it would give $80,000,000 a-year, and, in ten years, $800,000,000, independent of the re-investment of capital. It is clear that thus vast additional employment would be given to labour, freight to steamers, railroads and canals, markets for manufactures, and augmented revenue.

The homestead privilege will largely increase immigration. Now, beside the money brought here by immigrants, the census proves that the average annual value of the labour of Massachusetts *per capita* was, in 1860, $300 for each man, woman, and child. Assuming that of the immigrants at an average net annual value of only $100 each, or less than 33 cents a-day, it would make, in ten years, at the rate of 200,000 each year, the following aggregate:—

1st year	200,000	=	$20,000,000
2nd „	400,000	„	40,000,000
3rd „	600,000	„	60,000,000
4th „	800,000	„	80,000,000
5th „	1,000,000	„	100,000,000
6th „	1,200,000	„	120,000,000
7th „	1,400,000	„	140,000,000

8th year	1,600,000	=	$160,000,000
9th „	1,800,000	„	180,000,000
10th „	2,000,000	„	200,000,000
		Total	$1,100,000,000

In this table, the labour of all immigrants each year is properly added to those arriving the succeeding year, so as to make the aggregate, the last year, two millions. This would make the value of the labour of these two millions of immigrants, in ten years, $1,100,000,000, independent of the annual accumulation of capital, and the labour of the children of the immigrants after the first ten years, which, with their descendants, would go on constantly increasing.

But, by the actual official returns (see page 14 of Census), the number of alien immigrants to the United States, from December, 1850, to December, 1860, was 2,598,216, or an annual average of 259,821, say 260,000. The effect, then, of this immigration, on the basis of the last table, upon the increase of national wealth, was as follows: —

1st year	260,000	=	$26,000,000
2nd „	520,000	„	52,000,000
3rd „	780,000	„	78,000,000
4th „	1,040,000	„	104,000,000
5th „	1,300,000	„	130,000,000
6th „	1,560,000	„	156,000,000
7th „	1,820,000	„	182,000,000
8th „	2,080,000	„	208,000,000
9th „	2,340,000	„	234,000,000
10th „	2,600,000	„	260,000,000
		Total	$1,430,000,000

Thus the value of the labour of the immigrants from 1850 to 1860 was fourteen hundred and thirty millions of dollars, making no allowance for the accumulation of capital by annual re-investment, nor for the natural increase of population, amounting, by the census, in ten years, to about 24 per cent. This addition to our wealth by the labour of the children, in the first ten years, would be small; but in the second, and each succeeding decennium, when we count children and their descendants, it would be large and constantly augmenting. But the census shows that our wealth increases each ten years at the rate of 126·45 per cent. Now then, take our increase of wealth in consequence of immigration as before stated, and compound it at the rate of 126·45 per cent. every ten years, and the result is largely over three billions of dollars in 1870, and over seven billions of dollars ia 1880, independent of the effect of any immigration succeeding 1860. If these results are astonishing, we must remember that immigration here is augmented population, and that it is population and labour that create wealth. Capital, indeed, is the accumulation of labour. Immigration, then, from 1850 to 1860, added to our national wealth a sum more than one-third greater than our whole debt on the 1st of July last, and augmenting in a ratio much more rapid than its increase, and thus enabling us to bear the war expenses.

As the homestead privilege must largely increase

immigration, and add especially to the cultivation of our soil, it will contribute more than any other measure to increase our population, wealth, and power, and augment our revenue from duties and taxes.

We have seen that, by the Census (p. 195), the total value of the real and personal estate in the United States was—

In 1860	$16,159,616,068
In 1850	7,135,780,228

Increase from 1850 to 1860, 126·45 per cent.

At the same rate of increase, for the four succeeding decades, the result would be—

In 1870	$36,593,450,585
In 1880	82,865,868,849
In 1890	187,314,353,225
In 1900	423,330,438,288

If we subtract one-fourth from the aggregate, we will find that our public debt constitutes less than *one half of one per cent.* of the *increase* of our national wealth. This debt, then, does not exhaust our capital, but affects only a small diminution of the rate of augmentation.

If we would look at the causes of this vast increase of our national wealth, they will be found mainly in the enormous extent of our fertile lands, the vast emigration from Europe, and the constant addition of new States to the Union. Thus, from 1850 to 1860, four new States were added to the

Union. These four States were almost an untrodden wilderness in 1850, but in 1860 were rich and flourishing States, with a population of 638,965, and an aggregate wealth of $331,809,418. Within this decade, from 1860 to 1870, at least six new States will be added to the Union. This is evident from a reference to our present Territories, as follows: —

Dacotah . . .	95,316,480 acres.
Nebraska . .	48,636,800
Indian	56,924,000
Idaho	208,878,720
Washington .	44,796,160
Nevada . . .	52,184,960
Utah	68,084,480
Arizona . . .	80,730,240
New Mexico . .	77,568,640
Colorado . . .	66,880,000
Total . .	800,000,480 acres.

Here then are territories with an aggregate area of 800,000,480 acres, sufficient for 26 States of the size of New York. In all these territories but one, the precious metals are found in great abundance, and the railroad to the Pacific, with numerous branches through this vast region together with the great advantages of our new Homestead bill of last year, is settling these territories with unprecedented rapidity. Notwithstanding the war, immigration to the United States is progressing with more than its usual volume, caused by the very high wages for labour, the great benefits of our recent Homestead bill, and the exclusion, by recent act of Congress, of slavery from all this vast domain.

It will be observed, that, whilst the *lands* constituting these territories remain *public* lands, no estimate is made of them as wealth in the National census. It is only when these public lands become farms and private property, that they are valued as part of the wealth of the nation. This remark also applies to that 255,000,000 acres of public lands, in the sixteen *Land States* of the Union. Hence the amazing increase of wealth at each decade, in the new States and Territories. Thus, by table 35 of the Census of 1860, page 195, the rate of increase of wealth in the following States and Territories, from 1850 to 1860 was,

Territories.		
Washington	5000	per cent.
Nebraska	4800	do.
Utah	467	do.
New Mexico	302	do.
States.		
Kansas	8000	per cent.
Iowa	942	do.
California	837	do.
Minnesota	6000	do.
Michigan	330	do.
Oregon	471	do.
Illinois	457	do.
Wisconsin	550	do.

It is thus that the wave of population moves onward in our western States and Territories, that the axe and the plough are the pioneers of civilization, that farms, cities, and villages, the schoolhouse, and the church rise from the wilderness, as if by the touch of an enchanter's wand. That enchantment is the power of *freedom and education*, the effect of which (as compared with the deadly influence of slavery and ignorance), shall be illustrated in a succeeding letter. In that letter, by comparing the relative progress of our free and and slave States, as demonstrated by our Census, it will be proved, incontestably, that the total exclusion of slavery from our Union, will cause an addition to our national wealth vastly exceeding the whole public debt of our country, and soon leave us much richer than before the rebellion.

R. J. WALKER.

AMERICAN

FINANCES AND RESOURCES.

LETTER

No. III.

OF

HON. ROBERT J. WALKER, M.A.

COUNSELLOR AT LAW IN THE SUPREME COURT OF THE UNITED STATES,
LATE LAW REP. MI., SENATOR OF THE UNITED STATES,
SECRETARY OF THE TREASURY, COMMISSIONER TO CHINA,
GOVERNOR OF KANSAS, ETC., ETC.

LONDON:
WILLIAM RIDGWAY, 169, PICCADILLY, W.
1863.

10, Half Moon Street, Piccadilly.
Dec. 3, 1863.

IT is generally believed, even when the American rebellion should be suppressed, that there would be a great loss of wealth and resources on the part of the United States. As an economical question the great truth is not disputed by me, that, as a general rule, wars by a waste of property, by large expenditures, and by the withdrawal of so much labour from the pursuits of industry, impair the material interests of the nation. The influence of such considerations in the United States is not denied; but there is in the causes of this contest, as well as in its effects and consequences, results which will more than compensate for such losses. Slavery was the sole cause of this rebellion, and the result will be the reconstruction of the Union, with slavery everywhere extinguished. On this assumption, the question is, whether the substitution of free for slave labour throughout every State and Territory of the Union will not, as a question of augmented wealth and invigorated industry, far more than compensate for the losses incurred in the contest. Reasoning inductively, it might well be supposed that the willing labour of educated and energetic freemen, would be far more productive than the forced labour of ignorant, unwilling, and uneducated slaves. In the realm of science, as well as in the direction of labour, knowledge is power, education is wealth and progress; and that this is applicable to the masses who compose a community, and especially to the working classes, is demonstrated by our American official Census. In proof of this position, I will proceed by a reference to the official tables of our Census of 1860, to show not only in particular slave States, as compared with other free States, whether old or new, eastern or western, or making the comparison of the aggregate of all the slave with the free States, the annual product of the latter *per capita* is more than double that of the slave States. I begin with Maryland as compared with Massachusetts, because Maryland in proportion to her area, has greater natural advantages than any one of the slave or free States; and if the comparison with the free States is most unfavourable to her, it will be more so as to any other Southern State, as the Census shows, that, from 1790 to 1860, as well as from 1850 to 1860, Maryland increased in population per square mile more rapidly than any other Slave-holding State.

We must consider the area, soil, climate, mines, hydraulic power, location, shore line, bays, sounds, and rivers, and such other causes as affect the advance of wealth and population.

The relative progress of Maryland has been slow indeed. The population of the Union, by the census of 1790, was 3,929,827, of which Maryland, containing then 319,728, constituted a twelfth part

(12.29). In 1860, the Union numbered 31,445,080 and Maryland 687,034, constituting a forty-fifth part (45.76). In 1790, the free States numbered 1,968,455, Maryland's population then being equal to one-sixth (6.12); but, in 1860, the population of the free States was 18,920,078, Maryland's number then being equal to one twenty-seventh part (27.52). But, if Maryland had increased as rapidly from 1790 to 1860 as the whole Union, her proportion, one twelfth part, would have made her numbers in 1860, 2,620,315; and if her proportional increase had equalled that of the free States, her ratio, one sixth, would have made her population in 1860, 3,153,392.

I take the areas from the report (November 29, 1860) of the Commissioner of the General Land Office, where they are for the first time accurately given, "excluding the water surface." The population is taken from the census tables. I compare first Massachusetts and Maryland, because they are maritime and old States, and both in 1790 had nearly the same population, but, as will be shown hereafter, with vastly superior natural advantages in favour of Maryland.

Area of Maryland, 11,124 square miles; shore lines, by tables of United States Coast Survey, viz.: main shore, including bays, sounds, &c., 503 miles, islands 298, rivers to head of tide water 535; total, 1,336 miles.

Area of Massachusetts, 7,800 square miles;

shore lines, by tables of United States Coast Survey, viz.: main shore, including bays, sounds, &c. 435 miles, islands, 259, rivers to head of tide water 70; total, 764 miles. When we mark the Potomac and its tributaries, the lower Susquehanna, the deep and numerous streams of the Chesapeake, the commercial advantages of Maryland over Massachusetts are vast indeed. Looking at the ocean shore of Maryland, and also at the Chesapeake bay, the largest and finest estuary in the world, indented with numerous sounds and navigable inlets, three-fourths of its length for both shores being within Maryland, and compare this deep and tranquil and protected basin, almost one continuous harbour, with the rock-bound coast of Massachusetts, lashed by the stormy Atlantic, the superiority of Maryland is striking.

Mortality in Maryland, by the late census, viz., deaths from 1st June, 1859, to 31st May, 1860, 7,370 persons. Same time in Massachusetts, 21,303; making the ratio of deaths to the number living in Maryland, one to every 92, and in Massachusetts one to every 57; and the percentage of deaths in Maryland 1.09, and in Massachusetts 1.76. This rate of mortality for Massachusetts is confirmed by the late official report of their Secretary of State to the Legislature.

As to area, then, Maryland exceeds Massachusetts 43 per cent.; as to the shore line, that of Marylandis nearly double that of Massachusetts. As to climate that of Maryland, we have seen, is far the most salubrious. This is a vast advantage, not only in augmented wealth and numbers, from fewer deaths, but also as attracting capital and immigration. This milder and more salubrious climate gives to Maryland longer periods for sowing, working, and harvesting crops, a more genial sun, larger products and better and longer crop seasons, great advantages for stock, especially in winter, decreased consumption of fuel, a greater period for the use of hydraulic power, and of canals and navigable streams. The area of Maryland fit for profitable culture is more than double that of Massachusetts, the soil much more fertile, its mines of coal and iron, with the fluxes all adjacent, rich and inexhaustible; whereas Massachusetts has no coal, and no valuable mines of iron or fluxes. When we reflect that coal and iron are the great elements of modern progress, and build up mighty empires, this advantage of Maryland over Massachusetts is almost incalculable. The hydraulic power of Maryland also greatly exceeds that of Massachusetts. Such are the vast natural advantages of Maryland over Massachusetts. Now let us observe the results. Population of Maryland in 1790, 319,728; in 1860, 687,034; increase 367,300. Population of Massachusets in 1790, 378,717; in 1860, 1,231,065; increase, 852,348; difference of increase in favour of Massachusetts, 485,048; excess of Massachusetts over Maryland in 1790, 58,989, and in 1860, 544,031. This result is amazing, when we regard the far greater area of Maryland and her other vast natural advantages. The population of Maryland in 1790 was 28 to the square mile (28.74), and in 1860, 61 to square mile (61,76); whereas Massachusetts had 48 to the square mile in 1790 (48.55), and 157 to the square mile in 1860 (157.82). Thus Massachusetts had only 20 more to the square mile in 1790, and 96 more to the square mile in 1860. But if the areas of Maryland and Massachusetts had been reversed, Massachusetts, with the area of Maryland, and the population of Massachusetts of 1860 to the square mile, would have numbered then 1,755,661, and Maryland with the area of Massachusetts, and the population of Maryland of 1860 to the square mile, would have had then a population of only 481,728 upon that basis, leaving Massachusetts in 1860, 1,273,393 more people than Maryland.

By the census of 1790, Massachusetts was the fourth in population of all the States, and Maryland the sixth; but in 1860, Massachusetts was the seventh, and Maryland the nineteenth; and if each of the thirty-four States increases in the same ratio from 1860 to 1870, as from 1850 to 1860, Maryland will be only the twenty-fifth State.

These facts all conclusively attest the terrible effects of slavery on Maryland, and this is only one of the dreadful sacrifices she has made in retaining the institution. As to wealth, power, and intellectual development, the loss cannot be overstated.

Nor can manufactures account for the difference,

as shown by the still greater increase of the agricultural North-West. Besides, Maryland (omitting slavery) had far greater natural advantages for manufactures than Massachusetts. She had a more fertile soil, thus furnishing cheaper food to the working classes, a larger and more accessible coast, and nearly eight times the length of navigable rivers, greater hydraulic power, vast superiority in mines of coal and iron, a far more salubrious climate, cotton, the great staple of modern industry, much nearer to Maryland, her location far more central for trade with the whole Union, and Baltimore, her chief city, nearer than Boston to the great West, viz.: to the Ohio at Pittsburg and Cincinnati, the Mississippi at St. Louis, and the lakes at Cleveland, Toledo, and Chicago, by several hundred miles. Indeed, but for slavery, Maryland must have been a far greater manufacturing as well as commercial State than Massachusetts—and as to agriculture, there could be no comparison.

But Massachusetts did not become a manufacturing tate until afer the tariff of 1824. That measure, as well as the whole protective policy, Massachusetts earnestly opposed in 1820 and 1824, and Daniel Webster, as her representative, denounced it as unconstitutional. From 1790 to 1820 Massachusetts was commercial, not manufacturing, and yet, from 1790 to 1820, Massachusetts increased in numbers 144,442, and Maryland in the same time only 87,622. Yet, from 1790 to 1820, Massachusetts, the most commercial State, was far more injured by the embargo and the late war with England than any other State.

It is clear, then, that the accusation of the secession leaders that the North was built up at the expense of the South, by the tariff, can have no application to the progress of Massachusetts and Maryland, because the advance of the former over the latter preceded by more than thirty years the adoption of the protective policy, and a comparison of the relative advance of the free and slave States, during the same period, exhibits the same results.

There is one *invariable law*, whether we compare all the slave States with all the free States, small States with small, large with large, old with old, new with new, retarding the progress of the slaveholding States, ever operating, and differing in degree only.

The area of the nine free States enumerated in 1790, is 169,668 square miles, and of the eight slaveholding States 300,580 square miles, while the population of the former in 1790 was 1,968,455, and of the latter, 1,961,372; but, in 1860, these nine free States had a population of 10,594,168, and those eight slave States only 7,414,684, making the difference in favour of these free States in 1860 over those slave States, 3,179,844, instead of 7,083 in 1790, or a positive gain to those free States over those slave States of 3,172,761. These free States, enumerated in 1790 and 1860, were the six New

England States—New York, New Jersey, and Pennsylvania; and the slave States were, Delaware, Maryland, Virginia, North and South Carolina, Georgia, Tennessee, and Kentucky—yet we have seen that the area of those slave States was nearly double that of those free States, the soil much more fertile, the climate more salubrious, as shown by the census, that the shore line, including main shore, bays, and sounds, islands and rivers, to head of tide water, was, for those free States, 4,480 miles, and for those slave States, 6560 miles. Thus, it is clear, that the increase of population of these slave States should have far exceeded that of those free States. The population of these slave States per square mile in 1790 was six (6.52), and in 1860, 24 (24.66), and of those free States in 1790, was 11 per square mile (11.60), and in 1860, 62 per square mile (62.44). Thus, while the increase of those slave States from 1790 to 1860 was only 18 per square mile, that of those free States was nearly 51 per square mile (50.84), or in very nearly a triple ratio, while in wealth and education the proportionate progress was much greater.

No cause except slavery can be assigned for this wonderful difference, for the colonists of Maryland were distinguished for education, intelligence, and gentle culture. Lord Baltimore was a statesman and philanthropist, and his colony was a free representative government, which was the first to repudiate the doctrine of taxation without representation, and the first to introduce religious toleration. While Maryland has produced many of the most eminent soldiers, statesmen, and jurists, her relative decline in power, wealth and population, has been deplorable, and is attributable exclusively to the paralysing effect of slavery.

While the advance of Massachusetts, with her limited area and sterile soil, especially in view of the thousands of her native sons who have emigrated to other States, is one of the wonders of the world, yet, the relative increase of the population of New Jersey, from 1790 to 1860, compared with that of Maryland, is still greater than that of Massachusetts. The law is inflexible wherever slavery disappears. Population of New Jersey in 1790, 184-139, in 1860, 672,035, being an increase of 264 per cent. (264.96) for New Jersey, of 225 per cent. (225.06) for Massachusetts, and for Maryland 114 per cent. (114.88). The ratio of increase per square mile from 1790 to 1860 was: Massachusetts. 48.55 in 1790, and 157.82 in 1860; Maryland, 28.74 in 1790, and 61.76 in 1860; and New Jersey, 22.01 in 1790, and 80.70 in 1860. Thus, while Maryland from 1790 to 1860, little more than doubled her ratio of increase per square mile (28.74 to 61.76), and Massachusetts little more than tripled her ratio (48.55 to 157.82), New Jersey very nearly *quadrupled* hers (22.01 to 80.70). It must be conceded, however, that the natural advantages of New Jersey are far greater than those of Massachusetts, whose material and intellectual progress, in defiance of such serious obstacles, now is, and, most probably for ever will be, *without a parallel.* Now the area of New Jersey is but 8,320 square miles; the soil of Maryland is far more fertile, the hydraulic power much greater, the shore line much more than double, viz.: 531 for New Jersey, to 1,336 for Maryland; while New Jersey, with rich iron mines, has no coal, and one-third of her area is south of the celebrated Mason and Dixon's line, the northern boundary of Maryland. While the free States have accomplished these miracles of progress, they have peopled eleven vast Territories (soon by subdivision to become many more States), immigration to which has been almost exclusively from the North, as compared with the South.

The slave State which has increased *most* rapidly to the square mile of all of them from 1790 to 1860, has had a smaller augmentation per square mile than that free State which has increased most *slowly* per square mile during the same time of all the free States, and the result is the same as to wealth and education also. Under the *best* circumstances for the slave States, and the *worst* for the free States, this result proves the uniformity of the rule (like the great law of gravitation), knowing no exception to the effect of slavery, in depressing the progress of States in population, wealth, and education.

The isothermals of the great Humboldt, (differing so widely from parallels), which trace the lines of temperature on the earth's surface, prove, as to heat, the climate of the South (running a line from Charleston to Vicksburg) to be substantially the same as that of Greece and Italy—each, in its turn, the mistress of the world.

The census of 1860 exhibits our increase of population from 1790 to 1860 at 35.59 per cent., and of our wealth 126.45. Now, if we would increase the wealth of the country only one tenth in the next ten years, by the gradual disappearance of slavery (far below the results of the census), then, our wealth being now $16,159,616,068, the effect of such increase would be to make our wealth in 1870, instead of $36,593,450,585, more than sixteen hundred millions greater, and in 1880, instead of $82,865,-868,849, over three billions six hundred millions, or more than three times our present debt.

Before the close of this letter, it will be shown that the difference, *per capita*, of the annual products of Massachusetts and Maryland exceeds $150. As to the other Southern States, the excess is much greater. Now, if the annual products of the South were increased $150 each *per capita* (still far below Massachusetts) by the exclusion of slavery, then multiplying the total population of the South, 12,229,727, by 150, the result would be an addition to the annual value of the products of the South of $1,834,456,050, and in the decade, $18,344,580,-500. This change would not be immediate, but there can be no doubt that with the vastly greater natural advantages of the South, the superiority of free to slave labour, the immense immigration, especially from Europe to the South, aided by the Homestead bill, and the conversion of large plantations into small farms, an addition of at least one billion of dollars would be made in a decade, by the exclusion of slavery, to the value of the prod ucts of the South.

Having considered the relative progress in population of Massachusetts and Maryland, I will now examine their advance in wealth.

By tables 33 and 36, census of 1860, the value of the products of Massachusetts that year was $287,-000,000; and of Maryland, $66,000,000. Table 33 included domestic manufactories, mines, and fisheries (p. 59); and table 36, agricultural products. Dividing these several aggregates by the total population of each State, the value of that year's product of Massachusetts was $235, *per capita*, and of Maryland, $96, making the average annual value of the labour of each person in the former greatly more than double that of the latter, and the gross product more than quadruple. This is an amazing result, but it is far below the reality. The earnings of commerce and navigation are omitted in the census, which includes only the products of agriculture, manufactures, the mines, and fisheries. This was a most unfortunate omission, attributable to the secession leaders, who wished to confine the census to a mere enumeration of population, and thus obliterate all the other great decennial monuments which mark the nation's progress in the pathway of empire.

Some of these tables are given as follows:

First, as to Railroads.—The number of miles in Massachusetts in 1860 (including city roads) was 1,340, and the cost of construction $61,857,203 (table 38, pp. 230, 231). The value of the freight of these roads in 1860 was $500,524, 201 (p. 105). The number of miles of railroad in Maryland at the same time was 380, the cost of construction $21,387,157, and the value of the freight (at the same average rate) $141,111,348, and the difference in favour of Massachusetts $359,412,883. The difference must have been much greater, because a much larger portion of the freight in Massachusetts consisted of domestic manufactures, worth $250 per ton, which is $100 a ton above the average value.

The passengers' account, not given, would vastly swell the difference in favour of Massachusetts.

The tonnage of vessels built in Massachusetts in 1860 was 34,460 tons, and in Maryland, 7,798 tons (p. 107).

The number of banks in Massachusetts in 1860 was 174; capital, $64,519,200; loans, $107,417,-323. In Maryland, the number was 31; capital $12,568,962; loans, $20,898,762 (table 34, p. 193).

The number of insurance companies in Massachusetts 117; risks, $450,896,263. No statement given for Maryland, but comparatively very small, as the risks in Massachusetts were nearly one sixth of all in the Union.

Our exports abroad, from Massachusetts, for the fiscal year ending 30th June, 1860, were of the value of $17,003,277, and the foreign imports $41,187,539; total of imports and exports, $58,-190,816; the clearances 746,909 tons, the entries 849,449; total entered and cleared, 1,596,458 tons. In Maryland, exports $9,001,600, foreign imports $9,784,773; total imports and exports, $18,786,323; clearances, 174,000 tons; entries, 186,417; total of entries and clearances, 360,417 (table 14, Register of Treasury). Thus, the foreign imports and exports abroad, of Massachusetts, were much more than triple those of Maryland, and the entries and clearances very largely more than quadruple. The coastwise and internal trade are not given, as recommended by me when Secretary of the Treasury, but the tables of the railroad traffic indicate in part the immense superiority of Massachusetts.

These statistics, however, prove that, if the earnings of commerce and navigation were added, the annual value of the products of Massachusetts *per capita* would be at least $300, and three times that of Maryland. In estimating values *per capita*, we must find the earnings of commerce very large, as a single merchant, in his counting house, engaged in an immense trade, and employing only a few clerks, may earn as much as a great manufacturing corporation, employing hundreds of hands. Including commerce, the value *per capita* of the products and earnings of Massachusetts exceeds not only those of *any State in our Union,* BUT OF THE WORLD; and would, at the same rate, make the value of its annual products three hundred billions of dollars; and of our own country, upward of nine billions of dollars per annum. Such, under great natural disadvantages, is the grand result achieved in Massachusetts, by education, science, industry, free schools, free soil, free speech, *free labour,* free press, and free government. The facts prove that freedom is progress, that 'knowledge is power,' and that the best way to appreciate the value of property and augment wealth most rapidly, is to invest a large portion of it in schools, high schools, academies, colleges, universities, books, libraries, and the press, so as to make labour more productive, because more skilled, educated, and better directed. Massachusetts has achieved much in this respect; but when she shall have made high schools as free and universal as common schools, and the attendance on both compulsory, so as to qualify every voter for governing a State or nation, she will have made a still grander step in material and intellectual progress, and the results would be still more astounding.

By table 35 of the census, p. 195, the whole

value of all the property, real and personal, of Massachusetts, in 1860, was $815,237,433, and of Maryland, $376,919,944. We have seen that the value of the products that year in Massachusetts was $287,000,000 (exclusive of commerce), and of Maryland, $66,000,000. As a question, then, of profit on capital, that of Massachusetts was 35 per cent., and of Maryland 17 per cent. Such is the progressive advance (more than two to one) of free as compared with slave labour. The same law obtains in comparing all the free with all the slave States. But the proof is still more complete. Thus, Delaware and Missouri (alone of all the slave States) were ahead of Maryland in this rate of profit, because both had comparatively fewer slaves; and all the other slave States, whose servile population was relatively larger than that of Maryland, were below her in the rate of profit. The law extends to *counties*, those having comparatively fewest slaves increasing far more rapidly in wealth and population. This, then, is the formula as to the rate of profit on capital. First, the free States; next, the States and counties of the same State having the fewest relative number of slaves. The census, then, is an evangel against slavery, and its tables are revelations proclaiming laws as divine as those written by the finger of God at Mount Sinai on the tables of stone.

For seventy years we have had these census tables, announcing these great truths more and more clearly at each decade. They are the records of the nation's movement and condition, the decennial monuments marking her steps in the path of empire, the oracles of her destiny. They are prophecies, for each decade fulfills the predictions of its predecessor. They announce laws, not made by man, but the irrevocable ordinances of the Almighty. We cannot, with impunity, refuse to obey these laws For every violation, they enforce their own penalties. From these there is no escape in the present or the past, nor for the future, except in conformity to their demands. These laws condemn slavery; and the punishment for disobedience is recorded in the result of every census, and finally culminated in the rebellion. Slavery and freedom are antagonistic and discordant elements: the conflict between them is upon us; it admits of no neutrality or compromise, and one or the other system must perish.

We have seen that slavery is hostile to the progress of wealth and population: let us now ascertain its influence on moral and intellectual development.

By table 15 of the census of 1860, the result for that year was as follows: In Massachusetts, value of books printed, $397,500; jobs, $529,347; newspapers, $1,979,069; total, $2,905,916. Same year in Maryland, books printed, $58,000; jobs, $122,000; newspapers, $169,000; total, $350,155. By table 37, census of 1860, Massachusetts had 222 newspapers and periodicals, of which 112 were political, 31 religious, 51 literary, miscellaneous,

28. Maryland had only 57, all political. The whole number of copies issued in Massachusetts in 1860 was 102,000,760, and in Maryland, 20,721,472. Of periodicals, Massachusetts has monthly, 1 political, 10 religious, 18 literary, 7 miscellaneous; quarterly, religious 3, literary 2, miscellaneous 1, and 1 annual. Maryland had *none.* Not a religious, literary, scientific, or miscellaneous periodical or journal in the State! What terrible truths are unfolded in these statistics! None but a political party press in Maryland, all devoted, in 1860, to the maintenance, extension, and perpetuity of slavery, which had 57 advocates, and not one for science, religion, or literature.

We have seen that the circulation in 1860 of the press in Massachusetts exceeded that of Maryland by more than eighty-one millions of copies. These facts all prove that slavery is hostile to knowledge and its diffusion, to science, literature, and religion, to the press, and to free government.

For schools, colleges, libraries, and churches, I must take the tables of the census of 1850, those of 1860 not being yet published. There were in 1850 in Massachusetts, 3,679 public schools, 4,443 teachers, 176,475 pupils; native adults who cannot read or write, 1,861. In Maryland, 907 public schools, 1,005 teachers, 33,254 pupils; native adults who cannot read or write, 38,426, excluding slaves, to teach whom is criminal.

Thus, then, slavery is hostile to schools, withholding instruction from the children of the poor.

The number of public libraries in Massachusetts was 1,462, volumes 684,015. In Maryland, 124, and 125,042 volumes. Value of churches in Massachusetts, $10,206,000. In Maryland, $3,947,884, of which $2,541,240 is in Baltimore (which has very few slaves), and the remainder is mainly in the seven counties (from which slavery has nearly disappeared) adjoining Pennsylvania.

As to schools, colleges, books, libraries, churches, newspapers, and periodicals, it thus appears that Massachusetts is greatly in advance of Maryland.

Now then, let us contrast loyal Maryland with rebel South Carolina, the author of secession, and assuming for many years to instruct the nation. By the census of 1860, she had a population of 703,708, of whom 402,406 were slaves; and Maryland, numbering 687,049, had 87,189 slaves. Now, by the census of 1860, South Carolina had 45 journals and periodicals, and her annual circulation was 3,654,840 copies. The circulation therefore of Massachusetts exceeded that of South Carolina more than ninety-eight millions of copies, while Maryland exceeded South Carolina more than seventeen millions of copies. So much for South Carolina, as a great political teacher. As to schools in 1850: South Carolina had 724 public schools, 739 teachers, 17,838 pupils. Massachusetts, then, had 158,637 more pupils at public schools than South Carolina, and Maryland 15,416 more pupils at public schools than South Carolina.

The press of Massachusetts, we have seen, circulated in 1860 upward of one hundred and two millions of copies, equal to 279,454 per day, including journals and periodicals, each read, on an average, by at least two persons. This is independent of books and pamphlets, and of the very large circulation of papers from other States and from Europe. What a flood of light is thus shed daily and hourly upon the people of Massachusetts! This intellectual effulgence radiates by day and night. It is the sun in its meridian splendour, and the stars in an ever unclouded firmament. It has a centre and a circumference, but knows no darkness. Ignorance vanishes before it; wealth follows in its train; labour rejoices in its association, and finds its products more than doubled; freedom hails its presence, and religion gives it a cordial welcome; churches, schools, academies, colleges, and universities acknowledge its mighty influence. Science penetrates the secrets of nature, and unfolds each new discovery for the benefit of man. Coal, the offspring of the sun, develops its latent energy, and water contributes its untiring hydraulic power. Machinery takes more and more the place of nerves and muscles, cheapens clothing and subsistence and all the necessaries of life, and opens new fields of industry, and more profitable employment for labour. Steam and lightning become the slaves of man. He performs the journey of a day in an hour, and converses in minutes around the globe. The strength of man may not have been much increased, but his power is augmented a thousand-fold. His life may not have been materially lengthened, but, in the march of knowledge, a year now is as a century, compared with man's progress in the darkness of the middle ages. The eternal advance towards omniscience goes on, but is like that of the infinite approach of the asymptote, which never reaches the hyperbolic curve. The onward march of science is in a geometrical ratio, so that in time, the intellectual progress of a day in the future, must exceed that of a century in the past. Knowledge is enthroned as king, and grand truths and new ideas are his ministers. Science takes the diameter of the earth's orbit as a base line and unit of measurement, and with it spans immensity, and triangulates the nebulous systems amid the shadowy verges of receding space. Its researches are cosmical upon the earth and the heavens, and all the elements minister to its progress. Sink to the lowest mine, or fathom the ocean's depth, or climb the loftiest mountains, or career through the heavens on silken wings, and it is there also. On—on—on; nearer—nearer—still nearer it moves forever and forever, with accelerated speed, toward the infinite eternal. Such are the triumphs of knowledge; and he who diffuses it among our race, or discovers and disseminates new truths, advances man nearer to his Creator; he exalts the whole race; he elevates it in the scale of being, and raises it into higher and still higher spheres.

It is science that marks the speed of sound and

light and lightning, calculates the eclipses, catalogues the stars, maps the heavens, and follows, for centuries of the past and the future, the comet's course. It explores the animal, vegetable, and mineral kingdoms. With geology, it notes the earthquake upheaval of mountains, and, with mineralogy, the laws of crystallization. With chemistry, it analyzes, decomposes, and compounds the elements. If, like Canute, it cannot arrest the tidal wave, it is subjecting it to laws and formulas. Taking the sunbeam for its pencil, it heliographs man's own image, and the scenery of the earth and the heavens. Has science any limits or horizon? Can it ever penetrate the soul of man, and reveal the mystery of his existence and destiny? It is certainly exploring the facts of sociology, arranging and generalizing them, and deducing laws.

Man, elevated by knowledge in the scale of being, controls the forces of nature with greater power and grander results, and accumulates wealth more rapidly. The educated free labour of Massachusetts, we have seen, doubles the products of toil, *per capita*, as compared with Maryland, and quadruples them (as the census shows) compared with South Carolina. One day's labour of a man in Massachusetts is more than equal to two in Maryland, and four in South Carolina. So, if we take our savage tribes, with their huts and tents, their rude agriculture, their furs, their few and simple household manufactures, their hunting and fishing, the average product of their annual labour, at four cents a day each, would be $14.60 a year, or more than a fourth of that of South Carolina (56.91). So that Massachusetts, in material progress, is farther in advance of South Carolina than that State is of the savage Indians. Thus we have the successive steps and gradations of man: Massachusetts, with free labour and free schools, having reached the highest point of civilization: South Carolina, with slavery and ignorance (except the few), in a semi-barbarous stage; and the lowest savage condition, called barbarous, but nearer to South Carolina than that State to Massachusetts.

Slavery, then, the census proves, is hostile to the progress of wealth and population, to science, literature, and education, to schools, colleges, and universities, to books and libraries, to churches and religion, to the press, and therefore to free government; hostile to the poor, keeping them in want and ignorance; hostile to labour, reducing it to servitude, and decreasing two-thirds the value of its products; hostile to morals, repudiating among slaves the marital and parental condition, classifying them by law as chattels, darkening the immortal soul, and making it a crime to teach millions of human beings to read or write. And shall labour and education, literature and science, religion and the press, sustain an institution which is their deadly foe?

The discussion will be continued in my next letter.

R. J. WALKER.

AMERICAN

FINANCES AND RESOURCES.

LETTER

No. IV.

OF

HON. ROBERT J. WALKER, M.A.

COUNSELLOR AT LAW IN THE SUPREME COURT OF THE UNITED STATES,
LATE LAW REP. MI., SENATOR OF THE UNITED STATES,
SECRETARY OF THE TREASURY, COMMISSIONER TO CHINA,
GOVERNOR OF KANSAS, ETC., ETC.

LONDON:
WILLIAM RIDGWAY, 169, PICCADILLY, W.
1864.

10, Half Moon Street, Piccadilly.
Jan. 1st, 1864.

In my third and last letter on American Finances and Resources, the effect of the substitution of free for slave labour in the United States by the abolition of slavery was discussed. In that letter it was shown by the official American census of 1860, that the product that year, *per capita*, of Massachusetts was $235; *per capita*, Maryland $96; and of South Carolina $56. Massachusetts had no slaves; Maryland, 87,189; and South Carolina, 402,406. Thus we see the annual value of the products of labour decreased in proportion to the number of Slaves. In further proof of the position assumed in that letter, that the progress of of wealth, of population, and education in the United States was most injuriously affected by slavery, I now present other official facts from our census of 1860. My first comparison will be that of the free State of New York with slave-holding Virginia.

By the census, the population of Virginia in 1790 was 748,308, and in 1860, 1,596,318, making the ratio of increase 113.32 per cent. In 1790, New York numbered 340,120, and in 1860, 3,880,735, the ratio of increase being 1,040.99. (Table 1,

Prelim. Census Rep., p. 132.) Thus, the rate of increase in New York exceeded that of Virginia more than nine to one.

In 1790, the population of Virginia was largely more than double that of New York. In 1860, the population of New York was very largely more than double that of Virginia. In 1790, Virginia, in population, ranked first of all the States, and New York the fifth. In 1860, they had reversed their positions, and New York was the first, and Virginia the fifth. (Rep., p. 120.) At the same rate of progress, from 1860 to 1900, as from 1790 to 1860, Virginia, retaining slavery, would have sunk from the first to the twenty-first State, and would still continue, at each succeeding decade, descending the inclined plane toward the lowest position of all the States. Such has been, and still continues to be, the effect of slavery, in dragging down that once great State from the first toward the last in rank in the Union. But if, as in the absence of slavery must have been the case, Virginia had increased from 1790 to 1860 in the same ratio as New York, her population in 1860 would have been 7,789,141, and she must always have remained the first in rank of all the States.

Area.—The natural advantages of Virginia far exceed those of New York. The area of Virginia is 61,352 square miles, and that of New York, 47,000. The population of Virginia per square mile in 1790 was 12.19, and in 1860, 26.02. That of New York, in 1790, was 7.83, and in 1860, 84,36. Now, if New York, with her present numbers per square mile, had the area of Virginia, her population, in 1860, would have been 5,175,654, and that of Virginia, reduced to the area of New York, on the basis of her present numbers per square mile, would have been 1,320,000. This illustrates the immense effect of area, as one of the great elements influencing the progress of population. But, wonderful as are these results, the great fact is omitted in this calculation, that Virginia, in 1790, had largely more than double the population of New York. Thus, if we reverse the numbers of New York and Virginia in 1790, and take the actual ratio of increase of each for the succeeding seventy years, the population of Virginia, in 1860, would have been 728,875, and that of New York, as we have seen, would have been 7,789,141, making the difference exceed seven millions, or very largely more than ten to one. Reverse the areas also, and the difference would exceed eight millions.

Shore Line.—As furnishing cheap and easy access for imports and exports, creating marts for commerce with great cities, and affecting the interior most beneficially, the shore line, with adequate harbours, constitutes a vast element in the progress of states and empires. Now, by the last tables of the United States coast survey, the shore line of Virginia was 1,571 miles, and of New York 725 miles. The five great parallel tide-water rivers of Virginia, the Potomac, the Rappahannock, the York river, James river, and Roanoke (partly in North Carolina), with their tributaries, furnish easy access for hundreds of miles into the interior, with both shores of the noble Chesapeake bay for many miles, as well as its magnificent outlet and the main ocean for a considerable distance, all within the limits of Virginia. We have seen that the coast line of Virginia is largely more than double that of New York, and the harbours of Virginia are more numerous, deeper, and much nearer the great valley of the Ohio and Mississippi. By the coast-survey tables, the mean low water in the harbour of New York by Gedney's channel is 20 feet, and at high-water spring tides is 24.2; north channel, 24, mean low water, and 29.1 spring-tides, high water; south channel, 22 and 27.1; main ship channel, after passing S. W. spit buoy, on N. E. course, one mile up the bay, for New York, 22.5-27.06. By the same tables, from capes at entrance of Chesapeake bay to Hampton, at mean low water, 30 feet; spring tides, high water, 32.8. Anchorage in Hampton roads, 59-61.8. From Hampton roads to Sewell's point, 25-27.8. South of Sewell's point (one mile and a half), 21-23.8; up to Norfolk, 23-25.8. From Hampton roads to James river, entering to the northward of Newport News, middle ground, 22-24.8. From Hampton roads to James river, entering to the southward of Newport News, middle ground, 27-29.8. From abreast the tail of York spit, up to Yorktown, 33-35.8. Elizabeth river, between Norfolk and navy yard, 25.5-28.3.

When we leave the tide-water rivers for the interior navigable streams, Virginia has a vast advantage. New York has no such rivers above tide, but Virginia has the Ohio for hundreds of miles, with its tributaries, the Kanawha, Guyandotte, and Big Sandy. It is true, New York has several of the great lakes, and the vast advantage of connection with them through her great canal. But, in the absence of slavery, the canal projected by Washington (preceding that of New York) would have connected, through Virginia, the Chesapeake bay with the Ohio river. The James river, flowing into the Chesapeake, cuts the Blue Mountains, and the Kanawha, a confluent of the Ohio, cuts the Alleghany; thus opening an easy and practicable route for a great canal from the eastern to the western waters. The valley of the lakes, with which New York is connected by her canal, has an area of 335,515 square miles. The valley of the Mississippi, with which the Chesapeake would long since, in the absence of slavery, have been connected by the Virginia canal, has an area of 1,226,600 square miles. The shore line of the Mississippi and its tributaries, above tide water, is 35,644 miles. (Page 35 Compend. Census of 1850.) Our shore line of the lakes is 3,620 miles, including bays, sounds, and islands; and that of the British, 2,629. (Ib. 35.) The connection of the lakes with the Ohio and Mississippi would be the same for both States, the one being from the lakes to these rivers, and the other from the rivers to the lakes. The location of Virginia is more central than that of New York, and Virginia runs farther west by several hundred miles. We are so accustomed to look at the connection of New York with the West by her canal, and Virginia with no such union, that it is difficult to realize the great change if Virginia had been connected by her progressing work with the Ohio and Mississippi, and thence, by the present canals, with the lakes.

It is apparent, then, that, as regards easy access to the West, the natural advantages of Virginia surpass New York, and with greater facilities for artificial works. How many decades would be required, after emancipation, to bring the superior natural advantages of Virginia into practical operation, is not the question; nor do I believe that the city of New York will ever cease to be the centre of our own trade, and ultimately of the commerce of the world. But although Virginia, in adhering to slavery, has lost her supremacy in the Union, it is quite certain that, as a Free State, she would commence a new career of wonderful prosperity, that capital and population from the North and from Europe would flow there with a mighty current, her lands be doubled in value, and her town and city property far more than quadrupled.

Mines.—Virginia has vast mines of coal, the great element of modern progress. New York has none. It is coal that has made Great Britain a mighty empire, giving her power, by land and sea, equal to the manual force of all mankind. It is stated by the Commissioner of the General Land Office, in his report before referred to, of November, 1860, 'that an acre of coal, three feet thick, is equal to the product of 1,940 acres of forest trees; and each acre of a coal seam four feet in thickness, and yielding one yard of pure coal, is equivalent to 5,000 tons, and possesses, therefore, a reserve of mechanical strength in its fuel, equal to the life labour of more than 1,600 men.'

This statement of the Commissioner is made on the highest authority, and proves the vast natural advantages of Virginia over New York. Virginia, also, has far more abundant mines of iron, more widely diffused over the State, reaching from tide water to the Ohio. She has also these iron mines in juxtaposition with coal and all the fluxes. Virginia, also, has valuable mines of gold, lead, and copper. New York has no gold or copper mines, and produced in 1860 but $800 worth of lead. (Table 14.)

HYDRAULIC POWER.—Omitting Niagara, which thus far scorns the control of man, the hydraulic power of Virginia very far exceeds that of New York. It is to be found on the Potomac and its tributaries, and upon nearly every stream that flows into the Chesapeake or Ohio. The superior mildness of the climate of Virginia makes this power available there for a much greater portion of the year. The great falls of the Potomac, where Washington constructed the largest locks of the continent, has a water power unsurpassed, and is but twelve miles from tide water, at Washington. This point is a most healthy and beautiful location, surrounded by lands whose natural fertility was very great, and, in the absence of slavery, must have been a vast manufacturing city. This water power could move more spindles than are now worked on all this continent.

Agriculture and Manufactures.—The natural fertility of the soil of Virginia far exceeded that of New York, with a more genial sun, and much more favourable seasons for agricultural products, as well as for stock. The number of acres of land in Virginia susceptible of profitable culture, is nearly double that of New York, but much of it has been impoverished by slave labour, scratching and exhausting the soil, without manure or rotation of crops. The census shows that Virginia has all the products of New York, and cotton in addition. Virginia produced, in 1860, 12,727 bales of cotton (table 36), worth, at present prices, nearly $3,000,000. She also adjoins the States of North Carolina and Tennessee, producing, in 1860, 372,964 bales, worth, at present prices, nearly $90,000,000. Virginia is also much nearer than New York to all the other cotton States. With these vast advantages, with her larger area, more fertile soil, cheaper subsistence, her coal and iron and great hydraulic power, with so much cotton raised by herself and in adjacent States, Virginia should have manufactured much more cotton than New York. But, by the census (table 22), the value of the cotton manufacture of Virginia in 1850 was $1,446,109, and in 1860, $1,063,611—a decrease of one third. In New York, the value of the cotton manufacture in 1850 was $5,019,323, and in 1860, $7,471,961, an increase of over 48 per cent. So, if we look at the tables of mines, manufactures, and the fisheries, with the vastly superior advantages of Virginia, the whole product in 1860 was of the value of $51,300,000, and of agriculture $68,700,000; whilst in New York these values were respectively $379,623,560 and $226,376,440. (Tables of Census, 33 and 36.)

Climate and Mortality.—By table 6, page 22, of the Census, there were for the year ending June 1st, 1860, 46,881 deaths in New York, being 1 in every 82 of the population, and 1.22 per cent. The number of deaths in Virginia, in the same year, was 22,472, being 1 in every 70 of the population, or 1.43 per cent. There was, then, a slight difference in favour of New York. But Virginia is divided into four geographical sections; the tide-water, the Piedmont (running from the tide-water region to the Blue Mountains), the valley between these mountains and the Alleghanies, and the trans-Alleghany to the Ohio. These three last sections, containing three-fourths of the area and white population of the State, surpass New York in salubrity, with the most bracing and delightful climate. The climate of Virginia is far more favourable for stock and agricultural products than New York, with longer and better seasons, and is more salubrious than the climate of Europe (Comp. 1850).

Progress of Wealth.—We have seen how great was the advance in population of New York over Virginia, from 1790 to 1860, being in the ratio of more than 9 to 1. Now let us compare the relative progress of wealth. It is contended by the advocates of slavery, that it accumulates wealth more rapidly, and thus enriches the nation, although it may depress its moral and intellectual development, its increase of numbers and of power, and tarnish its reputation throughout the world. As population and its labour create wealth, it must be retarded by a system which, as we have seen in this case, diminishes the relative advance of numbers in the ratio of more than 9 to 1. But the census proves that slavery greatly retards the increase of wealth. By tables 33 and 36 of the census of 1860, it appears, omitting commerce, that the products of industry, as given, viz., of agriculture, manufactures, mines, and fisheries, were that year in New York $606,000,000, or $156 *per capita*; and in Virginia $120,000,000, or $75 *per capita*. This shows a total value of product in New York more than five times greater than in Virginia, and *per capita* more than 2 to 1. If we include the earnings of commerce, and all business not given in the census, I think it will be shown hereafter, that the value of the products and earnings of New York, in 1860, exceeded those of Virginia at least 7 to 1. As to the rate of increase, the value of the products of agriculture, manufactures, mines and fisheries of Virginia, in 1850, was $84,180,428 (table 9), and in New York $358,736,603, showing an increase in Virginia from 1850 to 1860 of $35,519,572, being 41 per cent. and in New York $249,263,397, being 70 per cent., exhibiting a difference of 29 per cent. Now the increase of population in Virginia from 1850 to 1860 was 12.29 per cent., and in New York 25.29 per cent., the difference being only 13 per cent. (Table 1, p. 131.) Thus, it appears, the increase of wealth in New York, exclusive of the gains of commerce, as compared with Virginia, was more than double the ratio of the augmentation of population. By the census table of 1860, No. 35, p. 195, 'The true value of the real and personal property, according to the eighth census was, New York, $1,843,338,517, and of Virginia $793,249,681.' Now we have seen the value of the products of New York in 1860 by the census was $606,000,000, and in Virginia $120,000,000. Thus, as a question of the annual yield of capital, that of New York was 34 per cent., and Virginia 15 per cent.; the annual product of capital being more than double in New York what it was in Virginia. The problem then is solved in Virginia, as it was in Maryland and South Carolina, and all the South compared with all the North, that slavery retards the progress of wealth and accumulation of capital, in the ratio of 2 to 1. Our war taxes may be very great, but the tax of slavery is far greater, and the relief from it, in a few years, will add much more to the national wealth than the whole deduction made by the war debt. Our total wealth, by the census of 1860, being, by table 35, $16,159,616,068, one per cent. taken annually to pay the interest and gradually extinguish the war debt, would be $161,596,160; whereas, judging by Virginia and New York, the diminished increase of the annual product of capital, as the result of slavery, is 2.10 per cent., or $453,469,250 per annum, equal in a decade, without compounding the annual results, to $4,534,692,500.

That our population would have reached in 1860 nearly 40,000,000, and our wealth have been more than doubled, if slavery had been extinguished in 1790, is one of the revelations made by the census; whilst in science, in education, and national power, the advance would have been still more rapid, and the moral force of our example and success would have controlled for the benefit of mankind the institutions of the world.

By table 36, p. 196, of the census of 1860, the *cash* value of the farms of Virginia was $371,096,211, being $11,91 per acre, and of New York $803,343,593, being $38.26 per acre. Now, by the table, the number of acres embraced in these farms of New York was 20,992,950, and in Virginia 31,014,950, the difference of value per acre being $25.36, or much more than 3 to 1 in favour of New York. Now, if we multiply this number of acres of farm lands of Virginia by the New York value, it would make the total value of the farm lands of Virginia $1,186,942,136, and the *additional* value caused by emancipation $815,845,925. But, stupendous as is this result in regard to lands, it is far below the reality. We have seen that the farm lands of Virginia, improved and unimproved, constituted 31,014,950 acres. By the census and the land-office tables, the area of Virginia is 39,265,280 acres. Deduct the farm lands, and there remain unoccupied 8,250,330 acres. Now, Virginia's population to the square mile being 26.02, and that of New York 84.36, with an equal density in Virginia, more than two-thirds of these Virginia lands, as in New York, must have been occupied as farms. This would have been equivalent, at two-thirds, to 5,500,000 acres, which, at their present average value of $2 per acre, would be worth $11,000,000; but, at the value per acre of the New York lands, these 5,500,000 acres would be worth $206,430,000. Deduct from this their present value, $11,000,000, and the remainder, $195,430,000, is the sum by which the unoccupied lands of Virginia, converted into farms, would have been increased in value by emancipation. Add this to the enhanced value of their present farms, $815,845,925, and the result would be $1,011,275,925, as the gain of Virginia in the value of lands by emancipation. To these we should add, from the same cause, the enhancement of the town and city property in Virginia to the extent of several hundred millions of dollars. In order to realize the truth, we must behold Virginia as she would have been, with New York railroads and canals, farms, manufactures, commerce, towns, and cities. Then we must consider the superior natural advantages of Virginia, her far greater area, her richer soil, her more genial sun, her greater variety of products, her mines of coal, iron, gold, copper, and lead, her petroleum, her superior hydraulic power, her much larger coast line, with more numerous and deeper harbours—and reflect what Virginia would have been in the absence of slavery. Her early statesmen, Washington, Jefferson, Madison, Monroe, Mason, Tucker, and Marshall, all realized this great truth, and all desired to promote emancipation in Virginia. But their advice was disregarded by her present leaders—the new, false, and fatal dogmas of Calhoun were substituted; and, as a consequence, Virginia, from the first rank (*longo intervallo*) of all the States, has fallen to the fifth, and, with slavery continued, will descend still more rapidly in the future than in the past.

By census table 36, p. 197, the value, in 1860, of the farm lands of all the Slave States, was $2,570,466,935, and the numbers of acres 245,721,-062, worth $10.46 per acre. In the Free States, the value of the farm lands was 4,067,947,286, and the number of acres 161,462,008, worth $25.19 per acre. Now if, as certainly in the absence of slavery would have been the case, the farm lands of the South had been worth as much per acre as those of the North, their total value would have been $6,189,713,551, and, deducting the present price, the *additional* cash value would have been $3,019,246,616.

But if, to this, we add the *increased* value of the *unoccupied* lands of the South, by multiplying them by the difference between their value per acre and that of the *unoccupied* lands of the North, the result is $2,240,000,000, which, added to that of the farm lands, makes $5,859,246,616 as the augmented value of the lands of the South caused by emancipation.

By census tables of 1860, 33 and 36, the total value of the products of agriculture, manufactures, mines, and fisheries in the Free States was $4,150,-000,000, and of the Slave States $1,140,000,000, making the products of the Free States in 1860 nearly 4 to 1 of the Slave States, and $217 *per capita* for the Free States, and for the Slave States $93 *per capita*. This is exclusive of commerce, which would greatly increase the ratio in favour of the North, that of New York alone being nearly equal to that of all the Slave States. Now, multiply the population of the Slave States by the value of the products *per capita* of the Free States, and the result is $2,653,631,032, making, by emancipation, the increased annual product of the Slave States $1,511,031,032, and in ten years, exclusive of the yearly accumulations, $15,110,310,320.

By the table 35, census of 1860, the total value of all the property, real and personal, of the Free States, was $10,852,081,681, and of the Slave States, $5,225,307,034. Now, the product, in 1860, of the Free States, being $4,150,000,000, the annual yield on the capital was 39 per cent.; and, the product of the Slave States being $1,140,000,000, the yield on the capital was 22 per cent. This was the gross product in both cases. I have worked out these amazing results from the census tables, to illustrate the fact, that the same law, by which slavery retarded the progress of wealth in Virginia, as compared with New York, and of Maryland and South Carolina, as compared with Massachusetts, rules the relative advance in wealth of all the Slave States, as compared with that of all the Free States. I have stated that the statistics of commerce, omitted in these tables, would vastly increase the difference in favour of the Free States as compared with the Slave States, and of New York as contrasted with Virginia. I shall now resume the latter inquiry, so as to complete the comparison between New York and Virginia. By commerce is embraced, in this examination, all earning not included under the heads of agriculture, manufactures, the mines, or fisheries.

Railroads.—The number of miles of railroads

in operation in New York, in 1860, including city roads, was 2,842 miles,* costing $138,395,055 ; and in Virginia, 1,771 miles, costing $64,958,807. (Census table of 1860, No. 38. pp. 230 and 233.) Now, by the same census report, p. 105, the value of the freights of the New York roads for 1860 was as follows: Product of the forest—tons carried, 373,-424; value per ton, $20; total value, $7,468,480. Of animals—895,519 tons; value per ton, $200; total value, $179,103,800. Vegetable food—1,-103,646 tons; value per ton, $50; total value, $55,-182,000. Other agricultural products—143,219 tons; value per ton, $15; total value, $2,148,055. Manufactures—511,916 tons; value per ton, $500; total value, $391,905,500. Other articles—930,-244 tons; value $10 per ton, total value, $9,302,-440. Grand total, 4,741,773 tons carried; value per ton, $163. Total values, $773,089,275. Deducting one quarter for duplication, makes 3,556,-330 tons carried on the New York roads in 1860; and the value, $579,681,790. The values of the freights on the Virginia roads, as estimated, is $60,-000,000, giving an excess to those of New York of $519,681,790, on the value of railroad freights in 1860. The passenger account, not given, would largely increase the disparity in favour of New York.

CANALS.—The number of miles of canals in New York is 1,038, and their cost $67,567,972. In Virginia, the number of miles is 178, and the cost

* Now over 3000 miles.

$7,817,000. (Census table 39, p. 238.) The estimated value of the freight on the New York canals is 19 times that of the freight on the Virginia canals. (Census.)

TONNAGE.—The tonnage of vessels built in New York in 1860 was 31,936 tons, and in Virginia 4,372. (Census, p. 107.)

BANKS.—The number of banks in New York in 1860 was 303; capital $111,441,320, loans $200,351,332, specie $20,921,545, circulation $29,959,506, deposits $101,070,273; and in Virginia the number was 65; capital $16,005,156, loans $24,975,792, specie $2,943,652, circulation $9,812,197, deposits $7,729,652. (Table 34, p. 193, Census.)

INSURANCE COMPANIES.—The risks taken in New York were $916,474,956, or nearly one third of those in the whole Union. Virginia, estimated at $100,000,000; difference in favour of New York $816,474,956. (Census, p. 79.)

EXPORTS AND IMPORTS, ETC.—Our exports abroad from New York for the fiscal year ending 30th June, 1860, were $145,555,449, and the foreign imports $248,489,877; total of both, $394,045,326. The clearances same year from New York were 4,574,285 tons, and the entries 4,836,448 tons; total of both, 9,410,733 tons. In Virginia, the exports the same year were $5,858,024, and the imports $1,326,249; total of both, $7,184,273; clearances, 80,381 tons, entries, 97,762 tons; total of both, 178,143 tons. (Table 14, Register of United States

Treasury.) Revenue collected from customs same year in New York, $37,788,969, and in Virginia $189,816, or 200 to 1 in favour of New York. (Tables, U. S. Com. of Customs.) No returns are given for the coastwise and internal trade of either State, but the tables of the railway and canal transportation of States show nearly the same proportion in favour of New York as in the foreign trade. Thus the *domestic* exports from New York for the above year abroad were $126,060,967, and from Virginia $5,833,370. (Same table, 14.) And yet Virginia, as we have seen, had much greater natural advantages than New York for commerce, as well as for mines, manufactures, and agriculture. But slavery has almost expelled commerce from Virginia, and nearly paralyzed all other pursuits.

These tables, taken from the census and the Treasury records, prove incontestably, that slavery retards the progress of wealth and population throughout the South, but especially in Virginia. Nor can the Tariff account for the results; for Virginia, as we have seen, possesses far greater advantages than New York for manufactures. Besides, the commerce of New York far surpasses that of Virginia, and this is the branch of industry supposed to be affected most injuriously by high tariffs, and New York has generally voted against them with as much unanimity as Virginia. But there is a still more conclusive proof. The year 1824 was the commencement of the era of high tariffs, and yet, from

1790 to 1820, as proved by the census, the percentage of increase of New York over Virginia was greater than from 1820 to 1860. Thus, by table 1 of the census, p. 124, the increase of population in Virginia was as follows:

From	1790	to	1800	17.63	per cent.
„	1800	„	1810	10·73	„
„	1810	„	1820	9.31	„
„	1820	„	1830	13.71	„
„	1830	„	1840	2.34	„
„	1840	„	1850	14.60	„
„	1850	„	1860	12.29	„

The increase of population in New York was:

From	1790	to	1800	72.51	per cent.
„	1800	„	1810	63,45	„
„	1810	„	1820	43.14	„
„	1820	„	1830	39,76	„
„	1830	„	1840	26.60	„
„	1840	„	1850	27.52	„
„	1850	„	1860	25.29	„

In 1790 the population of Virginia was 748,318, in 1820, 1,065,129, and in 1860, 1,596,318. In 1790 the population of New York was 340,120, in 1820, 1,372,111, and in 1860, 3,880,735. Thus, from 1790 to 1820, before the inauguration of the protective policy, the relative increase of the population of New York, as compared with Virginia, was very far greater than from 1820 to1860. It is quite clear, then, that the Tariff had no influence whatever in depressing the progress of Virginia as compared with New York.

We have heretofore proved by the census the same position as regards the relative progress of Maryland and Massachusetts, and the same principle applies as between all the Free, as compared with all the Slave States. In New York, we have seen that from 1790 to 1820, in the absence of high tariffs, and, even before the completion of her great canal, her advance in population was much more rapid than from 1820 to 1860. Indeed, it is quite clear that, so far as the Tariff had any influence, it was far more unfavourable to New York than to Virginia, New York being a much greater agricultural as well as commercial State.

Having shown how much the material progress of Virginia has been retarded by slavery, let us now consider its effect upon her moral and intellectual development.

Newspapers and Periodicals.—The number of newspapers and periodicals in New York in 1860 was 542, of which 365 were political, 56 religious, 63 literary, 58 miscellaneous; and the number of copies circulated in 1860 was 320,930,884. (Census tables, Nos. 15, 37.) The number in Virginia was 139; of which 117 were political, 13 religious, 3 literary, 6 miscellaneous; and the number of copies circulated in 1860 was 26,772,568. Thus, the annual circulation of the press in New York was twelve times as great as that of Virginia. As to periodicals: New York had 69 monthlies, of which 2 were political, 25 religious, 24 literary, and 18 miscellaneous; 10 quarterlies, of which 5 were religious, and 5 literary; 6 annuals, of which 2 were political, 2 religious, and 2 miscellaneous. Virginia had 5 monthlies, of which 1 was political, 2 religious, 1 literary, and 1 miscellaneous; and no quarterlies or annuals. The annual circulation of the New York monthlies was 2,045,000; that of Virginia was 43,900; or more than 43 to 1 in favour of New York.

As regards schools, colleges, academies, libraries, and churches, I must take the census of 1850, those tables for 1860 not being yet arranged and printed. The number of public schools in New York in 1850 was 11,580, teachers 13,965, pupils 675,221; colleges, academies, etc., pupils 52,001; attending school during the year, as returned by families, 693,329; native adults of the State who cannot read or write, 23,341. Public libraries, 11,013; volumes, 1,760,820. Value of churches, $21,539,561. (Comp. Census, 1850.)

The number of public schools in Virginia in 1850 was 2,937, teachers 3,005, pupils 67,438; colleges, academies, etc., pupils 10,326; attending school during the year, as returned by families, 109,775; native white adults of the State who cannot read or write, 75,868. Public libraries, 54; volumes, 88,462. Value of churches, $2,902,220. (Compend. of Census of 1850.) By table 155, same compend., the percentage of native free population in Virginia over 20 years of age who cannot read or write is 19.90, and in New York 1.87, in North Carolina 30.34, in Maryland, 11.10, in Massachusetts 0.32, or less than one-third of one per cent. In New England, the percentage of native whites who cannot read or write is 0.42, or less than one-half of one per cent.; and in the Southern States 20.30, or 50 to 1 in favour of New England. (Compend., table 571.) But, if we take the whole adult population of Virginia, including whites, free blacks, and slaves, 42.05 per cent., or nearly one-half, cannot read or write; and in North Carolina, more than one-half cannot read or write. We have seen, by the above official tables of the census of 1850, that New York, compared with Virginia, had nearly ten times as many pupils at schools, colleges, and academies, twenty times as many books in libraries, and largely more than seven times the value of churches; while the ratio of native white adults who cannot read or write was more than 10 to 1 in Virginia, compared with New York. We have seen, also, that in North Carolina nearly one-third of the native white adults, and in Virginia nearly one-fifth, cannot read or write, and in New England 1 in every 400, in New York 1 in every 131, in the South and South-west 1 in every 42 of the native white adults. (Comp. p. 153.)

My next comparison will be that of two great new Western States—Illinois, a Free State, and Missouri, slave-holding.

The comparison is just, for while Missouri has

increased since 1810, in wealth and population, much more rapidly than any of the Slave States, there are several Free States whose relative advance has exceeded that of Illinois. The rapid growth of Missouri is owing to her immense area, her fertile soil, her mighty rivers (the Mississippi and Missouri), her central and commanding position, and to the fact, that she has so small a number of slaves to the square mile, as well as to the free population.

The population of Illinois,, in 1810, was 12,282, and in 1860, 1,711,951 ; the ratio of increase from 1810 to 1860 being 13,838.70. (Table 1, Cens. 1860.) The population of Missouri in 1810, was 20,845, and in 1860, 1,182,012; the ratio of increase from 1810 to 1860 being 5,570.48. (Ib.) The rank of Missouri in 1810 was 22, and of Illinois 23. The rank of Missouri in 1860 was 8, and of Illinois, 4.

Area.—The area of Missouri is 67,380 square miles, being the 4th in rank, as to area, of all the States. The area of Illinois is 55,405 square miles, ranking the 10th. Missouri, then, has 11,875 more square miles than Illinois. This excess is greater by 749 square miles than the aggregate area of Massachusetts, Delaware, and Rhode Island, containing in 1860 a population of 1,517,902. The population of Missouri per square mile in 1810 exceeded that of Illinois .08; but, in 1860, the population of Missouri per square mile was 17.54, ranking the 22d, and that of Illinois, 30.90, ranking the 13th. Illinois, with her ratio to the square mile and the area of Missouri, would have had in 1860 a population of 2,082,042; and Missouri, with her ratio and the area of Illinois, would have had in 1860 a population of 971,803, making a difference in favour of Illinois of 1,110,239 instead of 529,939. The absolute increase of population of Illinois per square mile from 1850 to 1860 was 15.54, and of Missouri 7.43, Illinois ranking the 6th in this ratio and Missouri the 14th. These facts prove the vast advantages which Missouri possessed in her larger area as compared with Illinois.

But Missouri in 1810, we have seen, had nearly double the population of Illinois. Now, reversing their numbers in 1810, the ratio of increase of each remaining the same, the population of Illinois in 1860 would have been 2,905,014, and of Missouri, 696,983. If we bring the greater area of Missouri as an element into this calculation the population of Illinois in 1860 would have exceeded that of Missouri more than two millions and a half.

MINES.—By Census Tables, 9, 10, 13 and 14, Missouri produced, in 1860, pig iron of the value of $575,000; Illinois, none. Bar and rolled iron —Missouri, $535,000; Illinois, none. Lead—Missouri, $356,660; Illinois, $72,953. Coal—Missouri, $8,200; Illinois, $964,187. Copper—Missouri, $6,000; Illinois, none. As to mines, then,

Missouri has a decided advantage over Illinois. Indeed, the iron mountains of Missouri are unsurpassed in the world. That Illinois approaches so near to Missouri in mineral products, is owing to her railroads and canals, and not to equal natural advantages. The number of miles of railroad in operation in 1860 was, 2,868 in Illinois, and 817 in Missouri; of canals, Illinois, 102 miles; Missouri, none. (Tables 38, 39.) But if Missouri had been a free State, she would have at least equalled Illinois in internal improvemeuts, and the Pacific Railroad would have long since united San Francisco, St. Louis, and Chicago.

Illinois is increasing in a *progressive* ratio as compared with Missouri. Thus, from 1840 to 1850 the increase of numbers in Illinois was 78.81, and from 1850 to 1860, 101.01 per cent., while the increase of Missouri from 1840 to 1850 was 77.75 and from 1850 to 1860, 73.30. Thus, the ratio is augmenting in Illinois, and decreasing in Missouri. If Illinois and Missouri should each increase from 1860 to 1870, in the same ratio as from 1850 to 1860, Illinois would then number 3,441,448, and Missouri, 2,048,426. (Table 1.) In 1850, Chicago numbered 29,963, and in 1860, 109,260. St. Louis, 77,860 in 1850, and 160,773 in 1860. (Table 40.) From 1840 to 1850 the ratio of increase of Chicago was 570.31, and from 1850 to 1860, 264.65, and of St. Louis, from 1840 to 1850,

372.26 per cent., and from 1850 to 1860, 106.49. If both increased in their respective ratios from 1860 to 1870 as from 1850 to 1860, Chicago would number 398,420 in 1870, and St. Louis, 331,879. It would be difficult to say which city has the greatest natural advantages, and yet when St. Louis was a city, Chicago was but the site of a fort.

PROGRESS OF WEALTH.—By Census Table 36, the cash value of the farms of Illinois in 1860, was $432,531,072, and of Missouri, $230,632,126, making a difference in favour of Illinois, of $201,898,-946, which is the loss which Missouri has sustained by slavery in the single item of the value of her farm lands. Abolish slavery there, and the value of the farm lands of Missouri would soon equal those of Illinois, and augment the wealth of the farmers of Missouri over two hundred millions of dollars. But these farm lands of Missouri embrace only 19,-984,809 acres (Table 36), leaving unoccupied 23,-138,391 acres. The difference between the value of the unoccupied lands of Missouri and Illinois, is six dollars per acre, at which rate the increased value of the unoccupied lands of Missouri, in the absence of slavery, is $148,830,346. Thus it appears, that the loss to Missouri in the value of her lands, caused by slavery, is $340,729,292. If we add to this the diminished value of town and city property in Missouri, from the same cause, the total loss in that State in the value of real estate, exceeds

$400,000,000, which is nearly twenty times the value of her slaves. By Table 35, the increase in the value of the real and personal property of Illinois from 1850 to 1860, was $715,595,276, being 457,93 per cent., and of Missouri, $363,966,691, being 265.18 per cent. At the same rate of increase from 1860 to 1870, the total wealth of Illinois would then be $3,993,000,000, and of Missouri, $1,329,000,000, making the difference against Missouri, in 1870, caused by slavery, $2,664,000,000, which is more than double the whole debt of the nation, and more than twice the value of all the slaves in the Union.

The total wealth of the Union in 1860 exceeded $16,000,000,000. If this were increased $1,000,000,000 in time, by the augmented wealth of Missouri, and our revenue from duties and taxes should be $220,000,000, the increased income, being one-seventeenth of the whole, would exceed $12,000,000 per annum; or, if the increase of wealth should be only $200,000,000, then the augmented proportional annual revenue would be $2,750,000, or nearly one-eightieth part of the whole revenue.

By overthrowing the rebellion, the taxes to pay the national debt will be collected from all the States, instead of being confined to those that are loyal. The rebel Confederate debt, never having had any existence in law or justice, but having been created only to support a wicked rebellion, will of course be expunged by the reëstablishment of the Union. All the rebel States debt incurred since the revolt, for the purpose of overthrowing the Government, will, of course, have no legal existence. Under the Federal Constitution, no State Legislature can have any lawful existence, except in conformity with its provisions, accompanied by a prior oath of every member to support the Constitution of the United States. These assemblages, then, since the revolt in the several States, calling themselves State Legislatures, never had any legal existence or authority, and were mere assemblages of traitors. Such is the clear provision of the Federal Constitution, and of the law of nations and of justice. It would be strange, indeed, if conventicles of traitors in revolted States, could legally or rightfully impose taxes on the people of such States, loyal or disloyal, to overthrow the Government. Indeed, if justice could have her full sway, the whole debt of this Government, incurred to suppress this rebellion, ought to be paid by the traitors alone.

My next comparison will be that of the free State of Pennsylvania with Virginia.

Virginia was a considerable colony when Pennsylvania was occupied only by Indian tribes. In 1790, Virginia was first in rank of all the States, her number of inhabitants being 748,308. (Census Rep., 120, 121.) Pennsylvania then ranked the second, numbering 434,373 persons. (Ib.) In 1860 the population of Virginia was 1,596,318, ranking the fifth; Pennsylvania still remaining the second, and numbering 2,905,115. (Ib.) In 1790 the population of Virginia exceeded that of Pennsylvania 313,925; in 1860 the excess in favour of Pennsylvania was 1,308,797. The ratio of increase of population of Virginia from 1790 to 1860 was 113.32 per cent., and of Pennsylvania in the same period, 569.03. At the same relative ratio of increase for the next seventy years, Virginia would contain a population of 3,405,265 in 1930; and Pennsylvania 19,443,934, exceeding that of England. Such has been and would continue to be the effect of slavery in retarding the progress of Virginia, and such the influence of freedom in the rapid advance of Pennsylvania. Indeed, with the maintenance and perpetuity of the Union in all its integrity, the destiny of Pennsylvania will surpass the most sanguine expectations.

The population of Virginia per square mile in 1790 was 12.19, and in 1860, 26.02; whilst that of Pennsylvania in 1790 was 9.44, and in 1860, 63.18. (Ib.) The absolute increase of the population of Virginia per square mile, from 1790 to 1860, was 13.83, and from 1850 to 1860, 2.85; whilst that of Pennsylvania from 1790 to 1860, was 53.74, and from 1850 to 1860, 12.93. (Ib.)

Area.—The area of Virginia is 61,352 square miles, and of Pennsylvania 46,000, the difference being 15,352 square miles, which is greater, by 758 square miles, than the aggregate area of Massachusetts, Connecticut, and Delaware, containing in 1860 a population of 1,803,429. (Ib.) Retaining their respective ratios of increase per square mile from 1790 to 1860, and reversing their areas, that of Virginia in 1860 would have been 1,196,920, and of Pennsylvania 3,876,119. Reversing the numbers of each State in 1790, the ratio of increase in each remaining the same, the population of Pennsylvania in 1860 would have been 5,408,424, and that of Virginia, 926,603. Reversing both the areas and numbers in 1790, and the population of Pennsylvania would have exceeded that of Virginia in 1860 more than six millions.

SHORE LINE.—By the Tables of the Coast Survey, the shore line of Virginia is 1,571 miles, and of Pennsylvania only 60 miles. This vastly superior coast line of Virginia, with better, deeper, more capacious, and much more numerous harbours, unobstructed by ice, and with easy access for so many hundred miles by navigable bays and tide-water rivers leading so far into the interior, give to Virginia great advantages over Pennsylvania in commerce and every branch of industry. Indeed, in this respect, Virginia stands unrivalled in the Union. The hydraulic power of Virginia greatly exceeds that of Pennsylvania.

MINES.—Pennsylvania excels every other State in mineral wealth, but Virginia comes next.

SOIL.—In natural fertility of soil, the two States are about equal; but the seasons in Virginia are more favourable, both for crops and stock, than in Pennsylvania. Virginia has all the agricultural products of Pennsylvania, with cotton in addition. The area, however, of Virginia (39,265,280 acres) being greater by 9,825,280 acres than that of Pennsylvania (29,440,000 acres), gives to Virginia vast advantages.

In her greater area, her far superior coast line, harbours, rivers, and hydraulic power, her longer and better seasons for crops and stock, and greater variety of products, Virginia has vast natural advantages, and with nearly double the population of Pennsylvania in 1790. And yet, where has slavery placed Virginia? Pennsylvania exceeds her now in numbers 1,308,797, and increased in population from 1790 to 1860, in a ratio more than five to one. Such is the terrible contrast between free and slave institutions!

Progress of Wealth. — By Census Tables (1860) 33 and 36, it appears (omitting commerce) that the products of industry, as given, viz., of agriculture, manufactures, mines, and fisheries, were that year in Pennsylvania, of the value of $399,000,000, or $138 per capita; and in Virginia, $120,000,000, or $75 per capita. This shows a total value of product in Pennsylvania much more than three times that of Virginia, and, per capita, nearly two to one. That is, the average value of the product of the labour of each person in Pennsylvania is nearly double that of each person, including slaves, in Virginia. Thus is proved the vast superiority of free over slave labour, and the immense national loss occasioned by the substitution of the latter for the former.

As to the rate of increase; the value of the products of Virginia in 1850 was $84,480,428 (Table 9), and in Pennsylvania, $229,567,131, showing an increase in Virginia, from 1850 to 1860, of $35,519,572, being 41 per cent.; and in Pennsylvania, $170,032,869, being 51 per cent.; exhibiting a difference of 10 per cent. in favour of Pennsylvania. By the Census Table of 1860, No. 35, p. 195, the true value then of the real and personal property was, in Pennsylvania, $1,416,501,818, and of Virginia, $793,249,681. Now, we have seen, the value of the products in Pennsylvania in 1860 was $399,600,000, and in Virginia, $120,000,000. Thus, as a question of the annual yield of capital, that of Pennsylvania was 29 per cent., and of Virginia, 15 per cent. By Census Table 35, the total value of the real and personal property of Pennsylvania was $722,486,120 in 1850, and $1,416,501,818 in 1860, showing an increase, in that decade, of $694,015,698, being 96.05 per cent.; and in Virginia, $430,701,082 in 1850, and $793,249,681 in 1860, showing an increase of $362,548,599, or 84.17 per cent.

By Table 36, p. 196, Census of 1860, the *cash* value of the farms of Virginia was $371,092,211, being $11.91 per acre; and of Pennsylvania,

$662,050,707, being $38.91 per acre. Now, by this table, the number of acres embraced in these farms of Pennsylvania was 17,012,153 acres, and in Virginia, 31,014,950; the difference of value per acre being $27, or largely more than three to one in favour of Pennsylvania. Now, if we multiply the farm lands of Virginia by the Pennsylvania value per acre, it would make the total value of the farm lands of Virginia $1,204,791,804; and the *additional* value, caused by emancipation, $835,699,593. But the whole area of Virginia is 39,265,280 acres, deducting from which the farm lands, there remain unoccupied 8,250,330 acres. Now, if (as would be in the absence of slavery) the population per square mile of Virginia equalled that of Pennsylvania, three-fifths of these lands would have been occupied as farms; viz. 4,950,198, which, at the Pennsylvania value per acre, would have been worth $188,207,524. Deduct from this their present average value of $2 per acre, $9,800,396, and the remainder, $178,407,128, is the sum by which the unoccupied lands of Virginia, converted into farms, would have been increased in value by emancipation. Add this to the enhanced value of their present farms, and the result is $1,014,106,721 as the gain, on this basis, of Virginia in the value of her lands, by emancipation. To these we should add the increased value of town and city lots and improvements, and of personal property, and, with emancipation,

Virginia would now have an augmented wealth of at least one billion and a half of dollars.

The earnings of commerce are not given in the Census Tables, which would vastly increase the difference in the value of their annual products in favour of Pennsylvania as compared with Virginia. These earnings include all not embraced under the heads of agriculture, manufactures, the mines, and fisheries. Let us examine some of these statistics.

RAILROADS.—The number of miles of railroad in operation in Pennsylvania in 1860, including city roads, was 2,690.49 miles,* costing $147,283,410; and in Virginia, 1,771 miles, costing $64,958,807. (Census Table of 1860, No. 38, pp. 230, 232.) The annual value of the freight carried on these roads is estimated at $200,000,000 more in Pennsylvania than in Virginia, and the passenger account would still more increase the disparity.

CANALS.—The number of miles of canals in Pennsylvania in 1860 was 1,259, and their cost, $42,015,000. In Virginia the number of miles was 178, and the cost, $7,817,000. (Census Table 39, p. 238.) The estimated value of the freight on the Pennsylvania canals is ten times that of the freight on the Virginia canals.

TONNAGE.—The tonnage of vessels built in Pennsylvania in 1860 was 21,615 tons, and in Virginia, 4,372. (Census, p. 197.)

BANKS.—The number of banks in Pennsylvania

* Now 2,907 miles.

in 1860 was 90; capital, $25,565,582; loans, $50,327,127; specie, $8,378,474; circulation, 13,-132,892; deposits, $26,167,143:—and in Virginia the number was 65; capital, $16,005,156; loans, $24,975,792; specie, $2,943,652; circulation, $9,812,197; deposits, $7,729,652. (Census Table 35, p. 193.)

EXPORTS AND IMPORTS, ETC.—Our exports abroad from Pennsylvania, for the fiscal year ending 30th June, 1860, and foreign imports, were of the value of $20,262,608. The clearances, same year, from Pennsylvania, and entries were 336,848 tons. In Virginia the exports the same year, and foreign imports were of the value of $7,184,273; clearances and entries, 178,143 tons. (Table 14, Register of U. S. Treasury.) Revenue from customs, same year, in Pennsylvania, $2,552,924, and in Virginia, $189,816; or more than twelve to one in favour of Pennsylvania. (Tables U. S. Commissioner of Customs.) No returns are given for the coastwise and internal trade of either State; but the railway and canal transportation of both States shows a difference of ten to one in favour of Pennsylvania. And yet, Virginia, as we have seen, had much greater natural advantages than Pennsylvania for commerce, foreign and internal, her shore line up to head of tide water being 1,571 miles, and Pennsylvania only 60 miles.

We have seen that, exclusive of commerce, the products of Pennsylvania in 1860 were of the value of $399,600,000, or $138 per capita; and in Virginia, $120,000,000, or $75 per capita. But, if we add the earnings of commerce, the products of Pennsylvania must have exceeded those of Virginia much more than four to one, and have reached, per capita, nearly three to one. What but slavery could have produced such amazing results? Indeed, when we see the same effects in *all* the Free States as compared with *all* the Slave States, and in *any* of the Slave States, as compared with *any* of the Free States, the uniformity of results establishes the law beyond all controversy, that slavery retards immensely the progress of wealth and population.

That the Tariff has produced none of these results, is shown by the fact that the agriculture and commerce of Pennsylvania vastly exceed those of Virginia, and yet these are the interests supposed to be most injuriously affected by high tariffs. But there is still more conclusive proof. The year 1824 was the commencement of the era of high tariffs, and yet, from 1790 to 1820, as proved by the Census, the percentage of increase of Pennsylvania over Virginia was greater than from 1820 to 1860. Thus, by Table 1 of the Census, p. 124, the increase of population in Virginia was as follows:

From	1790	to	1800	17.63	per cent.
"	1800	"	1810	10.73	"
"	1810	"	1820	9.31	"
"	1820	"	1830	13.71	"
"	1830	"	1840	2.34	"
"	1840	"	1850	14.60	
"	1850	"	1860	12.29	"

The increase of population in Pennsylvania was:

From	1790	to	1800	38.67	per cent.
"	1800	"	1810	34.49	"
"	1810	"	1820	29.55	"
"	1820	"	1830	28.47	"
"	1830	"	1840	27.87	"
"	1840	"	1850	34.09	"
"	1850	"	1860	25.71	"

In 1790 the population of Virginia was 748,318; in 1820, 1,065,129, and in 1860, 1,596,318. In 1790 the population of Pennsylvania was 434,373; in 1820, 1,348,233, and in 1860, 2,906,115. Thus, from 1790 to 1820, before the inauguration of the protective policy, the relative increase of the population of Pennsylvania, as compared with Virginia, was very far greater than from 1820 to 1860. It is quite clear, then, that the tariff had no influence in depressing the progress of Virginia as compared with Pennsylvania.

Having shown how much the material progress of Virginia has been retarded by slavery, let us now consider its effect upon her moral and intellectual development.

Newspapers and Periodicals.—The number of newspapers and periodicals in Pennsylvania in 1860 was 367, of which 277 were political, 43 religious, 25 literary, 22 miscellaneous; and the total number of copies circulated in 1860 was 116,094,480. (Census Tables, Nos. 15, 37.) The number in Virginia was 139, of which 117 were political, 13 religious, 3 literary, 6 miscellaneous; and the number of copies circulated in 1860 was 26,772,568, being much less than one fourth that of Pennsylvania. The number of copies of monthly periodicals circulated in Pennsylvania in 1860 was 464,684; and in Virginia, 43,900: or much more than ten to one in favour of Pennsylvauia.

As regards schools, colleges, academies, libraries, and churches, I must take the Census of 1850, those tables for 1860 not being yet arranged or printed. The number of public schools in Pennsylvania in 1850 was 9,061; teachers, 10,024; pupils, 413,706; colleges, academies, &c., pupils, 26,142; attending school during the year, as returned by families, 504,610; native adults of the State who cannot read or write, 51,283; public libraries, 393; volumes, 363,400; value of churches, $11,853,291; percentage of native free population (adults) who cannot read or write, 4.56. (Comp. Census of 1850.)

The number of public schools in Virginia in 1850 was 2,937; teachers, 3,005; pnpils, 67,438; colleges, academies, &c., pupils, 10,326; attending school, as returned by families, 109,775; native white adults of the State who cannot read or write, 75,868; public libraries, 54; volumes, 88,462; value of churches, $2,902,220; percentage of native free adults of Virginia who cannot read or write, 19.90, (Comp. Census of 1850.) Thus, the church and educational statistics of Pennsylvania, and especially of free adults who cannot read or write, is as five to one nearly in favour of Pennsylvania.

When we recollect that nearly one third of the population of Pennsylvania are of the great German race, and speak the noble German language, to which they are greatly attached, and hence the difficulty of introducing common *English* public schools in the State, the advantage, in this respect, of Pennsylvania over Virginia is most extraordinary.

My last comparison will be that of our two smallest States—Rhode Island, a Free State, and Delaware, slave-holding.

In 1790 the population of Rhode Island was 69,110, and that of Delaware 59,096. In 1860 the former numbered 174,620, the latter 112,216. Thus, from 1790 to 1860, the ratio of increase of population of Rhode Island was 152.67 per cent., and of Delaware, 89.88. At the same relative rate of increase, for the next, as for the last seventy years, the population of Rhode Island in 1930, would be 441,212, and of Delaware, 213,074. Thus in 1790, Rhode Island numbered but 10,014 more than Delaware, 62,404 more in 1860, and, at the same ratio of increase, 228,138 more in 1930. Such has been and would be the effect of slavery in retarding the increase of Delaware, as compared with Rhode Island. (Census Table, 1860, No. 1.)

The population of Rhode Island per square mile in 1790, was 52.15, and in 1860, 133.71; that of Delaware, 27.87 in 1790, and 59.93 in 1860. The absolute increase of population of Rhode Island, per square mile, from 1790 to 1860, was 80.79, and from 1850 to 1860, 20.74; that of Delaware, from 1790 to 1860, was 25.05, and from 1850 to 1860, 9.76. (Ib.)

Area.—The area of Rhode Island is 1,306 square miles, and of Delaware, 2,120, being 38 per cent., or much more than one third larger than Rhode Island. Retaining their respective ratios of increase, per square mile, from 1790 to 1860, and reversing their areas, the population of Rhode Island in 1860, would have been 283,465, and of Delaware, 78,268.

In natural fertility of soil Delaware is far superior to Rhode Island, the seasons much more favourable for crops and stock, and with more than double the number of acres of arable land.

Progress of Wealth.—By Census Tables 33 and 36 (omitting commerce), it appears that the products of industry as given, viz., of agriculture, manufactures, mines, and fisheries, were that year, in Rhode Island, of the value of $52,400,000, or $300 per capita, and in Delaware, $16,100,000, or $143 per capita. That is, the average annual value of the product of the labour of each person in Rhode Island is greatly more than double that of the labour of each person in Delaware, including slaves. This, we have seen, would make the value of the products of labour in Rhode Island in 1930, $132,368,600, and in Delaware, only $30,469,582, notwithstanding the far greater area and superior natural advantages of Delaware as compared with Rhode Island.

As to the rate of increase: the value of the products of Delaware in 1850 was $7,804,992, in 1860, $16,100,000; and in Rhode Island, in 1850, $24,288,088, and in 1860, $52,400,000 (Table 9, Treas. Rep., 1856), exhibiting a large difference in the ratio in favour of Rhode Island.

By Table 36, p. 196, Census of 1860, the cash value of the farm lands of Rhode Island in 1860 was $19,385,573, or $37.30 per acre (519,698 acres), and of Delaware, $31,426,357, or $31.39 per acre (1,004,295 acres). Thus, if the farm lands of Delaware were of the cash value of those of Rhode Island per acre, it would increase the value of those of Delaware $5,935,385, whereas the whole value of her slaves is but $539,400.

But by Table 35, Census of 1860, the total value of the real and personal property in Rhode Island in 1860, was $135,337,588, and of Delaware, $46,242,181, making a difference in favour of Rhode Island, $89,095,497, whereas, we have seen, in the absence of slavery, Delaware must have far exceeded Rhode Island in wealth and population.

The earnings of commerce are not given by the census, but, to how vast an extent this would swell the difference in favour of Rhode Island, we may learn from the Census, Bank Table No. 34. The number of the banks of Rhode Island in 1860, was 91; capital, $20,865,569; loans, $26,719,877; circulation, $3,558,295; deposits, $3,553,104. In Delaware, number of banks, 12, capital, $1,640,675;

loans, $3,150,215; circulation, $1,135,772; deposits, $976,223.

Having shown how much slavery has retarded the material progress of Delaware, let us now consider its effect upon her moral and intellectual development.

NEWSPAPERS AND PERIODICALS.—The number of newspapers and periodicals in Rhode Island in 1860, was 26, of which 18 were political, 6 literary, and 2 miscellaneous. (Census, Table No. 37.) The number in Delaware was 14, of which 13 were political, and 1 literary. Of periodicals, Delaware had none; Rhode Island, 1. The number of copies of newspapers and periodicals issued in Rhode Island in 1860 was 5,289,280, and in Delaware only 1,010,776, or largely more than five to one in favour of Rhode Island.

As regards schools, colleges, academies, libraries, and churches, I must take the census of 1850, those tables for 1860 not being yet arranged or published. The number of public schools in Rhode Island in 1850 was 426, teachers 518, pupils 23,130; attending school during the year, as returned by families, whites, 28,359; native adults of the State who cannot read or write, 1,248; public libraries, 96; volumes 104,342; value of churches, $1,293,600; percentage of native free adults who cannot read or write, 149. Colleges and academies, pupils, 3,664. (Comp. Census of 1850.) The number of public schools in Delaware in 1850, was 194, teachers

214, pupils, 8,970; attending school during the year, whites, as returned by families, 14,216; native free adults of the State who cannot read or write, 9,777; public libraries, 17; volumes, 17,950; value of churches, $340,345; percentage of native free adults who cannot read or write, 23.03; colleges and academies, pupils, 764. (Comp. Census, 1850.)

The subject will be continued in my next number.

R. J. WALKER.

AMERICAN

FINANCES AND RESOURCES.

LETTER

No. V.

OF

HON. ROBERT J. WALKER, M.A.

COUNSELLOR AT LAW IN THE SUPREME COURT OF THE UNITED STATES,
LATE LAW REP. MI., SENATOR OF THE UNITED STATES,
SECRETARY OF THE TREASURY, COMMISSIONER TO CHINA,
GOVERNOR OF KANSAS, ETC., ETC.

LONDON:
WILLIAM RIDGWAY, 169, PICCADILLY, W.
1864.

10, Half Moon Street, Piccadilly.
Feb. 8th, 1864.

In my third and fourth letters on American Finances and Resources, the following comparisons were instituted.

Massachusetts and New Jersey, free States, with Maryland and South Carolina slave States; New York and Pennsylvania, free States, with Virginia slave State; Rhode Island, free State, with Delaware slave State; Illinois, free State, with Missouri slave State; the free States of 1790, with the slave States of that date; the free States of 1860, with the slave States of that date. These comparisons were based on the official returns of the Census of the United States, and exhibited in each case and in the aggregate the same invariable result, the vastly superior progress of the free States in wealth, population, and education.

I will now institute one other comparison, Kentucky, slave-holding, with Ohio a free State.

Kentucky—population in 1790, 73,077; Ohio, none. 1800: Kentucky, 220,955; Ohio, 45,365. 1860: Kentucky, 1,155,684; Ohio, 2,339,502. We must institute the comparison from 1800, as Ohio was a wilderness in 1790, when Kentucky had a population of 73,077. In Kentucky, the ratio of increase of population from 1800 to 1860 was 527,98 per cent, and in the same period in Ohio 5,057,08. Table 1, Census 1860: thus from 1800 to 1860 Ohio increased in nearly ten-fold the ratio of Kentucky.

Wealth. By Tables 33 and 36, Census of 1860, the value of the product of 1859 was as follows:—

Ohio . .	$337,619,000
Kentucky .	115,408,000

Per capita.

Ohio . .	$144,31
Kentucky .	99,92

Thus is it, that, whilst in 1790 and 1800 Kentucky was so very far in advance of Ohio, yet, in 1860, so vast was the advance of Ohio as compared with Kentucky, that the value of the product of Ohio was nearly triple that of Kentucky, and, *per capita*, much more than one-third greater. No reason can be assigned for these remarkable results, except that Kentucky was slave-holding, and Ohio a free State.

Their area is nearly the same, and they are adjacent States; the soil of Kentucky is quite equal to that of Ohio, the climate better for crops and stock, and the products more various.

We have seen the actual results in 1860, but if Kentucky had increased in population from 1800 to 1860 in the same ratio as Ohio, Kentucky then would have numbered 11,175,970, or nearly ten times her present population; and if the product had been the same as in Ohio, *per capita*, the value would have been

1,612,804,230, or more than 14 times greater than the result. Thus it is demonstrated by the official tables of the Census of the United States, that if Kentucky had increased in wealth and population from 1800 to 1860 in the same ratio as Ohio, the results would have been as follows:—

Kentucky: population in 1860, 11,175,970; actual population in 1860, 1,155,684; value of products in 1860, $1,612,804,230; actual value in 1860, $115,408,000.

Some attempt has been made to account for these marvellous results, by stating that Ohio has a border on one of the Lakes and Kentucky has not. But to this it may be replied, that Kentucky borders for twice the distance on the Ohio river, has a large front on the Mississippi river, and embraces within her limits those noble streams the Cumberland and Tennessee rivers, making, together with the Big Sandy, Licking, Kentucky, Green and Barren rivers, the natural advantages of Kentucky for navigation, superior to those of Ohio. But a conclusive answer to this argument is found in the fact, that, omitting all the counties of Ohio within the Lake region, the remainder, within the valley of the Ohio river, contain a population more than one-half greater than that of the whole state of Kentucky.

Lands.—The farm lands, improved and unimproved, of Ohio in 1860 were worth $666,564,171. The number of acres 20,741,138, value per acre $32,13. (Census of 1860, p. 197, table 36.) The farm lands of Kentucky, improved and unimproved, were worth $291,496,953, the number of acres 19,163,276, worth per acre $15,21. (*Ib.*) Difference in favour of Ohio, $375,067,165. But if to this we add the difference between the value of the Town and City lots and unoccupied lands of Ohio and Kentucky, the sum is $125,009,000, which added to the former sum ($375,067,165) makes the difference in favour of Ohio $500,076,165 when comparing the value of all her lands with those of Kentucky. We have seen that the value of the products in 1860 was, Ohio $337,619,000, Kentucky, $115,408,000. But these products embrace only agriculture, manufactures, the mines, and fisheries.

We have no complete tables for commerce in either State, but the canals and railroads are as follows:—Census of 1860, No. 38 pages 225, 226, 233.—Ohio: Miles of railroad, 3,016,83; cost of construction, $113,299,514. Kentucky: Miles of railroad, 569,93; cost of construction, $19,068,477. Estimated value of freight transported on these railroads in 1860; Ohio, $502,105,000; Kentucky, $48,708,000. On the 1st Jan. 1864, the number of miles of railroad in operation in Ohio was 3,356,74, costing $130,454,383, showing a large increase since 1860, whilst in Kentucky there was none. (Amer. R. R. Journal, page 61, vol. 37.) Canals in 1860 (census table 39): Ohio, 906 miles; Kentucky, two and a-half miles. These tables all prove how vast has been the increase of the wealth of Ohio as compared with Kentucky.

Let us now examine some of the educational statistics.

By Census table 37, giving the newspapers and periodicals in the United States in 1860, the whole number of that year was 4051, of which only 879 were in the slave States; total number of copies circulated that year in the United States, 927,951,548, of which number there were circulated in the slave States, only 167,917,188. This table shows the total number of newspapers and periodicals published in Ohio in 1859 was 340, and the number of copies circulated that year in that State was 71,767,742. In Kentucky, the number of newspapers and periodicals published in 1859 was 77, and the number of copies circulated that year was 13,504,044, whilst South Carolina, professing to instruct and control the nation, had a circulation of 3,654,840, although South Carolina in 1790 had a population of 249,073, when Ohio was a wilderness, and Kentucky numbered only 73,077.

As regards education, we must take the tables for the Census of 1850, those for 1860 not having been yet published.

By table 144, Census of 1850, the total number of pupils in public and private schools, colleges, and academies was for that year as follows: Ohio, 502,826. Kentucky, 85,914. Percentage of native free population who cannot read or write—table 155—Ohio, 3·24; Kentucky, 9·12; Slave States, native white adults who cannot read or write, ratio 17·23; free States, 4·12. (Table 157.) If we include slaves, more than one-half the adults of the slave States cannot read or write. Indeed it is made by law in the slave States a crime (severely punished,) to teach any slave to read or write. These tables also show that in South Carolina, the great leader of secession, (including slaves), more than three-fourths of the people can neither read nor write. Such is the State, rejoicing in the barbarism of ignorance and slavery, exulting in the hope of reviving the African slave trade, whose chief city witnesses each week the auction of slaves as chattels, and whose newspapers, for more than a century are filled with daily advertisements by their masters of run-away slaves, describing the brands and mutilations to which they have been subjected; that passed the first secession ordinance, and commenced the war upon the Union by firing upon the Federal flag and garrison of Sumter. Yet it is the pretended advocates of peace that justify this war upon the Union, and insist that it shall submit to dismemberment without a struggle, and permit slavery to be extended over nearly one-half the national territory, purchased by the blood and treasure of the nation. Such a submission to disintegration and ruin—such a capitulation to slavery, would have been base and cowardly. It would have justly merited for us the scorn of the present, the contempt of the future, the denunciation of history, and the execration of mankind. Despots would have exultingly announced that "man is incapable of self-government;" whilst the heroes and patriots in other countries, who, cheered and guided by the light of our example, had struggled in the cause of popular liberty, would have sunk despairing from the conflict. This is our *real offence* to European oligarchy, that we will crush this foul rebellion, extinguish the slavery by which it was caused, make the Union stronger and more harmonious, and thus give a new impulse and an irresistible moral influence and power to free institutions.

Let me recapitulate some of the facts referred to in these letters, and established by the census of the United States.

Area of the United States, 3,250,000 square miles, exceeding that of all Europe—all compact and contiguous, with richer lands, more mineral resources, a climate more salubrious, more numerous and better harbours, more various products, and increasing in wealth and population more rapidly than any other country.

	Miles.
Our ocean shore line, including bays, sounds, and rivers up to the head of tide water	33,663
Lake shore line	3,620
Shore line of Mississippi river and its tributaries above tide water . .	35,644
Shore line of all our other rivers above tide water is	49,857
Total . .	122,784

Our country then is better watered than any other, and has more navigable streams, and greater hydraulic power.

We have completed since 1790, 5,782 miles of canal, costing $148,000,000; and 33,860 miles of railroad (more than all the rest of the world), costing $1,625,952,215—(Amer. R. R. Il. Jour. 1864, No. 1448, Vol. 37, page 61.)

Our land lines of telegraph exceed those of all the rest of the world, the single line from New York to San Francisco being 3500 miles. Our mines of coal, according to Sir William Armstrong, the highest British authority, are 32 times as great as those of the United Kingdom.

Annual product of our mines of gold and silver, $100,000,000, estimated at $150,000,000 per annum by our Commissioner of the General Land Office, when the Pacific railroad shall be completed.

Public lands unsold, belonging to the Federal Government, 1,055,911,288 acres, being 1,649,861 square miles, and more than 32 times the extent of England.

Immigration to the United States from 1850 to 1860, 2,598,216, adding to our national wealth during that decade $1,430,000,000.

Education—granted by Congress since 1790 for the purposes of public schools—two sections (1280 acres) in every township (23,040 acres), in all 1,450,000,000 acres of public lands; one-eighteenth part given, being 80,555,555 acres, worth at the minimum price of $1.25 per acre, $100,694,443 — the real value, however, was much greater.

Granted by Congress for colleges and universities, 12,080,000 acres, including 3,553,824 given by the Federal Government to the State of Tennessee, worth at the minimum price of $1.25 per acre, $15,100,000, which is much below their true value.

Total in public lands granted by Federal Government for education 92,635,555 acres; minimum value, $115,794,443.

In 1836, after full payment of the entire principal and interest of the public debt, there remained in the Federal Treasury a surplus of $38,000,000; of which about one-half, $19,000,000, was devoted to educational purposes.

Total Federal appropriations since 1790 for education, $134,794,443.

This is exclusive of the many millions of dollars expended by the Federal Government for military and naval schools, &c. at West Point, Washington, Annapolis, and Newport. Besides these Federal donations, there has been granted by States, territories, counties, towns, and cities of the Union for education, since 1790 (partly estimated) $148,000,000. Grand total by States and Federal Government appropriated in the United States since 1790, for education, $282,794,443. This is independent of numerous private donations for the same purpose, that by Mr. Girard exceeding $1,500,000, and that by Mr. Smithson exceeding $500,000. It is then a fact that the Governments of the United States, State and Federal, since 1790, have appropriated for education more money than all the other Governments of the world combined during the same period. This is a stupendous fact, and one of the main causes of our wonderful progress and prosperity. We believe that "knowledge is power," and have appropriated nearly $300,000,000, during the last 74 years, in aid of the grand experiment. We believe that "man is capable of self-government," but only when educated and enlightened. We believe that the power and wealth and progress of nations increase in proportion to the education and enlightenment of the masses. We believe in intellectual as well as machine and muscular power, and that when the millions are educated, and work with their heads as well as their hands, the progress of the nation will be most rapid. Our patent office is a wonderful illustration of this principle, showing on the part of our industrial classes more valuable inventions and discoveries, annually, than are produced by the working men of all the rest of the world.

POPULATION.

In 1790 . . .	3,922,827
1800 . . .	5,305,937
1810 . . .	7,239,814
1820 . . .	9,638,191
1830 . . .	12,866,020
1840 . . .	17,069,453
1850 . . .	23,191,876
1860 . . .	31,445,080

Ratio of increase—from 1790 to 1800, 35·02; from 1800 to 1810, 36·45; from 1810 to 1820, 33·13; from 1820 to 1830, 33·49; from 1830 to 1840, 32·67; from 1840 to 1850, 35·87; from 1850 to 1860, 35·59. Thus it appears (omitting territorial acquisitions), that our ratio of increase was much greater from 1850 to 1860 than during any preceding decade. This was the result of augmented immigration, which is still to go on with increased power for many years. Making allowance for all probable contingencies, and reducing the decennial increase from 35·59, to three per cent. per annum, our able and experienced Superintendent of the Census, in his last official report, of 20th May, 1862, gives his own estimate of the future population of the United States:—

1870 . . .	42,328,432
1880 . . .	56,450,241
1890 . . .	77,263,989
1900 . . .	100,355,802

That, in view of our new homestead law—our high wages—the extinction of slavery—increased confidence in our institutions—and augmented immigration, these results will be achieved, can scarcely be doubted. As population becomes more dense in Europe, there will be an increased immigration to our Union, and each new settler writes to his friends abroad, and often remits money to induce them to join him in his Western home. The electric ocean telegraph will soon unite Europe with America, and improved communications are constantly shortening the duration of the voyage, and diminishing the expense. Besides, this war has made us much better known to the European *masses*, who, everywhere, with great unanimity and enthusiasm sustain our cause, and, with slavery extinguished, will still more prefer our institutions.

From all these causes, there will be an augmented exodus from Europe to America, when our rebellion is suppressed, and slavery overthrown. Besides, the President of the United States now proposes appropriations of money by Congress in aid of immigration, and such will become the policy of our Government. We have seen the official estimate made by our Superintendent of the Census, but if we take the ratio of increase of the last decade, the result would be as follows:—

1870	42,636,858
1880	57,791,315
1890	78,359,243
1900	106,247,297

The estimate of the Superintendent is therefore six millions less than according to the ratio from 1850 to 1860, and much less than from 1790 to 1860.

When we reflect that if, as densely settled as Massachusetts, our population would exceed 513,000,000, or if numbering as many to the square mile as England, our inhabitants would then be more than twelve hundred millions, the estimate of 100,000,000 for the year 1900 cannot be regarded as improbable.

Our national wealth was in	1850,	$7,135,780,228
„ „ „	1860,	$16,159,616,068

Increase from 1850 to 1860, 126·45 per cent.

At the same rate of increase for the four succeeding decades, the result would be—

In 1870 . . .	$36,593,450,585
1880 . . ,	82,865,868,849
1890 . . .	187,314, 53,225
1900 . . .	423,330,438,288

Tonnage—

1814	1,368,127 tons
1851 . . .	3,772,439 „
1861 . . .	5,539,812 „

At the same rate of increase as from 1851 to 1861, the result would be—

In 1871 . . .	8,134,578 tons
1881 . . .	11,952,817 „
1891 . . .	17,541,514 „
1901 . . .	25,758,948 „

Total number of copies of our newspapers and periodicals circulated in the United States in 1860, 927,951,548, exceeding that of all the rest of the world.

Let us now recapitulate the results from our Census, founded on a comparison of the Slave and Free States.

MASSACHUSETTS. FREE STATE.	MARYLAND. SLAVE STATE.
Area, 7,800 square miles.	. . 11,124 square miles.
Population in 1790, 378,717.	. . 319,728.
„ 1860, 1,231,066.	. . 687,049.
Products in 1859, $287,000,000.	$66,000,000.
„ per capita, $235.	$96.
Railroads 1340 miles.	380 miles.
„ cost $61,857,203.	$21,387,157.
Freight of 1860, $500,524,201.	$101,111,348.
Tonnage built in 1860, 34,460 tons.	. . 7,789.
Bank capital, $64,519,200.	$12,568,962.
Imports and exports, $58,190,816.	$18,786,323.
Value of property, $815,237,433.	$376,919,944.
Gross profit on capital, 35 per cent.	17 per cent.
Copies of press circulated in 1860, 102,000,760.	. . 20,723,472.
Pupils at public schools in 1860, 176,475.	. . 33,254.
Volumes in public libraries, 684,015	. . 125,042.
Value of churches, $10,206,000.	$3,947,884.

NEW YORK. FREE STATE.	VIRGINIA. SLAVE STATE.
Area, 47,000 square miles.	. . 61,352.
Population in 1790, 340,120.	. . 748,308.
„ 1860, 3,880,735.	. . 1,596,318.
Product of 1859, $606,000,000.	$120,000,000.
Per capita, $156.	$75.
Gross profit on capital, 34 per cent.	. . ·15.
Value per acre of farm lands, $38,26.	$11,91.
Railroads 2,842 miles.	. . 1,771.
„ cost of construction, $138,395,055.	$64,958,807.
Freight in 1860, $579,681,790.	$110,000,000.
Canals, 1,038 miles.	. . 178.
„ cost $67,567,972.	$7,817,000.

Tonnage built in 1860, 31,936.	. 4,372.
Bank capital, $111,441,320.	$16,005,156.
Exports & imports, 1860, $394,045,326	7,184,273.
Copies of press circulated in 1860, 320,980,884.	. . 26,772,518.
Pupils at public schools in 1860, 675,221.	. . 67,428.
Vols. in public libraries, 1,760,820.	. . 88,462.
Value of churches, $21,539,561.	$2,002,220.
Per centage of native free population who cannot read or write, 1·87.	. . 19·90.

Compare the column as regards Virginia with the returns for Pennsylvania, and the result is nearly as remarkable as that of New York.

Pennsylvania, area 46,000 population in 1790, 434,373: in 1860, 2,900,115. Products of 1859, $399,600,000 per capita $138 profit on capital 22 per cent. Value of farm lands per acre $38,91. Railroads, 2,690 miles, costing $147,483,410. Canals, 1,259 miles, costing $42,015,000. Tonnage built in 1860, 21,615 tons. Bank capital $25,565,582. Exports and imports, $20,262,608. Copies of press circulated in 1860, 116,094,480. Pupils at public schools, 413,706. Volumes in public libraries, 363,400. Value of churches $11,853,291.

Illinois—Free State.	Missouri. Slave State.
Area, 55,405 square miles.	. 67,380.
Population 1810, 12,282.	. . 20,845.
„ 1860, 1,711,951.	. . 1,182 012.

Ratio of increase from 1810 to 1860, 13,838 per cent.	. . 5,570.
Railroads in operation in 1860, 2,868 miles.	. . 817.
Ditto, 1st Jan. 1864, 3,080 miles.	. . 914.
Value farm lands 1860, $432,531,072,	$230,632,126.
Canals, 102 miles. . .	. . none.
Ratio of increased value of property from 1850 to 1860, 458 per cent.	. . 265.
At same ratio from 1860 to 1870, as from 1850 to 1860, total wealth in 1870 would be $3,993,000,000	$1,329,000,000.

R. Island—Free State.	Delaware—Slave State.
Area, 1,306 square miles.	. . 2,120.
Population in 1792, 69,110.	. . 59,096.
" in 1860, 174,520.	. . 112,216.
Product in 1859, $52,400,000.	$16,100,000.
Value of property in 1860, $135,000,000.	$46,242,181.
Bank capital, $20,865,569.	$1,640,675.
Copies of press issued in 1860, 5,289,280.	. . 1,010,776.
Pupils at public schools, 23,130.	. . 8,970.
Volumes in public libraries, 104,342.	. . 17,950.
Pupils at colleges and academies, 3,664.	. . 764.
Per centage of native free adults who cannot read or write, 1.49.	. . 23·03.
Value of churches, $1,293,700.	$340,345.

N. Jersey—Free State.	S. Carolina—Slave State.
Area, 8,320 square miles.	. . 24,500.
Population in 1790, 184,139.	. . 249,073.
" in 1860, 672,035.	. . 703,708.

Ratio of increasef rom 1790 to 1860, 265 per cent.	. . 182.
Population per square mile in 1860, 80·77.	. . 28·72.
Increase of population per square mile from 1790 to 1860, 58·64.	. . 18·55.
Ditto from 1850 to 1860, 21·93.	. . 1.44.
Population in 1860, remaining the same per square mile if area equal to that of S. Carolina, 1,978,650.	Population in 1860, remaining the same per *square mile,* if area equal to that of N. Jersey, 238,950.
Product of 1859, $167,398,003.	$46,445,782.
Per capita, $249.	$66.
Farm lands 1860, improved and unimproved acres, 2,983,531.	. . 15,595,860.
Value in 1860, $180,250,338.	$139,652,508.
Agricultural products of 1860, $86,398,000.	$39,645,728.
Product per acre, $28·96.	$2·54.
Improved lands, 1,944,445 acres.	. . 4,572,060.
Product per acre, $44·43.	$8·67.
Value of farm lands per acre, $60·42.	$8·95.
	Value of farm lands if worth as much per acre as those of N. Jersey, $942,660,377.
Copies of press issued in 1860, 12,801,412.	. . 3,654,840.
Per centage of native free adults who cannot read or write, 5·10.	. . 12·73.
Per centage of native white children at school, 80·56.	. . 26·025.
Pupils at colleges, academies, and public schools, 88,244.	. . 26·025.
Value of churches, $3,712,863.	$2,181,476.

Michigan—Free State.	Florida—Slave State.
Area, 56,243.	. . 59,268.
Population, 1810, 4,762.	. . 16,989. } Spanish.
„ 1820, 8,765	. . 23,801. }
„ 1830, 31,639	. . 34,730.
„ 1860, 749,113	. . 140,425.
Population per square mile in	
1810, 0·08	. . 0·28.
1820, 0·15	. . 0·38.
1830, 0·56	. . 0·58,
1860, 13·32	. . 2·37.
Absolute increase of population from 1830 to 1860, 717,474	. . 105,695.
Relative rank in 1830, 25	. . 26.
„ 1860, 16	. . 31.
Absolute increase of population from 1850 to 1860 per *square mile*, 6·25	. . 0·89.
Value of total product of 1859, $99,200,000	$12,300,000.
Of agriculture alone, $64,000,000	$9,600,000,
Total product per capita, $132·04	$87·59.
Farm lands improved and unimproved in 1860, acres 6,931,442	. . 2,849,572.
Improved farm lands, 1860, acres 3,419,861	. . 676,464.
Value of lands improved and unimproved in 1860, $163,279,087	$16,371,684.
Product per acre, $9·23	$3·01.
„ of improved land, $18·71	$14·18.
Value of farm lands, 1860, per acre, $23·55	$5·74.
	Value of farm lands of Florida, if worth as much *per acre* as those of Michigan, $67,105,222.

	Product of Florida lands if equal *per acre* to those of Michigan in 1859, $26,300.549.
Copies of press issued in 1860, 11,606,596	. . 1,081,601.
Percentage of native free adults, who cannot read or write, 2·84	. . ·198.
Public libraries, volumes 107,943	. . 2,660.
Pupils in public schools, academies and colleges, 112,382	. . 3,129.
Percentage of native white children at school, 99·53	. . 35·77.
WISCONSIN—FREE STATE.	TEXAS—SLAVE STATE.
Area, 53,924 square miles	. . 274,356.
Population in 1840, 30,749	. . 80,983. (Republic.)
„ 1860, 775,881	. . 604,215.
Population per square mile in 1840, 0·57	. . 0·29.
Population per square mile in 1860, 8.99	. . 2·20.
Increase per square mile from 1840 to 1860, 8·42	. . 1·91.
Absolute increase of population from 1850 to 1860 per square mile, 8·99	. . 1·41.
Value of total product of 1859, $101,375,000	$52,749,000.
Of agriculture alone, $72,875,000	$46,499,000.
Total product per capita, $130·39	. . 87·30.
Farm lands improved and unimproved, acres 7,899,170	. . 23,245,433.
Improved farm lands, 1860, acres 3,746,036	. . 2,649,207.
Value of lands improved and unimproved in 1860, $131,117,082	$104,007,689.

Product per acre of improved and unimproved lands in 1859, $9·22	$2·00.
Product per acre of improved lands in 1859, $19·45	$17·55.
Value of farm lands per acre, $16·59	$4·47.
	Value of farm lands of Texas, if worth as much per acre as those of Wisconsin, $385,641,733.
	Product of Texas lands in 1859, if equal per acre to those of Wisconsin, $214,212,892.
Copies of press issued in 1860, 10,798,670	. . 7,855,808.
Percentage of native free adults who cannot read or write, 1·04	. . 11·84.
Public libraries, volumes, 21,020	. . 4,230.
Pupils in colleges and public schools, 61,615	. . 11,500.
Percentage of native white children at school, 74·90	. . 45.82.
INDIANA. FREE STATE.	TENNESSEE. SLAVE STATE.
Area, 33,809 square miles.	. . 45,600.
Population, 1790, none.	. . 35,791.
" 1800, 4,875.	. . 105,602.
" 1860, 1,350,428.	. . 1,109,801.
Product of 1859, 175,690,628.	$99,894,070.
Agricultural, $132,440,682.	$82,792,070.
Total product, per capita, $130·10.	$90·01.
Product of agriculture per capita. $90·68.	$74·60.
Population per square mile in 1800, 0·14	. . 2·31.

Population per square mile, 1860, 39·63.	. . 24·34.
Absolute increase of population, from 1850 to 1860, per square mile, 10·72.	. . 2·35.
Relative rank in 1800, 20th.	. . 15th.
Do. in 1860, 6th.	. . 10th.
Farm lands improved and unimproved acres, 16,315,776.	. . 20,355,934.
Improved do. 8,161,717.	. . 6,897,974.
Value of farm lands, $344,903,776.	. . 272,555,054.
Do. per acre, $21·13.	. . 13,39.
Value of product per acre improved and unimproved farm lands, $8·17.	$4·06.
Do. of improved farm lands, $16·26.	$12· .
Volumes in public libraries, 68,403.	. . 22,896.
Pupils at public schools and colleges, 168,754.	. . 115,750.
FREE STATES, 1790.	SLAVE STATES OF 1790.
Namely Massachusetts (then including Maine,) Rhode Island, Connecticut, New Hampshire, Vermont, New York, New Jersey, and Pennsylvania.	Namely, Delaware, Maryland, Virginia, North Carolina, South Carolina, Georgia, Kentucky and Tennessee.
Area, 169,668 square miles.	. . 300,580.
Population in 1790, 1,968,455.	. . 1,961,372.
,, 1860, 10,594,168.	. . 7,414,684.
Population per square mile in 1790, 11·60.	. . 6·50.
Do. in 1860, 62·44.	. . 24·66.
Increase of population per square mile, from 1790 to 1860, 50·84.	. . 18·14.
FREE STATES OF 1860.	SLAVE STATES OF 1860.
Area, 835,631.	. . 888,591.

Farm lands, 161,462,000.	. . 248,721,062.
Value, $4,067,947,286.	. . 2,570,466,935.
Value per acre, $25·19.	. . 10·46.
Total product of 1859, namely, of agriculture, manufactures, mines and fisheries, $4,150,000,000.	$1,140,000,000.
Per capita, $217.	$93.
Copies of press issued in 1860, 760,034,360.	. . 167,917,188.
By table 157, (Census of 1850), ratio of native white adults who cannot read or write, 4·12 per cent.	. . 17·23 (more than four to one.)
Same tables for Census of 1860, partially estimated, 3·21.	. . 17·03 (more than 5 to 1).
	Whole additional value of *all* the lands of the Slave States, whether farm lands or unoccupied, if worth as much per acre as those of the Free States, $5,859,246,616.
	Total value of products of the Slave States in 1859, if equal per capita to those of the Free States, $2,653,631,032.
	Deduct actual products of 1859, $1,140,000,000.
	Absolute increase of 1859, if Free States, $1,513,631,032.
	That is, the *additional* value of the actual

	products of the Slave States, caused by emancipation, $1,513,631,032.
Total value of all the property, real and personal of the free States in 1860, $10,852,081,081.	Ditto, of all the Slave States including slaves $5,225,307,034.
Annual gross profit of capital, 39 per cent.	. . 22.
	If we could add the annual earnings of commerce (not included in the census tables), the yearly product of the Free States per capita would be almost triple that of the Slave States, the commerce of N. York alone being nearly equal to that of the entire South.
Total agricultural product of free States in 1859, $2,527,676,000.	$862,324,000 (Slave States).
Agricultural product of Free States per capita in 1859, $131·48.	Ditto of Slave States per capita in 1859, $70·56.
Do. per acre in 1859, improved and unimproved lands, $15·65.	$3·58.
Do. per acre, improved lands, $28·68.	11·55.

It is thus demonstrated by the official statistics of the census of the United States from 1790 to 1860, that the total annual product of the Free States *per capita*, exceeds that of the Slave States, largely more than two to one, and, including commerce, very nearly three to one. As regards education also we see, that the ratio in favour of the Free States is more than four to one in 1850, (4·12 to 17·23), and, in 1860, more than five to one, (3·21 to 17·03). And even as regards agricultural products, we have seen, that those of the Free States were $2,527,676,000 per annum, and of the Slave States, only $862,234,000. The value of the lands of the Free States was $25·19 per acre, of the Slave States only $10·46 per acre; the product of the improved lands of the Free States was $28·68 *per acre*, and of the Slave States $11·55, whilst, *per capita*, the result was $131·48, to $70·56.

These facts prove how much greater the crops of the Slave States would be, if their farms, (including cotton), were cultivated by free labour. It is also thus demonstrated, how completely the fertile lands of the South are exhausted and reduced in value by slave culture. Having thus proved deductively, the ruinous effects of Slavery, I will proceed, in my next letter, inductively, to exhibit the causes which have produced these remarkable results.

R. J. WALKER.

APPENDIX.

BY ROBERT J. WALKER.

We have seen by the census tables, if the product *per capita* of the Slave States in 1859, had been equal to that of the Free States for that year, that the ADDITIONAL value produced in 1859 in the Slave States, would have been $1,531,631,000. Now as our population augmented during that decade 35.59 per cent., this *increased* value, at that ratio, in 1869 would have been $2,052,332,272. If multiplying the amount *each year* by three only, instead of $3\frac{559}{1000}$ the result, during that decade, would have been as follows:—

Product of	1860 . . .	$1,559,039,962
,,	1861 . . .	1,605,811,060
,,	1862 . . .	1,654,085,391
,,	1863 . . .	1,703,707,952
,,	1864 . . .	1,754,819,198
,,	1865 . . .	1,807,464,773
,,	1866 . . .	1,861,688,716
,,	1867 . . .	1,917,539,377
,,	1868 . . .	1,975,065,558
,,	1869 . . .	2,034,317,524
Total augmented product of the decade		$17,873,539,511

That is, the total *increased* product of the Slave States, during the decade from 1859 to 1869, would have been $17,873,539,511, if the production in the Slave States had been equal, *per capita*, to that of the Free States. This, it will be remembered, is gross product. This, it will be perceived, is far below the actual result, as we can see by comparing the real product of 1869, $2,052,332,272, as before given, with the $2,034,317,524, as the result of a multiplication by three each year.

The ratio of the increase of our *wealth*, from 1850 to 1860, as shown by the census, was much greater than that of our population—namely, 126.45 per cent., instead of 35.59 per cent. Multiplying by this ratio (126.45), the result would be an *additional* product in 1869, in the Slave States, of $3,427,619,475. But our wealth increases in an augmented ratio during each decade.

Thus, the ratio of the increase of our wealth, as shown by the census, was as follows:—

From 1820 to 1830	. . . .	41 per cent.
„ 1830 to 1840	. . . .	42 „
„ 1840 to 1850	. . . .	64 „
„ 1850 to 1860	. . . .	126.45 „

Thus, the increase of our wealth from 1840 to 1850, was more than 50 per cent. greater than from 1830 to 1840; and from 1850 to 1860, nearly double that from 1840 to 1850. At the same duplicate ratio, from 1850 to 1870, the result would be over 250 per cent. That such would have been a close approximation to the true result, is rendered still more probable by the fact, that the product of 1859, as shown by the census, was 250 per cent. greater than that of 1849.

If, then, instead of 126.45 per cent. we were to assume 250 per cent. as the ratio, the result would be in 1869, $5,297,708,612, as the *increased* product of the Slave States that year, if the ratio *per capita* were equal to that of the Free States. If we carry out these ratios from 1859 to 1869, either of 126.45, or of 250 into the aggregate of the decade, the results are startling. Assuming, however, that of the population only, we have seen that the aggregate result in the decade from 1859 to 1869 was over seventeen billions of dollars, or largely more than ten times our debt, incurred by this rebellion.

When, then, I reassert the opinion, heretofore expressed by me, that as the result of the superiority of free over slave labour, our wealth in 1870, and especially in each succeeding decade, as a consequence of the entire abolition of Slavery in the United States, will be far greater, notwithstanding the debt, than if the rebellion had never occurred, there is here presented conclusive official proof of the truth of this statement. We have seen that our wealth increased from 1850 to 1860, 126.45 per cent., whilst that of England, from 1851 to 1861, augmented only at the rate of 37 per cent.

Applying these several ratios to the progress of the wealth of the United Kingdom and the United States, respectively, in 1870, 1880, 1890, and 1900, the result is given below.

We have seen by the census, that our national wealth was in—

1850	$7,135,780,228
1860	16,159,616,068

Increase from 1850 to 1860, 126.45 per cent.
England „ 1851 to 1861, 37 per cent.
Assuming these ratios, the result would be as follows :—

United Kingdom,	1861,	wealth	$31,500,000,000
„	1871,	„	43,155,000,000
„	1881,	„	59,122,350,000
„	1891,	„	80,997,619,500
„	1901,	„	110,966,837,715

United States,	1860,	wealth,	$16,159,616,068
„	1870,	„	36,593,450,585
„	1880,	„	82,865,868,849
„	1890,	„	187,314,353,225
„	1900,	„	423,330,438,288

Thus, it appears by the census of each nation, that, each increasing in the same ratio respectively as for the last decade, the wealth of the United States in 1880 would exceed that of the United Kingdom $23,743,518,849 ; that in 1890 it would be much more than double, and in 1900, approaching quadruple that of the United Kingdom.

When we reflect that England increases in wealth much more rapidly than any other country of Europe, the value of these statistics may be estimated, as proving how readily our national debt can be extinguished without oppressive taxation.

These are the results, founded on the actual statistics, without estimating the enormous increase of our national wealth, arising from the abolition of Slavery. We have seen that, by the official tables of the census of 1860, the value of the *products* of the United States, so far as given, for the year 1859, was $5,290,000,000. But this is very short of the actual result. The official report (pages 59, 190, 198 to 210), shows that this included *only* the products of "agriculture, manufactures, mines, and fisheries." In referring to the result as to "*manufactures*," at page 59 of his official report before given, the Superintendent says,—"If to this amount were added the very large aggregate of mechanical productions below the annual value of $500, of which no official cognizance is taken, the result would be one of *startling magnitude.*"

1. This omission alone, for gross product, is estimated at $500,000,000.

2. Milk and eggs, fodder, wood, poultry and feathers, omitted, gross products, estimated at $350,000,000.

3. Gross earnings of trade and commerce, including freights, &c., by land and water, $1,000,000,000.

4. Gross earnings of all other pursuits and business, including all other omissions, $1,000,000,000.

Total gross products of 1860, as thus estimated, $8,140,000,000, of which the amount for the Free States, as estimated, is $6,558,334,000, and for the Slave States, $1,581,666,000.

I have heretofore referred to the vast influence of *education* as one of the principal causes of the greater product *per capita* in the Free than in the Slave States, of the much larger number of patents, of inventions, and discoveries, in the former than in the latter.

At the April Meeting of 1844, upon the request of the Society, I delivered at Washington (D. C.) the Introductory Address for the National Institute, in which, up to that date, an account was given by me of "the various improvements and discoveries made by our countrymen in the inductive sciences." On reference to that address, which was published at its date (April, 1844), with their *bulletin*, it will be seen that, from the great Franklin down to Kinnersley, Fitch, Rumsey, Fulton, Evans, Rush, the Stevens of New Jersey, Whitney, Godfrey, Rittenhouse, Silliman, J. Q. Adams, Cleveland, Adrain, Bowditch, Hare, Bache, Henry, Pierce, Espy, Patterson, Nulty, Morse, Walker, Loomis, Rogers, Saxton, and many others; these men, with scarcely an exception, were from the Free States.

EXTRACT.

"And, first, of electricity. This has been cultivated with the greatest success in our country, from the time when Franklin with his kite drew down electricity from the thunder cloud, to that when Henry showed the electrical currents produced by the distant lightning discharge. In Franklin's day the idea prevailed that there were two kinds of electricity, one produced by rubbing vitreous substances, the other by the friction of resinous bodies. Franklin's theory of one electric fluid in all bodies, disturbed in its equilibrium by friction, and thus accumulating in one and deserting the other, maintains its ground, still capable of explaining the facts elicited in the progress of modern discovery. Franklin believed that electricity and lightning were the same, and proceeded to the proof. He made the perilous experiment, by exploring the air with a kite, and drawing down from the thunder cloud the lightning's discharge upon his own person. The bold philosopher received unharmed the shock of the electric fluid, more fortunate than others who have fallen victims to less daring experiments. The world was delighted with the discoveries of the great American, and for a time electricity was called Franklinism on the continent of Europe; but Franklin was born here, and the name was not adopted in England. While Franklin made experiments, Kinnersley exhibited and illustrated them, and also rediscovered the seemingly opposite electricities of glass and resin. Franklin's lightning rod is gradually surmounting the many difficulties with which it contended, as experience attests the greater safety of houses protected by the rod, properly mounted, whilst the British attempt to substitute balls for points has failed. This question, as to powder magazines, has lately excited much controversy. Should a rod be attached to the magazine, or should it be placed upon a post at some distance? This question has been solved by Henry. When an electrical discharge passes from one body to another, the electricity in all the bodies in the neighbourhood is affected. Henry magnetized a needle in a long conductor, by the discharge from a cloud, more than a mile from the conductor. If a discharge passes down a rod, attached to a powder house, may it not cause a spark to pass from one receptacle for powder to another, and thus inflame the whole? The electrical plenum, which Henry supposed, is no doubt disturbed, and to great distances; but the effect diminishes with the distance. If all the principal conductors about a building can be connected with a lightning rod, there is no danger of a discharge; for it is only in leaving or entering a conductor that electricity produces heating effects; but if not, the rod is safer at a moderate distance from the building. The rate at which electricity moved was another of the experiments of Franklin. A wire was led over a great extent of ground, and a discharge passed through it. No interval could be perceived between the time of the spark passing to and from the wire at the two ends. Not long since, Wheatston of England, aided by our own great mechanic, Saxton, solved the problem. This has induced Arago, of France, to propose to test the rival theories of light, by similar means—to measure thus a velocity, to detect which has heretofore required a motion over the line of the diameter of the earth's orbit.

In galvanism, our countrymen have made many important discoveries. Dr. Hare invented instruments of such great power as well to deserve the names of calorimeter and deflagrator. The most refractory substances yielded to the action of the deflagrator, melting like wax before a common fire. Even charcoal was supposed to be fused in the experiments of Hare and Silliman, and the visionary speculated on the possibility of black as well as white diamonds. Draper, by his most ingenious galvanic battery, of two metals and two liquids, with one set of elements, in a glass tube not the size of the little finger, was able to decompose water. Faraday, of England, discovered the principle, that when a current of electricty is set in motion, or stopped in a conductor, a neighbouring conductor has a current produced in the opposite direction. Henry proved that this principle might be made available to produce an action of a current upon itself, by forming a conductor in the whirls of a spiral, so that sparks and shocks might be obtained by the use of such spirals, when connected with a pair of galvanic plates, a current from which could give no sparks and no shocks. Henry's discoveries of the effects of a current in producing several alternations in currents in neighbouring conductors,—the change of the quality of electricity which gives shocks to the muscles into that producing heat, and *vice versâ*,—his mode of graduating these shocks,—his theoretical investigations into the causes of these alterations,—are abstruse, but admirable; and his papers have been republished throughout Europe. The heating effects of a galvanic current have been applied by Dr. Hare to blasting. The accidents which so often happen in quarries may be avoided by firing the charge from a distance, as the current which heats the wire, passing through the charge, may be conveyed, without perceptible diminution, through long distances. A feeble attempt to attribute this important invention of Dr. Hare to Colonel Pasley, an English engineer, has been abandoned. This is the marvellous agent by which our eminent countryman, Morse, encouraged by an appropriation made by Congress, will, by means of his electric telegraph, soon communicate information forty miles, from Washington to Baltimore, more rapidly than by whispering in the ear of a friend sitting near us. A telegraph on a new plan at that time, invented by Mr. Grout, of Massachusetts, in 1799, asked a question and received an answer in less than ten minutes through a distance of ninety miles. The telegraph of Mr. Morse will prove, I think, superior to all others; and the day is not distant when, by its aid, we may perhaps ask questions and receive replies across our continent, from *ocean to ocean*, thus uniting with steam in enlarging the limits over which our Republic may be safely extended.*

* This address was made and published several months before any electric telegraph line was in operation, and is believed to be the first prediction of the success of this principle, as CONTINENTAL or OCEANIC.

Many of our countrymen have contributed to the branch which regards the action of electrified and magnetic bodies. Lukens' application of magnetism to steel, (called *touching*,) the compass of Bissel for detecting local attraction, of Burt for determining the variation of the compass, and the observations on the variations of the needle made by Winthrop and Dewitt, deserve notice and commendation. Not long since, Gauss of Germany, invented instruments by which the changes of magnetic variation and force could be accurately determined. Magnetic action is ever varying. The needle does not point in the same direction for even a few minutes together. The force of magnetism, also, perpetually varies. True as the needle to the pole, is not a correct simile for the same place, and, if we pass from one spot to another, is falsified at each change of our position; for the needle changes its direction, and the force varies. Enlarged and united observations, embracing the various portions of the world, must produce important results. The observations at Philadelphia, conducted by Dr. A. D. Bache, and now continued by him under the direction of the Topographical Bureau, are of great value, and will, it is hoped, be published by Congress. Part of them have already first seen the light in Europe—a result much to be regretted, for we are not strong enough in science to spare from the national records the contributions of our countrymen.

These combined observations, progressing throughout the world, are of the highest importance. The University of Cambridge, the American Philosophical Society, and Girard College, have erected observatories; and one connected with the Depot of Charts and Instruments has been built last year in this city by the Government, and thoroughly furnished with instruments for complete observations. The names of Bache, Gillis, Pierce, Lovering, and Bond, are well known in connection with these establishments.

A magnetic survey of Pennsylvania has been made by private enterprise, and the beginning of a survey in New York. Loomis has observed in Ohio, Locke in Ohio and Iowa, and to him belongs the discovery of the position of the point of greatest magnetic intensity in the Western World. Most interesting magnetic observations (now in progress of publication by Congress) are the result of the toilsome, perilous, and successful expedition, under Commander Wilkes, of our navy, by whom was discovered the Antarctic continent, and a portion of its soil and rock brought home to our country.

The analogy of the auroral displays with those of electricity in motion, were first pointed out by Dr. A. D. Bache, whose researches, in conjunction with Lloyd of Dublin, to determine whether differences of longitude could be measured by the observations of small simultaneous changes in the position of the magnetic needle, led to the knowledge of the curious fact, that these changes, which had been traced as simultaneous, or nearly so, in the continent of Europe, did not so extend across the Atlantic.

Kindred to these two branches, are electro-magnetism and magneto-electricity, connected with which, as discoverers, are our countrymen Dana, Green, Hare, Henry, Page, Rogers, and Saxton. The reciprocal machine for producing shocks, invented by Page, and the powerful galvanic magnet of Henry, are entitled to respectful notice. This force, it was thought, might be substituted for steam; but no experiments have as yet established its use, on any important scale, as a motive power. The fact that an electrical spark could be produced by a peculiar arrangement of a coil of wire, connected with a magnet, is a recent discovery; and the first magneto-electric machine capable of keeping up a continuous current was invented by Saxton.

Electricity and magnetism touch in some points upon heat. Heat produces electrical currents; electrical currents produce heat. Heat destroys magnetism. Melted iron is incapable of magnetic influence. Reduction of temperature in iron so far decreases the force, that a celebrated philosopher made an elaborate series of experiments to ascertain whether a great reduction of temperature might not develope magnetic properties in metals other than iron. This branch of thermo-electricity has received from us but little attention. Franklin's experiments, by placing differently coloured cloths in the snow, and showing the depth to which they sunk, are still quoted, and great praise has been bestowed abroad on a more elaborate series of experiments, by a descendant of his, Dr. A. D. Bache, proving that this law does not hold good as to heat, unaccompanied by light. The experiments of Saxton and Goddard demonstrate that solid bodies do slowly evaporate. It is proper here to mention our countryman, Count Rumford, whose discoveries as to the nature and properties of heat, improvement in stoves and gunnery, and in the structure of chimneys and economy of fuel, have been so great and useful.

Light accompanies heat of a certain temperature. That it acts directly to increase or decrease magnetic force, is not yet proved; and the interesting experiments made by Dr. Draper, in Virginia, go to show that it is without magnetic influence. The discussion of this subject forms the branch of optics, touching physical science on the one side, the most refined, and the highest range of mathematics on the other. Rittenhouse first suggested the true explanation of the experiment, of the apparent conversion of a cameo into an intaglio, when viewed through a compound microscope, and anticipated many years Brewster's theory. Hopkinson wrote well on the experiment made by looking at a street lamp through a slight texture of silk. Joscelyn, of New York, investigated the causes of the irradiation manifested by luminous bodies, as for instance the stars. Of late, photographic experiments have occupied much attention, and Draper has advanced the bold idea, supported by experiment, that the agent in the so-called photography, is not light, nor heat, but an agent differing from any other known principle. Henry has investigated the luminous emanation from lime, calcined with sulphur, and certain other substances, and finds that it differs much from light in some of its qualities.

Astronomy is the most ancient and highest branch of physics. One of our earliest and greatest efforts in this branch was the invention of the mariner's quadrant, by Godfrey, a glazier of Philadelphia. The transit of Venus, in the last century, called forth the researches of Rittenhouse, Owen, Biddle, and President Smith, near Philadelphia, and of Winthrop, at Boston. Two orreries were made by Rittenhouse, as also a machine for predicting eclipses. Most useful observations, connected with the solar eclipses, from 1832 to 1840, have been made by Paine, of Boston. We have now well supplied observatories at West Point, Washington, Cambridge, Philadelphia, Hudson, Ohio, and Tuskaloosa, Alabama, and the valuable labours of Loomis, Bartlett, Gilliss, Bond, Pierce, Walker, and Kendall, are well known. Mr. Adams, so distinguished in this branch and that of weights and measures, laid last year the corner-stone of an observatory at Cincinnati, where will soon be one of the largest and most powerful telescopes in the world. Most interesting observations as to the great comet of 1843 were made by Alexander, Anderson, Bartlett, Kendall, Pierce, Walker, Downes, and Loomis, and valuable astronomical instruments have been constructed by Amasa Holcomb, of Massachusetts, and Wm. J. Young, of Philadelphia.

It is difficult to class the brilliant meteors of November the 13th, 1833. If such meteors are periodic, the discovery was made by Professor Olmsted; and Mr. Herrick, of New Haven, has added valuable suggestions. The idea that observers, differently placed, of the time of appearance and disappearance of the same meteor, would give the means of determining differences of longitude, was first applied in our own country, where the difference of longitude of Princeton and Philadelphia was determined by observations of Henry and Alexander, Espy and Bache. In meteorology our countrymen have succeeded well. Dr. Wells, of South Carolina, elaborated his beautiful and original theory of the formation of dew, and supported it by many well-devised and conclusive experiments. The series of hourly observations, by Professor Snell and Capt. Mordecai, are well known; and the efforts of New York and Pennsylvania, of the medical department of the army, and its present enlightened head, Dr. Lawson, have much advanced this branch of science. The interesting question, does our climate change, seems to be answered thus far in the negative, by registers kept in Massachusetts and New York. There are two rival theories of storms. That of Redfield, of a rotary motion of a wide column of air, combined with a progressive motion in a curved line. Espy builds on the law of physics, examines the action of an upmoving column of air, shows the causes of its motion and the results, and then deduces his most beautiful theory of rain and of land and water-spouts. This he puts to the test of observation; and in the inward motion of wind towards the centre of storms, finds a striking verification of his theory. This theory is also sustained by the overthrow or injury, in the recent tornado at Natchez, of the houses whose doors and windows were closed, while those which were open mostly escaped unhurt. Mr. Espy must be considered, not only here, but throughout the world, as at the head of this branch of science. This subject has been greatly advanced by Professor Loomis, whose paper has been pronounced, by the highest authority, to be the best specimen of inductive reasoning which meteorology has produced. The most recent and highly valuable meteorological works of Dr. Samuel Forry are much esteemed. Many important discoveries in pneumatics were made by Dr. Franklin and Count Rumford, and the air pump was also greatly improved by Dr. Prince, of Salem.

Chemistry, in all its departments, has been successfully pursued among us. Dana, Draper, Ellet, Emmet, Hare, the Mitchells, Silliman, and Torrey, are well known as chemical philosophers; and Booth, Boyé, Chilton, Keating, Mather, R. Rogers, Seybert, Shepherd, and Vanuxem, as *analysts*; and F. Bache, Webster, Greene, Mitchell, Silliman, and Hare, as authors. In my native town of Northumberland, Pennsylvania, resided two adopted citizens, most eminent as chemists and philosophers, Priestly and Cooper. The latter, who was one of my own preceptors, was greatly distinguished as a writer, scholar, jurist, and physician, as well as a chemist. Priestly, although I do not concur in his peculiar views of theology, was certainly one of the most able and learned of ecclesiastical writers, and possessed also a mind most vigorous and original. His discoveries in pneumatic chemistry have exceeded those of any other philosopher. He discovered vital air, many new acids, chemical substances, paints, and dyes. He separated nitrous and oxygenous airs, and first exhibited acids and alkalies in a gaseous form. He ascertained that air could be purified by the process of vegetation, and that light evolved pure air from vegetables. He detected the powerful action of oxygenous air upon the blood, and first pointed out the true theory of respiration. The eudiometer, a most curious instrument for fixing the purity of air, by measuring the proportion of oxygen, was discovered by Dr. Priestly. He lived and died in my native town, universally beloved as a man, and greatly admired as a philosopher. Chemistry has actively advanced among us during the present century. Hare's compound blow-pipe came from his hand so perfect, in 1802, that all succeeding attempts of Dr. Clark, of England, and of all others, in Europe and America, to improve upon it or go beyond the effects produced, have wholly failed. His mode of mixing oxygen and hydrogen gases, the instant before burning them, was at once simple, effective, and safe. The most refractory metallic and mineral substances yielded to the intense heat produced by the flame of the blow pipe. In chemical analysis, the useful labors of Keating, Vanuxem, Seybert, Booth, Clemson, Litton, and Moss, would fill many volumes. In organic chemistry, the researches of Clark, Hare and Boyé were rewarded by the discovery of a new ether, the most explosive compound known to man. Mitchel's experiments on the penetration of membranes by gases, and the ingenious extension of them by Dr. Rogers, are worthy of all praise. The softening of India rubber, by Dr. Mitchell, renders it a most useful article. Dyer's discovery of soda ash yielded him a competence. Our countrymen have also made most valuable improvements in refining sugar, in the manufacture of lard oil, and stearin candles, and the preservation of timber by Earle's process. Sugar and molasses have been extracted in our country from the corn stalk, but with what, if any profit, as to either, is not yet determined. No part of mechanics has produced such surprising results as the steam engine, and our countrymen have been among the foremost and most distinguished in this great and progressive branch. When Rumsey, of Pennsylvania, made a steamboat which moved against the current of the James river four miles an hour, his achievement was so much in advance of the age, as to acquire no public confidence. When John Fitch's boat stemmed the current of the Delaware, contending successfully with sail boats, it was called, in derision, the *scheme boat*. So the New Yorkers, when the steamboat of their own truly great mechanic, Stevens, after making a trip from Hoboken, burnt accidentally one of its boiler tubes, it was proclaimed a failure. Fulton also encountered unbounded ridicule and opposition, as he advanced to confer the greatest benefits on mankind, by the application of steam to navigation. So Oliver Evans, of Pennsylvania, (who has made much such useful improvements in the flour mill,) was pronounced insane, when he applied to the Legislatures of Pennsylvania and Maryland for special privileges in regard to the application of steam to locomotion on common roads. In 1810, he was escorted by a mob of boys, when his amphibolas was moved on wheels by steam more than a mile through the streets of Philadelphia, to the river Schuylkill, and there, taking to the water, was paddled by steam to the wharves of the Delaware, where it was to work as a dredging machine. Fulton's was the first successful steamboat, Stevens's the first that navigated the ocean, Oliver Evans's the first high-pressure engine applied to steam navigation. Stevens's boat, by an accident, did not precede Fulton's, and Stevens's engine was wholly American, and constructed entirely by himself, and his propeller resembled much that now introduced by Ericsson. Stevens united the highest mechanical skill with a bold, original, inventive genius. His sons, (especially Mr. Robert L. Stevens, of New York,) have inherited much of the extraordinary skill and talent of their distinguished father. The first steamboat that ever crossed the ocean was built by one of our countrymen, and their skill in naval architecture has been put in requisition by the Emperor of Russia and the Sultan of Turkey. The steam machines invented by our countrymen to drive piles, load vessels, and excavate roads, are most ingenious and useful. The use of steam, as a locomotive power, upon the water and the land, is admirably adapted to our mighty rivers and extended territory. From Washington to the mouth of the Oregon is but one half,* and to the mouth of the Del Norte but one fourth, of the distance of the railroads already constructed here; and to the latter point, at the rate of motion (thirty miles an hour) now in daily use abroad, the trip would be performed in two days, and to the former in four days. Thus, steam, if we measure distance by the time in which it is traversed, renders our whole Union, with its most extended limits, smaller than was the State of New York ten years since. Steam cars have been moved, as an experiment, both here and abroad, many hundred miles, at the rate of sixty miles an hour; but what will be the highest velocity ultimately attained in common use, either upon the water or the land, is a most important problem, as yet entirely unsolved. Our respected citizens, Morey and Drake, have endeavoured to substitute the force of explosion of gaseous compounds for steam. The first was the pioneer, and the second has shown that the

* Now only one tenth.

problem is still worth pursuing to solution. An energetic western mechanic made a bold but unsuccessful effort to put in operation an engine acting by the expansion of air by heat; and a similar most ingenious attempt was made by Mr. Walter Byrnes, of Concordia, Louisiana; as also to substitute compressed air, and air compressed and expanded, as a locomotive power. All attempts to use air as a motive power, except the balloon, the sail vessel, the air gun, and the windmill, have thus far failed; but what inventive genius may yet accomplish in this respect, remains yet undetermined. There is, it is true, a mile or more of pneumatic railway used between Dublin and Kingstown. An air pump driven by steam exhausts the air from a cylinder in which a piston moves; this cylinder is laid the whole length of the road, and the piston is connected to a car above, so that, as the piston moves forward on the exhaustion of the air in front of it, the car is also carried forward. The original idea of this pneumatic railway was derived from the contrivance of an American, quite unknown to fame, who, as his sign expressed it, showed to visitors a new mode of carrying the mail,* more simple, and quite as valuable, practically, as this atmospheric railway. The submerged propeller of Ericsson, and the submerged paddle wheel, the rival experiments of our two distinguished naval officers, Stockton and Hunter, are now candidates for public favour; and the Princeton on the ocean as she moves in noiseless majesty, at a speed never before attained at sea, seems to attest the value of one of these experiments, whilst the other is yet to be determined. The impenetrable iron steam vessel of Mr. Stevens is not yet completed, nor have those terrific engines of war, his explosive shells, yet been brought to the test of actual conflict.

In curious and useful mechanical inventions, our countrymen are unsurpassed, and a visit to our new and beautiful Patent Office will convince the close observer that the inventive genius of America never was more active than at the present moment. The machines for working up cotton, hemp, and wool, from their most crude state to the finest and most useful fabrics, have all been improved among us. The cotton gin of Eli Whitney has altered the destinies of one-third of our country, and doubled the exports of the Union. The ingenious improvements for imitating medals, by parallel lines upon a plain surface, which, by the distances between them, give all the effects of light and shade that belong to a raised or depressed surface, invented by Gobrecht and perfected by Spencer, has been rendered entirely automatic by Saxton, so that it not only rules its lines at proper distances and of suit-

* This idea unquestionably originated in the United States, but has been improved last year; and introduced by Mr. Rammel, of England.

able lengths, but when its work is done it stops. In hydraulics, we have succeeded well; and the great aqueduct over the Potomac at Georgetown, constructed by Major Turnbull, of the Topographical Corps, exhibits new contrivances, in overcoming obstacles never heretofore encountered in similar projects, and has been pronounced in Europe one of the most skilful works of the age.

The abstract mathematics does not seem so well suited to the genius of our countrymen as its application to other sciences. Those among us who have most successfully pursued the pure mathematics, are chiefly our much esteemed adopted citizens, such as Nulty, Adrain, Bonnycastle, Gill, and Hassler. Bowditch was an American, and is highly distinguished at home and abroad. Such men as Plana and Babbage rank him among the first class, and his commentary on the "Mécanique Céleste" of Laplace, has secured for him a niche in the temple of fame, near to that of its illustrous author. Anderson and Strong are known to all who love mathematics, and Fischer was cut off by death in the commencement of a bright career. And may I here be indulged in grateful remembrance of two of my own preceptors, Dr. R. M. Patterson and Eugene Nulty. The first was the Professor at my Alma Mater (the University of Pennsylvania) in natural philosophy and the application of mathematics to many branches of science. He was beloved and respected by all the class, as the courteous gentleman and the profound scholar; and the mint of the United States, now under his direction, at Philadelphia, has reached the highest point of system, skill, and efficiency. In the pure mathematics Nulty is unsurpassed at home or abroad. In an earlier day, the elder Patterson, Ellicot, and Mansfield, cultivated this branch successfully in connection with astronomy.

A new and extensive country is the great field for descriptive natural history. The beasts, birds, fishes, reptiles, insects, shells, plants, stones, and rocks, are to be examined individually and classed; many new varieties and species are found, and even new genera may occur. The learned Mitchell, of New York, delighted in these branches. The eminent Harlan, of Philadelphia, and McMurtrie, were of a later and more philosophic school. Nuttall, of Cambridge, has distinguished himself in natural history, and Haldeman is rising to eminence.

Ornithology is one of the most attractive branches of natural history. Wilson was the pioneer; Ord, his biographer, followed, and his friend Titian Peale; Audubon is universally known, and stands pre-eminent; and the learned Nuttall, and excellent and enthusiastic Townsend are much respected. Most of these men have compassed sea and land, and encountered many perils and hardships to find their specimens. They have explored the mountains of the North, the swamps of Florida, the prairies of the West, and accompanied the Exploring Expedition to the Antarctic, and round the world. As botanists, the Bartrams, Barton, and Collins, of Philadelphia, Torrey, of New York, Gray and Nuttall of Cambridge, Darlington, of Westchester, are much esteemed. The first botanical garden in our country was that of the Bartons, near Philadelphia; and the first work on botany was from Barton, of the same city. Logan, Woodward, Brailsford, Shelby, Cooper, Horsefield, Colden, Clayton, Muhlenburg, Marshal, Cutler, and Hosack, were also distinguished in this delightful branch.

A study of the shells of our country has raised to eminence the names of Barnes, Conrad, Lea, and Raffinesque. The magnificent fresh water shells of our western rivers are unrivalled in the old world, in size and beauty. How interesting would be a collection of all the specimens which the organic kingdom of America presents, properly classified and arranged according to the regions and States whence they were brought. Paris has the museum of the natural history of France, and London of Great Britain; but Washington has no museum* of the United States, though so much richer in all these specimens.

In mineralogy, the work of Cleveland is most distinguished. Shepherd, Mather, Troost, Torrey, aud a few others, still pursue mineralogy for its own sake; but, generally, our mineralogists have turned geologists, studying rocks on a large scale, instead of their individual constituents, and vying with their brethren in Europe in bold and successful generalization, and in the application of physical science to their subject. Maclure was one of the pioneers, and Eaton and Silliman contributed much to the stock of knowledge. This school has given rise to the great geological surveys made or progressing in several of the States. Jackson, in Maine; Hitchcock, in Massachusetts; Vanuxen, Conrad, and Mather, in New York; the Rogers, in New Jersey, Pennsylvania, and Virginia; Ducatel, in Maryland; Owen and Locke, in the West; Troost, in Tennessee; Horton, in Ohio; the courageous, scientific, and lamented Nicolet, in Missouri, Iowa, and Wisconsin, have made contributions, not only to the geology of our country, but to the science of geology itself, which are conceded to be among the most valuable of the present day. The able reports of Owen and Nicolet were made to Congress, and deserve the highest commendation.

In geographical science, the explorations of Lewis and Clarke; of Long, Nicolet, and the able and intrepid Fremont; the effective State survey of Massachusetts; the surveys of our public

* We now have several such museums in Washington.

lands; the determination of the boundaries of our States, and especially those of Pennsylvania, by Rittenhouse and Elliot; of part of Louisiana, by Graham and Kearney; of Michigan, by Talcott; and of Maine, by Graham; have gained us great credit. The national work of the coast survey, begun by the late Mr. Hassler, and prosecuted through all discouragements and difficulties by that indomitable man, has reflected honour upon his adopted country, through the Government which liberally supported the work, and through whose aid it is now progressing, under new auspices, with great energy.* The lake survey is also now advancing under the direction of Captain Williams, of the Topographical Corps. Among the important recent explorations, is that of the enlightened, untiring, and intrepid Fremont, to Oregon, which fixes the pass of the Rocky Mountains within twenty miles of the northern boundary of Texas. Lieutenant Fremont is a member of the Topographical Corps, which, together with that of Engineers, contains so many distinguished officers, whose labours, together with those of their most able and distinguished chiefs, Colonel Totten and Colonel Abert, fill so large a portion of the public documents, and are so well known and highly appreciated by both Houses of Congress and by the country. The Emperor of Russia has entered the ranks of our Topographical Corps, and employed one of their distinguished members, Captain Whistler, to construct his great railroad from St. Petersburg to Moscow. The travels of our countrymen, Stephens, to Yucatan and Guatemala, to Egypt, Arabia, and Jerusalem; and of Dr. Grant to Nestoria, have increased our knowledge of geography and of antiquities, and have added new and striking proofs of the truths of Christianity.

Fossil geology occupied much of the time and attention of the great philosopher and statesman, Jefferson, and he was rewarded by the discovery of the megatherium. The mastodon, exhumed in 1801, from the marl pits of New York, by Charles Wilson Peale, has proved but one of an order of animal giants. Even the tetracaulodon, or tusked mastodon, of Godman, upon which rested his claims to fame, is not the most curious of this order, as the investigations of Hayes and Horner have proved. This order has excited the attention, not only of such minds as Cooper, Harlan, and Hays, but has also occupied the best naturalists of France, Britain, Germany, and Italy.

Fossil conchology has attracted the attention of Conrad, the Lees' and the Rogers', not only calling forth much ingenuity in description and classification, but also throwing great light upon the relative ages of some of the most interesting geological forma-

* Our Coast Survey, as commenced by Hassler, and being completed by Bache, is admitted in Europe to be the best in the world.

tions. The earthquake theory of the Rogers' is one of the boldest generalizations, founded upon physical reasoning, which our geologists have produced. In the parallel ridges into which the Apalachian chain is thrown, they see the crests of great earthquake waves, propagated from long lines of focal earthquake action, more violent than any which the world now witnesses. The geologist deals in such sublime conceptions as a world of molten matter, tossed into waves by violent efforts of escaping vapours, cooling, cracking, and rending, in dire convulsion. He then ceases to discuss the changes and formation of worlds, and condescends to inform us how to fertilize our soil, where to look for coal and iron, copper, tin, cobalt, lead, and where we need not look for either. He is the Milton of poetry, and the Watt of philosophy. And here let me add, that the recent application of chemistry to agriculture is producing the most surprising results, in increasing and improving the products of the earth, and setting at defiance Malthus' theory of population.

In medicine, that great and most useful branch of physics, our countrymen have been most distinguished. From the days of the great philosopher, physician, patriot, and statesman, Benjamin Rush, down to the present period, our country has been unsurpassed in this branch; but I have not time even to give an outline of the eminent Americans, whose improvements and discoveries in medicine have contributed so much to elevate the character of our country, and advance the comfort and happiness of man. Rush, one of the founders of this branch in America, was one of the signers of our Declaration of Independence, and his school of medicine was as independent and national as his course in our revolutionary struggle. Statistics are chiefly concerned, as furnishing the facts connected with government and political economy, but they are also ancillary to physics. The statistical work of Mr. Archibald Russell, of New York, which immediately preceded the last census, contained many valuable suggestions, some of which were adopted by Congress; and had more been incorporated into the law, the census would have been much more complete and satisfactory. The recent statistical work of Mr. George Tucker of Virginia, on the census of 1840, is distinguished by great talent and research, and is invaluable to the scholar, the philosopher, the statesman, and philanthropist.

THE END.

Made in United States
North Haven, CT
05 November 2026

21766941R00215